LATE SUMMER FLOWERS

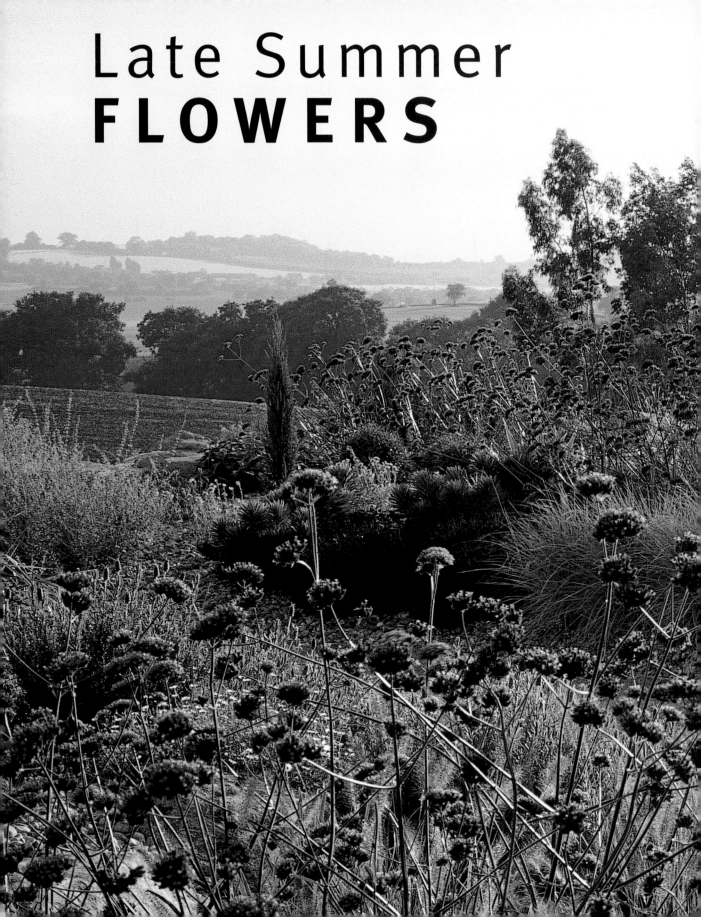

Late Summer
FLOWERS

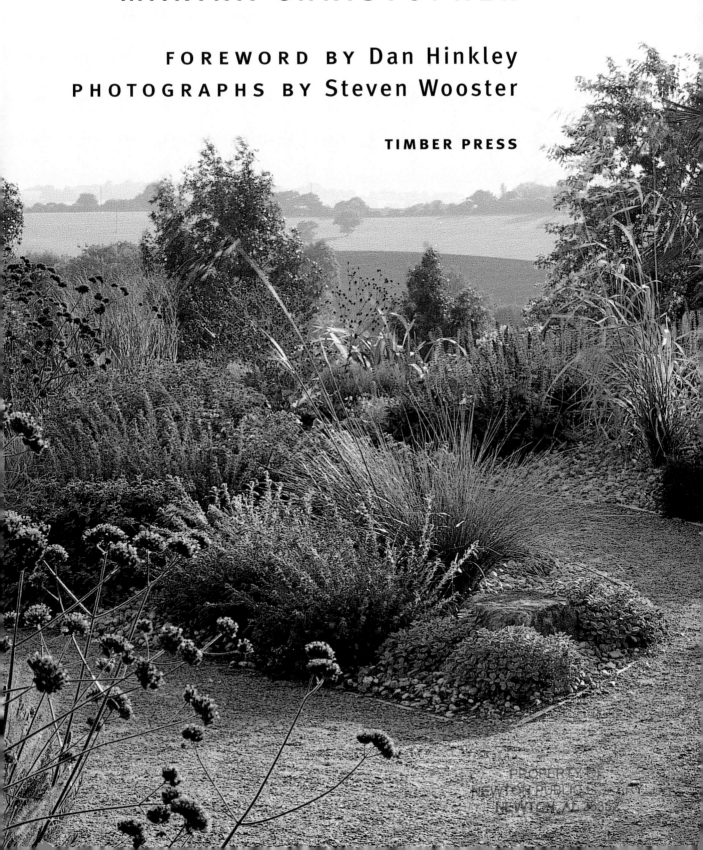

MARINA CHRISTOPHER

FOREWORD BY Dan Hinkley
PHOTOGRAPHS BY Steven Wooster

TIMBER PRESS

For My Mother

LATE SUMMER FLOWERS
Copyright © Frances Lincoln Ltd 2006
Text copyright © Marina Christopher 2006
Photography copyright © Steven Wooster 2006 except for *Agastache*
'Painted Lady' (p. 101) and *Centaurea* 'Phoenix Bronze' (p. 113)
© Clive Nichols; *Verbascum* 'Patricia' (p. 103) © Anne Green-Armytage;
and *V.* 'Clementine' (p. 104) © Howard Rice.

Published in North America in 2006 by
Timber Press, Inc.
The Haseltine Building
133 S.W. Second Avenue, Suite 450
Portland, Oregon 97204-3527, U.S.A.
www.timberpress.com

ISBN-13: 978-0-88192-756-6
ISBN-10: 0-88192-756-2

A catalog record for this book is available from the Library of Congress.

Conceived, edited and designed for Frances Lincoln by
Berry & Co (Publishing) Ltd
47 Crewys Road
Childs Hill
London NW2 2AU

Editor Susan Berry
Designer Anne Wilson
Indexer Marie Lorimer

Printed and bound in Singapore by Tien Wah Press Pte. Ltd.

9 8 7 6 5 4 3 2 1

Page 1: *Verbena macdougalii.*
Title page: Drifts of *Verbena bonariensis* AGM and grasses
predominate in a gravel garden.
Right: Elegant arching flowerheads of *Miscanthus sinensis* 'Roland'.

CONTENTS

Foreword by Dan Hinkley

In 1993, I stumbled upon a colorful quartet of British horticulturists in the mountains of South Korea, all of us happening to be there to explore its rich native flora. Physically dwarfed, perhaps, by the other members of the team on this trip, Marina Christopher made up for her diminutive size by a spunky spirit, great sense of humor and encyclopedic knowledge of plants. It was inevitable that we would become fast friends.

In retrospect, that trip was pivotal for me on many different levels. When I consider the numerous plant genera we experienced in their natural habitat, I wonder if this book – devoted to late-blossoming perennials – did not begin its evolution somewhere along our shared trail. I recall vast fields of cultivated *Angelica gigas* with enormous carmine umbels atop 6ft stems, surrounded by the flicker of visiting pollinators in early evening light. Graceful white spires of numerous species of *Cimicifuga* were still in blossom, adding fragrance and floral presence to the natural vignette long after other flowers had departed for the year. Marina and I shared the pleasure of seeing *Chrysanthemum morifolium*, the predecessor of all modern chrysanthemum hybrids, adding its simple charms to the autumn landscape near the ocean beaches. And, of course, the most sturdy and dependable of the late-season perennials, the aconitums, were in peak blossom, with somber helmets of purple or light blue hooded flowers carried along upright stems as well as on, in several species, a framework that climbed and twined through the diverse understorey of shrubs.

Long after that trip, Marina and I continued a friendship, based partly on the fact that we could commiserate with one another on the challenges faced in making a living by making plants. On yearly trips visiting her in Hampshire, I came to note two things that distinguished Phoenix Perennials from Heronswood, my own nursery. Marina possessed an extraordinary eye for talented garden plants: those that are straightforward and no-nonsense, many of which bring the garden to life in late summer. In fact, her refined palette ultimately came to influence my own garden and nursery inventory. The other more painful difference was that Marina grew each and every plant to perfection. In fact, so seductive is the quality of her plants that I continue to find myself buying the same plant over and again on each subsequent visit to her nursery.

What these attributes say about Marina's delightful and inspiring account of late-blossoming perennials is that it is based not just on a genuine fondness for plants and appreciation for gardening, but also on that most rare of ingredients in contemporary garden writing: indisputable hands-on knowledge. There are few gardeners whose validation of a plant's worthiness I would take so seriously.

Clouds of lilac-pink flowers hover over a froth of delicate green leaves in the diminutive *Thalictrum kiusianum*. A choice plant for a cool, humus-rich shady border.

Introduction

For the purposes of this book a late-summer perennial may best be described as a plant that reliably produces flowers and interesting or unusual seed-heads, or an architectural silhouette, that contribute positively to the garden after midsummer's day on a year in, year out basis. What constitutes a positive contribution is highly subjective – what may appeal greatly to one person may be an anathema to another. It is important to appreciate your garden without being dominated by current ideas and trends in the media world of gardening – after all it is your plot to cherish, as you think fit.

In this book everything bar shrubs and trees will be considered, although I focus on true perennials; I have little experience with trees and shrubs anyway and will leave them to more expert attention.

The majority of gardens in Britain are at their finest in spring and summer, while the latter months of the year pass with just a whimper. However, there are large numbers of spectacular late-flowering plants that are better represented in the gardens of our northern European counterparts. This may well be owing to the shorter growing season in these areas and the better use of the months when growth is possible. There is no doubt that the general climate is changing and seasons are not so distinct. In Britain, the autumn months are lengthening and relatively frost-free weather can now be experienced into December. If the peak of flowering terminates in June, there are then many months when the garden may be lacklustre and uninteresting. The increased use of late-summer perennials will help to renew inspiration in the months of the year when shadows are lengthening.

Exuberant late-summer flowers and grasses spill over and soften the edges of the hard landscaping of the path. Pale pink saponaria, rusty red heleniums, broccoli-like heads of sedum and fiery tapers of *Persicaria amplexicaulis* jostle with structural giants such as Joe pye-weed (*Eupatorium*) and ironweed (*Vernonia crinita*) in late summer.

Creating a border satisfactory at all seasons is an almost impossible task and is rarely successful. It is better to dedicate an area to later flowering perennials preferably where the late-summer sunlight can cast its ethereal golden light through foliage and flowerheads. Grasses, flowers with spires such as *Verbascum* and *Veronicastrum*, or spheres of *Echinops* and *Centaurea*, or flat plates like those of *Achillea*, can appear magical when backlit by the setting sun.

There are many ways to extend the flowering season. A large number of the daisy family (*Asteraceae*) bloom naturally at this time, notably *Aster* species (Michaelmas daisies) and *Helianthus* (sunflowers). Others have flowered earlier in the year but can bloom again with judicious pruning and cutting back. Good examples of this would be *Nepeta racemosa* 'Walker's Low' and several *Salvia nemorosa* cultivars. Annuals sown late will give colour well into the autumn months. Plants like *Phlox paniculata* can be managed with selective pruning so as to produce flowers over a longer season. Understanding the biology of the plant material can greatly assist the gardener in extending the season. Leaving elegant seed-heads and the architectural silhouettes of many umbellifers will also provide food and shelter for birds, small mammals and insects.

I am particularly interested in the concept of the garden as an ecosystem where the relationship between plants, animals, man and their environment allows healthy growth and development, without recourse to chemicals and artificial fertilizers. Inevitably not all plants will be suitable for a site and it is important to understand which group of plants will perform well on a particular soil. There are microclimates and niches in all gardens and if you exploit these areas you can increase the diversity of plants you grow.

Right: Ornamental grasses dominate the autumn months with overtones of buff and straw. Here, stands of *Calamogrostis* x *acutiflora* 'Karl Foerster' combine seamlessly with globular *Echinops* seed-heads and arching flowerheads of *Miscanthus sinensis* cultivars, with the veil-like *Deschampsia* in the foreground.

Overleaf: *Achillea* 'Walther Funcke' (page 12); *Echinacea angustifolia* (page 13).

PLANTING FOR LATE SUMMER FLOWERS

The Late Summer Line-up

Many plants naturally bloom later in the year, so to create a successful late-summer border with the minimum of effort it would be prudent to use a large percentage of them. Given unlimited time and a lot of extra work, an autumn border could be produced with plants that do not usually perform at this time of year, but skilled and clever manipulation would be needed to obtain the desired effect, and much of the result would be at the mercy of the vagaries of the weather. Therefore in this chapter I will be reviewing the natural autumn line-up and will consider in a later section how to manipulate the seasons through judicious sowing, pruning and deadheading. A combination of the two can produce a diverse and colourful extravaganza to end the growing season, enhancing the autumn colours provided by trees and shrubs during the fall.

WHAT TO CHOOSE?

Gardeners have access to a multitude of plant material from all over the world mainly thanks to the endeavours of plant hunters past and present. In areas where the temperature and seasons show little variation from one month to the next, plants can germinate, grow and flower at any time of the year. However, a large proportion of the world exhibits distinct seasons, whether this is ruled by temperature, daylight or rainfall, or a combination of all three.

It is interesting to muse why flowers do not all bloom at the same time as soon as the conditions are suitable and it is the phrase when "the conditions are suitable" that is the crux of the matter. Many continental areas, such as the Mediterranean, have hot, dry summers, which would desiccate new growth and

A profusion of late-summer daisies. Golden-yellow rudbeckias and buff and yellow achilleas mix well with flamboyant orange and burgundy dahlias. The occasional rose and kniphofia punctuate this hot, fiery border.

shrivel flowers. In terrain like this there is a spring and autumn flush of growth. Some plants emerge fast in spring, flower and seed before the drought, their seed lying dormant until the autumn cool and moisture. Others begin growth as soon as the first good rainfall relieves the heat of the summer and complete their life-cycle before the onset of winter.

The purpose of any plant is to produce progeny for the next season in the form of seed, offsets, plantlets or bulbs but, in the main, seed is the primary method of propagation. Once the seed has developed and ripened there is little need for more flower, which is why deadheading is so effective in continuing flower production – until there is ripe seed, the plant will continue to produce more inflorescences, even if it results in it flowering itself to death! Selective plant breeding regimes by man have resulted in many cultivars that do not produce seed, or are sterile, another factor that lengthens the flowering period. (This does occasionally occur in the wild when two species hybridize and produce a sterile hybrid, but many eventually die out unless they can reproduce by vegetative means.)

In other regions, such as the North American prairies, there may be such competition between species that a longer time is required until a plant has built up enough energy to burst into flower. Many of the North American sunflowers are large, leafy herbaceous perennials that need time to grow and emerge above the general height of other prairie plants. Ripe seed can be carried away from the parent by the wind to find a suitable place to lodge and germinate. In the case of plants which produce seed attractive as food to birds and animals, there is often an edible casing around the seed and, on digestion, the intact seed is passed out with the faeces, ensuring a moist and fertile beginning for a new plant. Only a tiny percentage of the seed generated in any one year will ever reach maturity, so there is a lot of wastage.

Areas such as the permafrost regions of the Soviet states and Canada will only become suitable for growth late in the year when the frost has left the surface, and there is limited time in which a plant can reach maturity before the ground becomes

Helenium 'Moerheim Beauty' AGM, an old cultivar with reddish-brown flowers, continues to be a great plant for the perennial border.

solid again with the onset of winter. Thus, there are many reasons why some plants flower and seed later than others and it is by exploiting these differences in flowering time that a gardener can select plants that remain in bloom for so much of the year.

MAJOR PLAYERS

Certain genera dominate at the end of the summer and I shall concentrate on the key family groups, as each has its own particular needs and attributes. Many of them are North American natives, especially members of *Asteraceae* (previously known as *Compositae*), the daisy family.

Asteraceae

It is difficult to imagine an autumn border without at least one representative of this family. Asters, chrysanthemums, dahlias, echinaceas, heleniums and rudbeckias are but a small scratch on the surface of this vast family. There are tender daisies, such as the South African osteospermum and the cosmos from Mexico, which barely survive a hard frost, while others such as *Taraxacum* (yes, the dreaded dandelion) seem almost impossible to kill! Plants hailing from temperate Asia and Siberia, such as *Ligularia*, are tolerant, hardy and easily grown when provided with enough moisture. They have worldwide distribution and may be annuals, biennials, perennials, shrubs or even trees in some tropical areas. There are many botanical tomes, which can be used for reference (see page 201) to understand the botany more fully. For the purposes of this book, though, I will attempt to keep the botanical usage to a minimum but I do provide a useful glossary on page 200.

A typical daisy structure is made up of many individual flowers in a capitulum, which, at first sight, appears to be the flowerhead. On closer inspection it can be seen that there is an outer ring of ray florets and an inner ring of disc florets. These are all attached at their base to the swollen end of the flower stalk – the receptacle. Disc florets usually consist of both sexes and are identical, radiating from the centre. Ray florets do not always have reproductive parts and are characterized by having one side of the corolla extended into a ray, which looks similar

to a petal in other plant families. These are usually showy and colourful – you have only to think of bright yellow sunflowers, rusty red heleniums or the ranges of flower colour in the asters to get the picture. Not all the *Asteraceae* have this simple form but there are always exceptions to the rules. For instance, both *Ageratum* and *Eupatorium* are familiar garden plants, which do not have ray florets but only disc florets. Another characteristic of this family is white, sticky latex or sap, which exudes when stems or leaves are damaged. A good example of this is the familiar dandelion (*Taraxacum* sp.).

Many daisies start to mature from the disc florets on the outside of the circle towards the centre. This can be seen clearly in some of the echinaceas, the cone flowers of North America. Here, the disc florets are arranged in a cone on top of the receptacle and a small ring of fertile disc florets can be recognized by the ripe pollen, often yellow, which appears as a ring round the cone. This is a feature of *Rudbeckia occidentalis* 'Green Wizard', which has a black cone with no ray florets so the maturing of the pollen is more obvious. My main interest in the *Asteraceae* as garden plants is in the ability to attract insects especially in the late summer. Many daisies are fragrant and produce plentiful amounts of pollen, which becomes a magnet for butterflies. A substantial planting of echinaceas or asters will attract large numbers of butterflies, particularly Small Tortoiseshell, Peacock and Painted Lady. Thistles are well known for being caviar to bees and hoverflies. Another daisy with only disc florets, Joe pye-weed is an essential component of the late-summer border for providing nectar for overwintering butterflies.

As many of the *Asteraceae* flower so late in the year, there is a long part of the season where there is little to see in the way of flower. A border which is supposed to look good all season may well suffer if there is a large number of late-flowering plants that do not provide added interest with foliage or stems or growth habit. Therefore if you are trying to combine a border for all seasons try to choose plants that have good foliage as well. There are lots of dahlias such as *Dahlia* 'Bishop of Llandaff' AGM and *D.* 'David Howard' AGM which have good purple foliage and many of the thistles have handsome, jagged grey-green foliage, such as *Echinops ritro* 'Veitch's Blue', *Cynara cardunculus* AGM and

Onopordum acanthium. Some asters, such as *A. laevis* 'Calliope', have beautiful black stems and healthy green leaves; *A. lateriflorus* also has a number of cultivars, such as 'Prince' and 'Lady in Black', with lush purple-black foliage that is a prominent feature in the border. Achilleas can lend dissected grey-green foliage, such as *Achillea* 'Moonshine' AGM, which has yellow flowers; *Anthemis punctata* subsp. *cupaniana* AGM has lovely mounds of silvery-grey foliage with white, yellow-centred daisies. Artemisias can sport almost silvery-white scented foliage; it is often better to remove the flowers so as not to spoil the effect of the shining filigree mound. Ligularias require moist soil, preferably in dappled shade. Some such as *Ligularia dentata* are grown for their foliage rather than flowers. Notable cultivars are 'Desdemona' AGM, 'Othello' and 'Britt-Marie Crawford'. Others may be grown for their form rather than their flowers or foliage. Santolina can be topiarized – more often seen as great globes such as at West Green House at Hartley Wintney in Hampshire, UK, but other shapes could be enforced upon them. In fact when there are large numbers of santolinas planted together the odour of their flowers can be overwhelming. I once spent many days looking for something dead around a bed full of flowering santolinas until I realized it was the inflorescence itself. Small wonder they are fertilized by flies!

Another feature of some of this family is the great height they can reach in a single season. Who can fail to be impressed when looking up at *Helianthus salicifolius* at a mere 3m (10ft) or an annual giant sunflower at 4m (13ft) plus. I never fail to be amused when gazing up at the flamboyant, grossly over-large heads of a strain of giant sunflowers grown at Bramdean House in Hampshire, which are secured to huge stakes, as their stems are so large. A real "Jack and the Beanstalk plant"! *Coreopsis tripteris* is a mere dwarf at 2.4m (8ft), along with several other perennial *Helianthus* and *Rudbeckia* all attaining about 2m (6ft 6in) in a single season. *Leucanthemella serotina* with its pure white daisies and yellow eye on 2m (6ft 6in) stems is a sight to behold before autumn storms ravage the pristine petals and rip the leaves from the stems after shredding them. *Silphium*, another North American native can also tower 2m (6ft 6in) or more in height. They are rather coarse in leaf and not entirely suitable for

Opposite: An aster relative, *Vernonia crinita*, adds rosy-purple jewels of colour among tall grasses and herbaceous giants in the late summer.

the smaller garden but all have their charm. *Silphium laciniatum*, *S. perfoliatum* AGM and *S. terebinthinaceum* are all available at specialist nurseries or can be grown from seed. *Ligularia*, *Sinacalia tangutica* and *Vernonia crinita* often manage 1.5m (5ft) in the growing season, depending on the rainfall and moisture content of the soil. The majority of these giants are in the yellow to orange spectrum, a colour range often spurned by a large section of the gardening community. Maybe there will be a gradual change in the perceived colour taste of the gardening elite and we will see more of these colours being used. Backlit by low autumnal sunlight, and supported with clumps of majestic buff, tawny, rusty and yellowing grasses such as molinias and *Miscanthus*, these yellow giants can indeed be an imposing sight.

Achilleas are almost unique in the presentation of their flowers in horizontal plates and combine well with plants producing spikes like foxgloves, or spheres such as globe thistles, as well as perfect partners for grasses. They are available in a vast range of colours and sizes but can be capricious and short-lived if conditions are not ideal. They prefer an alkaline soil with good drainage and full sun – shades of white, cream and yellow appear to be more tolerant of conditions than varieties with orange, red and terracotta hues. Many of the coloured forms also tend to fade to unpleasant mustard tones, wrecking aesthetic colour combinations with impunity. Well, you can't have everything.

Apiaceae

Another family that is well represented in the latter half of the year is the *Apiaceae* (previously known as *Umbelliferae*). Not primarily for flowering at this late stage, it is good for foliage effects, seed-heads, structure and substance that often persists well into the winter months. As a focal point, the stark silhouettes of cow parsleys covered in hoar-frost with a backdrop of a wintry ice-blue sky are hard to beat. Seed-heads left intact provide much needed food for birds and small mammals, while the hollow stems can be used as winter homes for beneficial insects such as ladybirds and bees.

The main characteristics of the *Apiaceae* are the formation of the flowers in umbels (which, incidentally, gave rise to the original family name of *Umbelliferae*). An umbel is a flat-topped

Above: Silvery-green flowers of *Eryngium yuccifolium*, a New World eryngo from the United States.

inflorescence made up of several flowers; each flower supported by a pedicel (a stem supporting a flower or seed), which all originate from the same point on the main stem. The majority of cow parsleys have small yellow or white flowers that smell slightly foetid and are often pollinated by flies or beetles. The root system is usually a taproot, often edible, such as in carrots or parsnips, or sometimes used as an aphrodisiac, like candied *Eryngium maritimum* roots. The base of the leaves sheaths the stem and the leaves are usually dissected, especially in older foliage. The stems between the leaf nodes are hollow and great for making blow-pipes – and also provide good homes for insect larvae. The whole plant has a characteristic herby smell and many indeed are important commercial crops used for culinary purposes. Imagine cooking without parsley, dill, fennel, chervil, coriander and angelica! Young seedlings of the *Apiaceae* are distinct from many families in their narrow linear cotyledons (primary or seed leaves) and are best sown fresh.

Below: From front to back, soft pink *Saponaria lempergii* 'Max Frei' and *Molinia caerulea* subsp. *arundinacea* 'Transparent' with *Echinacea purpurea*, *Eryngium giganteum* 'Silver Ghost' AGM and *Monarda* 'Scorpion'.

Umbellifers are being used more extensively nowadays, with the movement towards more naturalistic plantings. Seed production is often profuse and seedlings should be kept in check lest giant archangelicas or bronze fennel overrun the border. There is definitely a place for these majestic structural plants along with other members of the family such as astrantias, eryngiums and bupleurums.

Several of the large cow parsleys are monocarpic (a plant that germinates, flowers, sets seed and then dies). They may be annual, biennial or live many years before flowering. One impressive monocarpic umbellifer is *Peucedanum verticillare*, which emerges in spring with pinkish-purple-tinged foliage. If it has taken several years before it flowers, it may reach as much as 3m (10ft) before its pale yellow umbels open to display horizontal flowerheads at angles to the stout stem. Its skeleton will persist well into the winter until it is either cut down or is battered into submission by winter gales. Many of the angelicas provide a strong and substantial presence in the border, among them *Angelica archangelica* and *A. gigas*, which is grown as a commercial crop in Korea for the production of an aphrodisiac concoction. Few herbaceous plants could compete in size with *Heracleum mantegazzianum*, although it must be noted that it is illegal to sell this plant as it causes serious photodermatitis in bright sunlight. Photosensitivity is a feature of many of the larger cow parsleys; indeed Socrates expired from dabbling with hemlock (*Conium maculatum*), which possesses poisonous alkaloids.

Eryngiums, astrantias and bupleurums are also members of the *Apiaceae* and play an important part in decorative horticulture. They all have attractive bracts that superficially resemble petals, while the centre of the "flower" is actually the umbel containing many small flowers. Astrantias and eryngiums are widely used in floristry as both are good as cut flowers. The flowers of New World eryngiums are packed together in green, red or reddish-brown thimble-shaped umbels with fibrous roots; they prefer a relatively rich soil that is not too dry. The more familiar Old World eryngiums have green, grey-green or steely-blue massed inflorescences usually surrounded by sharp, spiny bracts. The colloquial name "sea holly" is an apt description for some of these species. They prefer good drainage, and full sun will intensify the blue or purplish-blue coloration in the bracts, leaves, stems and flowers in species such as *Eryngium bourgatii, E. alpinum, E. planum* and hybrids such as *E.* x *oliverianum* AGM, *E.* x *tripartitum* AGM and *E.* x *zabelii* along with their named cultivars. They have long taproots, which can be used for taking root cuttings when the plant is in its dormant season. These coloured eryngos are highly ornamental and are good material for cut flowers and dried interior decoration. Most of the eryngiums are perennial but there are annual and biennial members of the family too.

Astrantias range in colour from greenish-white through white, pink and ruby red towards reddish purple, and they are perennials. There are many cultivars and seed strains of astrantias which are remontant (they flower more than once in a season). In recent years there have been many excellent introductions from breeding programmes such as *Astrantia major* 'Roma', a sterile, large pink-flowered masterwort selected by Piet Oudolf from seedlings from *A. m.* 'Ruby Wedding', a fine burgundy form. They prefer a moisture-retentive soil and will thrive in sun or dappled shade. The white and green forms, such as *A. m.* subsp. *involucrata* 'Shaggy' and *A. m.* subsp. *i.* 'Moira Reed', are much sought for their fine structure and for use as a cut flower by flower arrangers.

Bupleurums are far less known in subtle shades of green and bronze. All of them work well in naturalistic plantings and most will flower in the latter half of the year. They have a similar flower shape to astrantias but are oh-so-understated.

Lamiaceae

Other plant families also form a substantial proportion of the familiar garden flora. One of these is the *Lamiaceae* (originally *Labiatae* before the botanists changed the name!). This includes most of the aromatic herbs, such as lavender, marjoram, thyme, mint, catmint, rosemary and sage. Not only are they a significant component of many gardens, they are also of great commercial importance for medical, perfumery, culinary and decorative purposes. The majority of culinary herbs hail from the Mediterranean and will tolerate drought during the summer but are less tolerant of being waterlogged during the winter months.

Opposite: Pink and yellow do not always sit well together but in this majestic flowering specimen of *Peucedanum verticillare*, the soft yellow flowering umbels contrast well with the strong architectural pink stems.

Above: A small (20cm/8in) Mediterranean herb, *Origanum amanum* AGM is ideal for a well-drained and sheltered sunny position.

This gives rise to the idea that they are not hardy, but warm, wet winters will cause more casualties than cold, dry seasons. Therefore they are reasonably cold-hardy but not tolerant of too much moisture in winter. Considering the terrain from which they come that is hardly surprising. The salvias and agastaches from Mexico and southern states of North America have similar preferences. My own nursery and garden is on a reasonably light but sticky clay, which holds more moisture in winter than a lot of these plants can tolerate. I have discovered that by raising the level of the beds by just a few inches, and by incorporating plenty of bulky organic material and grit, I can grow many of these herbs with little difficulty unless the winter is particularly wet. For the members of this family from really arid regions, I use raised beds (approximately 45cm/18in high) with a high percentage of grit (60–80 per cent) and compost to give adequate drainage.

The botanical characteristics of this family are familiar to many of us who use them in the kitchen for enhancing and flavouring meals. They have square stems, decussate and opposite leaves, which are usually simple; the volatile oils they possess in small glands give them the aromatic qualities. The flowers are bisexual and are characteristically bi-labiate or two-lipped (hence the original family name of *Labiatae* – from labia or lip). The seeds are usually large bony nutlets, which are a pleasure to collect during seed harvesting as they emerge from the spent flowers cleanly and easily. There can be little doubt as to what is the seed part, whereas in other families identifying the germ is far more difficult. There is often a clear distinction between the upper and lower lip of the flower, with the lower lip acting as a landing stage for pollinating insects. Humming birds pollinate some New World *Lamiaceae* in their native habitats.

For the late-summer garden *Lamiaceae* family members are particularly useful. Many of them have long flowering seasons, which start towards the end of May and continue until the first significant frosts. Cutting back catmints and some sages after the initial flush of flowers usually ensures that a second flush, albeit less flamboyant than the first, will appear towards the end of the summer and into the autumn season. There is also a wide range of colour and form in the family, so choosing different members of it can provide height and breadth in the border. The *Lamiaceae*, as with the *Asteraceae*, are attractive to beneficial insects, to bees, hoverflies, butterflies and day-flying as well as nocturnal moths. It is also true to say that rabbits are deterred from eating most aromatic *Lamiaceae*, although the same is not always true for deer who confound the gardener by changing their garden delicacies during the season.

There are a number of *Lamiaceae* that are tender but provide excellent foliage. One of these is *Plectranthus*, which originates mainly from Africa, although one of the most familiarly used garden plants is *Plectranthus argentatus* AGM from Queensland, Australia. These are best used in containers, where they can stand outside during the summer months and then be taken into a conservatory or cool glasshouse for winter. Luckily they are easy to grow from cuttings in spring and will quickly make up into good-sized plants. I have recently acquired *Plectranthus neochilus*, which has a handsome mound of light green leaves and is covered with small spikes of mid-blue flowers by early autumn. There are many more of these plants appearing on the market with good foliage all summer and the bonus of attractive spires of blooms late in the season.

A large number of the *Lamiaceae* are adapted to drought conditions during the summer months. Leathery leaves, such as those of *Salvia officinalis*, do not desiccate quickly and grey-green or silver foliage, like that of many lavenders and *Phlomis*, reflects some of the heat away from the plant. Herbs, for example, like thyme and rosemary have slender, narrow leaves, often with a slightly inrolled margin, which helps to prevent water loss. It is interesting to note that when these plants are container grown, they often require more water than other plants; I often wonder whether plants that grow in adverse conditions develop a specialized root system which enables them to make efficient use of the water supply available. This would then explain their susceptibility to winter wet.

It is difficult to discuss the *Lamiaceae* without giving a special mention to the salvias, which appear as annuals, biennials, perennials, sub-shrubs and shrubs. They are also available in a vast spectrum of colours and are a valuable addition to the waning season. There are a number of salvias, often of borderline hardiness, which lend a strong vertical accent to the herbaceous

Above: Spikes of *Salvia nemorosa* 'Rosenwein' showing pale pink flowers contrasting with the deep pink calyces.

bed in late summer and autumn. Many of these originate in South America, such as *Salvia guaranitica* and its many fine cultivars including 'Blue Enigma' AGM, 'Argentine Skies', 'Black and Blue' and a handsome hybrid 'Purple Majesty'. *Salvia uliginosa* AGM, another native of South America, graces the border in late summer with long wands of pale blue held well above the foliage, uplifting many of the russet hues of autumn. On a trip to Australia, I was amazed at its frequent use in gardens and how stunning it looked with *Gaura lindheimeri* AGM and roses.

Compton D'Arcy and Rix collected *Salvia patens* 'Guanajuato' on their 1991 plant expedition in Mexico. It is like a taller version of *Salvia patens* AGM with enormous blue flowers and thick square stems up to 2–3m (6–10ft) with a dark central blotch in the otherwise green diamond-shaped leaves. Grown well, this can be a marvellous specimen plant but it often requires some support during windy weather. Not all salvias are giants, many could be considered alpines, such as the Turkish *Salvia caespitosa,* and others are grown primarily for their foliage. Who could fail to be impressed by the handsome rosette of *Salvia aethiopis* or the less divided leaves of *S. argentea* AGM with their tomentose silvery-white foliage resembling nothing more than a recumbent sheep! Martyrs to the attentions of slugs, these are indeed difficult plants to grow well but worth all the effort.

Colour is another important factor in choosing a salvia for a particular site in the garden. There is a wide range of colours available although not all plants will be hardy. The collections by Compton, D'Arcy and Rix in Mexico yielded several hybrids (around the town of Jame) between *S. greggii* and *S. microphylla,* referred to as *S.* x *jamensis* hybrids. Several seed-grown hybrids from this collecting trip were named: 'Los Lirios' AGM, 'La Tarde', 'La Luna', 'El Durazno' and 'La Siesta', to list some of them. Since their introduction there have been many more named x *jamensis* cultivars ranging through white, pale pink to peach, magenta and purple with a few vibrant reds added for good measure. Already well known are the sub-shrubby salvias like *Salvia microphylla* var. *microphylla* 'Newby Hall' AGM and

Tawny grasses provide the backdrop for *Salvia nemorosa* 'Amethyst' AGM in late summer.

S. m. var. *m.* 'La Foux', both basically red flowered, with more of the orange spectrum in 'Newby Hall' and more blue in 'La Foux'.

Many of the familiar garden salvias are perennial such as *Salvia officinalis* and all its coloured cultivars, and the hardy *nemorosa*, *sylvestris* and x *superba* group. In the latter salvias, the colour range is more in the blue, indigo, pink and purple spectrum, often with an attractive contrasting calyx, which really enhances the flower spikes. This is particularly true of *Salvia nemorosa* 'Caradonna', a recent cultivar with good purplish-blue flowers and an almost black calyx and stem. Ernst Pagels, a nurseryman from Leer in north-west Germany, was responsible for the introduction of a large number of excellent *Salvia nemorosa* cultivars, which have proved their garden worthiness by remaining widely available at nurseries. His introductions include 'Ostfriesland' AGM, 'Wesuwe', 'Lubecca' AGM and 'Amethyst' AGM. He is also responsible for extensive breeding work in some of our most majestic grasses, *Miscanthus*, which are also major players in the late-summer garden. More recent introductions of hardy salvias, and indeed most perennials, have tended towards more dwarf and compact varieties that flower well in a container and thus help sales for nurserymen. The proliferation of these "stunted" cultivars is a development which certainly worries me, as so many of these plants are not suitable for garden plantings. I accept that many gardeners have smaller plots nowadays but a host of short plants will only exaggerate the size of the area.

There are many tender and annual salvias that have been used as bedding plants, often in municipal displays of formal plantings with cultivars that have been selected for compact flower spikes and larger flowers to make more of a visual impact. I believe that some of the excellent colours bred in recent years could be used successfully among perennials rather than as massed bedding plants. The pure white form of *Salvia coccinea* could be combined with more strident-coloured flowers or used against dark foliaged plants for a more integrated approach. I recently became acquainted with *Salvia algeriensis*, an annual sage from Algeria, which grows rapidly to as much as 90cm (36in) high with large lavender and buff-lipped flowers. Placed well, it could be a perfect accompaniment for other perennials. Biennials such as the familiar *Salvia sclarea* var. *turkestanica*, with its huge, showy lilac-purple hop-like bracts as it comes up to flower, make a real statement in a border although it is wise to place it where the foliage will not be bruised. Among descriptions of its odour when crushed are "smelly armpits" and "cat's urine" but the smell is a selling point for some of my customers! There is also a white form called 'Vatican White'. Other fine biennials or short-lived perennials include *Salvia argentea* AGM and *S. aethiopis* which have pale bicoloured blooms of lavender-blue and white.

Salvias are so diverse, floriferous and interesting that there has been much written about them (see also pages 170–5).

Poaceae

The grasses (*Poaceae*) form the backbone of many naturalistic plantings. They are in nature the most successful of all plant

species, covering a surface area greater than any other family. Economically they are vitally important in providing a source of nutrition for most of the human population in grains such as rice, wheat, barley and rye. What would cows and sheep eat if there was no grass?

Ornamental grasses generally flower in late summer and through the autumn with their skeletal forms persisting through the winter months. Not only are the flowering plumes spectacular but many grasses exhibit good autumn colours in rich reds, russets, gold, yellow and straw, which are particularly breathtaking when backlit by a low seasonal sun.

The family is characterized by parallel venation in the leaves and stems are usually round, often hollow with solid hard nodes. Flowers appear in spikelets and are usually pollinated by wind so

Grasses dominate the autumn border with tones of straw, buff, pink and green. Seed-heads of *Veronicastrum* (left foreground), globe thistles, *Veratrum nigrum*, *Digitalis ferruginea* AGM and E*ryngium* add texture, while small jewels of colour are provided by *Thalictrum*, *Astrantia* and *Knautia macedonica*.

Above: The crimped flowerheads of *Miscanthus sinensis* 'Roland'.

Opposite: Elegant spires of *Digitalis ferruginea* AGM provide strong vertical accents in late summer.

copious quantities of pollen are produced, the bane of hay fever sufferers! Many grasses are able to spread by underground rhizomes that can root at the nodes as they grow and produce new shoots. Couch grass (*Agropyron repens*) is one of the most successful of the rhizomatous weed grasses and a curse to most gardeners. Unfortunately, some of the grasses first developed for ornamental use exhibited these characteristics such as 'Gardener's Garters' (*Phlaris arundinacea* 'Picta') and this prejudiced their use in many gardens. Other species seed freely and can quickly colonize large areas but are usually easier to control than rhizomatous species. Examples include *Stipa tenuissima* and *Anemanthele lessoniana* (syn. *Stipa arundinacea*). There are many excellent clump-forming grasses that do not invade the garden and it is the responsibility of nurserymen to ensure that more of these non-invasive types are available. Others should carry a Government Health Warning!

Some of the main grass families used in ornamental plantings include *Deschampsia, Molinia, Miscanthus, Panicum, Pennisetum* and *Stipa*. Old growth is cut down in early spring and as the year progresses the plants grow and look just like grass! A border that has 10–25 per cent ornamental grass content flowering in autumn will show little of its potential until late July and August, but with the grass foliage playing an important supporting role in the general greenery and health of the bed. As summer progresses the grasses will begin to dominate the scene until they put on their dramatic if muted display in late summer. Their grace and mobility in the slightest breeze gives an extra dimension to the late-summer border and I would certainly not wish to be without them.

Scrophulariaceae

Flowers massed in spires and spikes give important vertical structure to the naturalistic or herbaceous border. The Scrophulariaceae, the snapdragon or figwort family, are well represented in the late-summer line-up with towering verbascums, foxgloves and veronicastrums contrasting with the more diminutive penstemons, antirrhinums and toadflaxes. For sheer flower power they are of great importance, as many genera bloom for several months until the first hard frosts.

"Scrophs", as we call them in the trade, exhibit a wide variation in flower shape and size although they are usually zygomorphic (which means that the flower can be divided symmetrically in one plane only; consider a single foxglove or snapdragon inflorescence and cut it in two to leave identical mirror images – excruciating word, simple explanation). Seed is usually small, and there is plenty of it; it is formed in hard capsules, so many of this family like foxgloves and toadflaxes will happily seed around. Flowers are often tubular or bell-shaped and pollinated by insects. I get great pleasure from watching the bees pollinating the foxgloves, disappearing up each trumpet in turn, accompanied by much buzzing and humming, to re-emerge a few seconds later with haunches covered with pollen. Mind you, many of my bees are now cheating, biting their way through the neck of the flower and stealing the nectar without participating in the assault course up the trumpet!

Many members of this family have flowers in rather muted tones, which associate well with fall colours in russets, gold and straw. Several verbascum hybrids have buff, apricot and cream flowers combining seamlessly with ornamental grasses. Rusty foxgloves such as *Digitalis ferruginea* AGM and *D. parviflora* have brown or russet flowers, mimicking faded seed-heads of veronicas and veronicastrums. Penstemons exhibit a large range of shades and can contribute splashes of colour at low level. In general flowers in this family are relatively small but massed together in spikes or spires. Seldom gaudy or ostentatious, the *Scrophulariaceae* provide the background in which other plants can strut their stuff.

Bulbs

Many bulbs produce showy displays in late summer and autumn and a garden would be much poorer without them. Bulbs are classified into several families but for the purpose of this book I have taken the liberty of lumping them together as they are a major player in the late-summer line up. Not all are in flower in late summer and autumn but may contribute to the general appearance of the border with structural seed-heads and skeletons. Drumstick alliums are a case in point. *A. cristophii* AGM

and *A. schubertii* have spectacular dried flowerheads, which, like tumbleweeds, roll away when the seed is ripe. This usually occurs in late summer or autumn and until then their bleached seedheads are an interesting structural component in the border.

Other drumstick alliums, although not so dramatic, produce a framework of tall lollipops accentuating their earlier glory. Some ornamental onions do flower during late summer and autumn. *Allium sphaerocephalon* produces numerous egg-shaped heads of purple flowers in late July and combines particularly well with grasses such as *Deschampsia cespitosa* 'Goldtau'. *Allium cernuum*, the nodding onion, flowers in July and onwards with fairly large blooms of rosy purple dangling in loose clusters on swaying stems. *Tulbaghia* sp. flower throughout the latter part of the season if the weather is favourable.

Bulbous plants are useful components of the ornamental garden as they tend to take up little space, conducting their growth and flowering in a relatively short time and then disappearing

Below: Groupings of autumn bulbs such as *Colchicum* 'Rosy Dawn' AGM and *Cyclamen hederifolium* AGM can liven up a woodland border or a shady corner in early autumn.

underground safely within their storage organ or bulb. Not so with all of them. Crinums and *Amaryllis* produce copious mounds of foliage, as do colchicums and many of the large kniphofias. The dying leaves do not contribute to the ornamental garden but should not be removed as nutrients from the decaying foliage are required for the bulbs. It is best to find a place for them where the foliage is not so noticeable but the flowers can be admired.

The heady scent of lilies is redolent of balmy summer evenings and whether container-grown or planted in the garden they add an extra sensory dimension. Many bulbs have sweetly scented flowers, including *Amaryllis*, some tulbaghias (besides the strong onion odour from the roots) and some of the species *Gladiolus*, a far cry from the blowsy cut flowers used by florists.

It is important to note where bulbs are placed in the border when it comes to clearing the debris from the previous season. Spearing or slicing precious bulbs with a garden tool is disheartening and can be avoided with care and an accurate planting plan. Healthy stands of agapanthus, *Nerine bowdenii* AGM or *Sternbergia lutea* can be a real showstopper late in the season while clumps of *Crocosmia*, *Schizostylis* and *Kniphofia* uplift the late-summer border. The range of bulbs available to the gardener ensures flowers throughout every month of the year.

These five families or groups of plants contribute the bulk of plant material flowering in the latter half of the year but there are many other families that act as a supporting role to the dominant characters. They enhance, augment and complement the stars of autumn planting.

The selection of groups playing a major or minor function is highly subjective and I have based my choice partly on the sheer numbers of plants involved and those that I consider to play an important role in gardens I admire or have designed for late-summer interest. I make no apologies for my preference but am fully aware that this list is not exhaustive.

Above: Slender spikes of *Kniphofia* 'Buttercup' AGM mix well with grasses and crocosmias in August and September.

MINOR PLAYERS

I have a passion for plants that produce life-giving nectar for beneficial insects, especially towards the end of the growing season when insects need to store highly nutritious food to survive the winter months. Perhaps it is because I enjoy my food so much that I wish my garden helpers to benefit from the plants they pollinate and keep free from unwanted pests.

Dipsacaceae

The scabious family (*Dipsacaceae*) has a large number of plants with a long flowering or late season which are ambrosia to bees and butterflies. Free-draining alkaline soils in sun appear to be the optimal requirements for the majority of this family, conditions that I do not have on my nursery. However, I have discovered *Succisa* and the related genus *Succisella*, which have small button-like scabious flowers on wiry stems, flowering from 30–90cm (12–36in) in late summer. A colour range through white, cream, primrose, pink, rose and blue is available and the insects love them. Not the most spectacular perennials but good as companion plants and they do tolerate a moisture-retentive soil, are hardy and will even thrive in dappled shade.

Teasels are strongly architectural specimens often with vicious spines and thorns ready to slash unsuspecting passers-by. Usually biennial, producing a prickly rosette in the first year, they elongate to as much as 2.4m (8ft) in the following season. They will thrive in poor soil in full sun providing nectar for insects, especially bees when in flower, and seed for many small birds through the winter. I love to watch the antics of charms of goldfinches feasting greedily on these architectural giants. No less imposing in height are many of the *Cephalaria* sp., some of which also have persistent skeletons through the dormant months such as *C. dipsacoides* and *C. radiata*. They have scabious-like flowers of cream or primrose and can be used at the back of the border with coarse-leaved giants such as *C. gigantea* or nearer the front for species such as *C. dipsacoides*, which is just as tall but has a structure of strong wiry branches that can frame the plants behind it, similar to the effect of *V. bonariensis* AGM.

The genera usually considered to represent scabious are *Knautia* and *Scabiosa*, which thrive on calcareous soils in sun with

Fragrant spires of *Actaea simplex* Atropurpurea Group 'Brunette' AGM combine with *Sanguisorba officinalis* and the graceful *Molinia caerulea* subsp. *arundinacea* 'Transparent'.

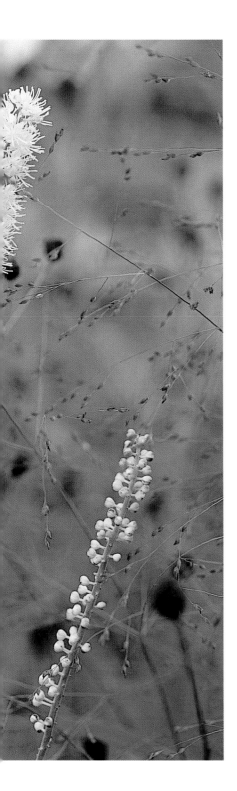

good drainage. I can grow them reasonably successfully on my raised gritty beds, especially the smaller flowered species such as *S. columbaria* and *K. macedonica*. *Scabiosa caucasica* and its cultivars with large blue, cream or white salvers do not flourish so well. By experimenting with different varieties and species I have a good collection of this family, which flower over many months, providing nectar for many hungry beneficials.

Rosaceae

Herbaceous perennials of the *Rosaceae* (Rose family) generally flower in midsummer and beyond. Notable examples are *Geum*, *Potentilla* and *Filipendula*. Other less familiar genera, such as *Gillenia* and *Sanguisorba*, are at their peak later in the season with some varieties of burnet blooming as late as October. *Gillenia* is a North American woodland genus although it appears to thrive in the UK in more open and sunny habitats in moisture-retentive soil. *Gillenia trifoliata* AGM sports delicate white flowers in midsummer giving way to delightful russet seed-pods through autumn with good red and bronze foliage tones. *Gillenia stipulata* extends the season and is a similar plant with more lax growth.

The real gems of the *Rosaceae* for late-seasonal interest are, for me, the sanguisorbas. There are few species but in recent years additional wild collections notably from Korea, China and Japan have extended the flowering season by many weeks. A fine collection from China by Dan Hinkley, inspirationally referred to as *Sanguisorba* sp. DJHC535, waves its small red buttons aloft through September and October and is perhaps the latest flowering of the *officinalis* form of burnet. An introduction from Korea collected in 1993 by Compton, D'Arcy, Christopher and Coke is similarly imposing in early autumn. Akin to *Sanguisorba tenuifolia* 'Alba' with its splendid, slender, white catkin-like tassels, this lovely 1.8m (6ft) perennial possessed the moniker *Sanguisorba sp.* CDC late-flowering form. Recently more happily renamed *Sanguisorba* 'Korean Snow', it is truly beautiful reflected in water on a still autumn day.

Nurserymen and gardeners growing several burnets together in a small area are finding great promiscuity among the species and some wonderful hybrids have appeared in recent years. Many sanguisorbas have small, slightly insignificant flowers compared to the mass of glossy pinnate foliage but have a quiet subtlety that I adore. A good nursery friend with a wonderful turn of phrase described the flowers of a form of *Sanguisorba officinalis* as being "like a swarm of small raspberries" – how succinct. I would not be without them.

Ranunculaceae

The buttercup family (*Ranunculaceae*) is much in evidence early in the year with spectacular displays of *Helleborus*, *Hepatica* and *Trollius*. Autumn-flowering species are generally not so dramatic but provide good structural features. Nobody could deny that the inflorescence of the late-summer flowering monk's-hood, such

Right: *Scabiosa caucasica* 'Miss Willmott' AGM is a magnet for bees and butterflies.

Opposite: Pink stems and a froth of cream flowers atop this noble giant, *Thalictrum pubescens*, in late July. The skeleton persists well into the early winter months.

as *Aconitum carmichaelii* Wilsonii Group is anything less than impressive as is a vigorous clump of Japanese anemones in full bloom. Thalictrums, however, are often wind pollinated and have relatively small flowers with a froth of dangling stamens and copious pollen released by the gentlest breezes, as in *T. lucidum* or *T. pubescens* (syn. *T. polygamum*). Some are pollinated by insects and tend to have coloured sepals around the stamens, rather like a Victorian crinoline, and are mildly scented to attract their pollinators. These include familiar species like *Thalictrum rochebruneanum* and *T. delavayi* AGM. Many meadow rues are tall, between 90cm–1.8m (36in–6ft), with delicate pinnate leaves reminiscent of an aquilegia, indeed *T. aquilegiifolium* is named for this very reason. Some species have an almost bluish-green bloom on stems and leaves, especially conspicuous in *Thalictrum chelidonii*. The winter skeletons of aconitums and meadow rues stand like sentinels against the cold, clear winter skies.

Another valuable and imposing member of the buttercup family to flower through the latter half of the year is *Actaea*. *Actaea simplex* and its varieties and cultivars are probably the most familiar bugbanes used in gardens. They prefer moisture-retentive soil in sun or dappled shade producing lusty mounds of dissected foliage and strong flowering stems with large white or cream fragrant spikes to 1.8m (6ft) or more from late summer onwards. Dark-bronze foliaged forms are extremely popular, requiring full sun and moist acid soil to develop the finest bronzed coloration, which acts as a magnificent foil for the contrasting white flowers. 'Hillside Black Beauty', 'Brunette' AGM and 'James Compton' are all good examples of dark-foliaged forms and 'Pink Spike' has pink-tinged buds and flowers. Other fine varieties with greener leaves include 'Mountain Wave', 'Prichard's Giant' and 'Scimitar'. I feel that they are underused in gardens and hope this will change. Smaller specimens of *Actaea,* but no less worthy or beautiful, include *A. matsumurae* and its cultivars. 'White Pearl' has beautiful green foliage with creamy white spikes to 1.2m (4ft) while 'Elstead Variety' has dark stems and similar upright flowering candles. There are other species, some with yellowish tinged blooms and some that have a foetid smell but all are good, useful garden-worthy plants for late-seasonal interest. Use them.

Creating the Habitat

I have always supported the premise that a garden full of beneficial insects helps to create an environment that is balanced and ecologically sound. There may be unwelcome outbursts of aphids or other deleterious insects but with good populations of beneficials, these outbursts can usually be contained.

In general, I prefer an organic approach to gardening and rarely use noxious chemicals. However, I am not a purist and if one insect pest becomes a problem I will try to use biological control and, if that fails, integrated pest management. I would resort to chemicals only to clear an outbreak that might threaten the healthy balance. Birds are also of great importance in a garden and will remove thousands of insect pests during a single day. I am fortunate in living in a rural area surrounded by trees and shrubs, many of them native. These provide nesting sites and cover for all manner of wildlife, good and not so good for a gardener. I fervently believe that a balance should be sought where the gardener and the wildlife can co-exist to mutual satisfaction.

I am aware that I am privileged in where I live and that suburban and city dwellers have far more to contend with in lack of verdancy. Soils are often compacted and damaged around built-up areas and the surrounding spaces are often planted with non-native species, which do not encourage our native insects and birds to the same extent as the true countryside. Over-enthusiastic feeding and watering can lead to lush growth and susceptibility to damage by mechanical means, such as wind, which can cause secondary fungal and bacterial infections. Bruised foliage and stems release odours, which may be detected by unwanted aphids. Once they have located a damaged plant, it will be only a matter of hours until there is a substantial aphid infestation, as they can breed so rapidly. There is no doubt that the aphid is a severe pest in suburban locations.

An exuberant late-summer bed with the egg-shaped purple flowers of *Allium sphaerocephalon* emerging through clumps of blue and white agapanthus and gypsophila. Repeat planting lends cohesion to the border.

Plant breeding has led to many flowers being sterile, which, although beneficial to the gardener by reducing the amount of deadheading, usually means that little pollen or nectar is produced. This obviously is not so attractive to beneficial insects. I know that I am constantly referring to insects but in sheer numbers they far outweigh any other wildlife and are probably the most important factor in our garden environment. Many gardeners are totally unaware of their invisible populations but part of my enjoyment in the garden is the continual background humming and buzzing which for me denotes a healthy site.

In recent years there has been a move towards gardens using native wildflowers as the sole source of plant material to attract indigenous wildlife. Indeed, in an earlier incarnation, my original nursery concentrated on wildflowers to encourage

Drifts of *Verbena bonariensis* AGM, *Gaura lindheimeri* AGM, teasels and clumps of *Calamagrostis* x *acutiflora* and *Molinia* cv link this naturalistic planting.

beneficial insects. Sadly, in those days, "wildflowers" were considered synonymous with "weeds" and it was a decade later that this direction in gardening became popularized and implemented by more than the small minority of the "hair shirt" brigade. I have never restricted my choice of insect-attracting plants to British natives as I am aware from observation that many "foreign" plants play a major part in providing sustenance. Nobody could deny that *Buddleja* sp., opportunistic shrubby plants from Asia, America and Africa that colonize the most inhospitable crevices between buildings and on wasteland, are the focal point for many nectaring butterflies. especially towards the end of the summer season. My choice of plants encompassed species from all over the temperate world that would satisfy the appetites of my voracious six-legged friends.

In this chapter, I summarize a few methods of creating different habitats within a garden situation to successfully grow a wider range of ornamental plants. The underlying soil and its condition will exert the most influence on what will grow best but there are many methods of tweaking the nutritional value, moisture-content and structure of the earth to allow scope for experimentation with a different floral selection. You can also create other features which will help to extend the range of plants grown.

Soil type

Selecting and growing plants that attract beneficial insects is one way of creating a habitat in a garden situation. However, there are many factors that can influence the success or failure of such a project. A basic understanding of the soil type and its drainage is most important in the selection of suitable plant material. There is little point in trying to grow a subject that hails from a hot, arid environment in cold, boggy ground or a moisture-loving shade plant in an exposed sunny position with sharp drainage. Many plants are tolerant and forgiving of a vast range of conditions, which allows the gardener a wide choice of material to exploit.

In general, the underlying soil type will be the greatest influence on the plants that can be grown successfully. If, for instance a gardener detests or reviles acid-loving flora, it would be sensible to obtain a plot of land that is alkaline or neutral. Small alterations of the pH can be achieved by various means but they usually take some time or are expensive to implement, such as removing the inherent earth and replacing it with topsoil of a different character. Why make more difficulties by changing the natural habitat and order in such a bullish fashion? If, as I mentioned before, a floral type is anathema to the gardener then every effort to obtain a garden with suitable soil should be made and the problem will not arise.

Removing and replacing earth is indeed a drastic measure to alter the structure and pH of a piece of land, but most gardeners do change the structure and condition of their soil in more subtle ways. Different habitats can be created by these less extreme methods and a wider range of plant material grown in

consequence. Adding a mulch, be it organic or inert, will alter the nature of the ground by changing the transfer of moisture to the atmosphere. Plants require moisture in the form of water, oxygen and light to photosynthesize and grow. The use of a mulch retains moisture in the ground and enables plant roots to access and assimilate the water more easily (see also pages 61–4).

Drainage

This is one of the most important aspects of a garden and can be responsible for the success or failure of its plant community. The majority of garden plants currently grown for ornamental use in temperate climates prefer good drainage and plenty of light. Reasonable drainage is especially important in winter as many plants are cold-tolerant but not wet-tolerant in the colder months. A garden that is waterlogged in winter will have many more casualties than would a cold, dry site. If a garden is sited in an area with a high water-table or if it is waterlogged in winter, there are still many plants that are adapted to these conditions but it will restrict the choice available to the gardener. If a garden is to be built from scratch it is relatively easy to install a drainage system, either tile drains or a perforated polythene pipe. In areas of thick clay, mole drains can be used to break up the subsoil and carry excess water away from the surface. It is best to use experienced drainage companies for this task as a waterlogged site can lead to great expense, disappointment and disturbance in an established garden.

Improving drainage is a key step in creating a different habitat on a particular plot. Adding organic material either as mulch or by digging it in will also alter the properties of the soil and enable a wider range of plants to be grown successfully. Clay soils are often referred to as heavy or cold soils as they have a multitude of small pores that have a high water-holding capacity coupled with slow drainage. Earth with a high water content takes a lot longer to warm up in spring than a quick free-draining soil, which contains a high proportion of dry air space, allowing plant roots to penetrate easily. The pore structure of clay soils is easily

An ethereal look and magical mood can be achieved when grasses are backlit by low sun.

damaged in winter and wet conditions. If there is too much surface activity, either human or machine, it puddles the clay particles, reducing the number of drainage pores, and causing waterlogging of the soil. (This feature of clay has been used to good effect in creating ponds and pools for livestock to drink fresh clean water throughout the year and so generating another habitat for a different range of plants.)

Free-draining soils allow plants to grow more quickly in spring as the soil begins to warm but they can be at a disadvantage during periods of drought during the summer months when there is little water accessible to the roots. Clay soils hold more life-giving water during these times but extreme drought can prove disastrous for a wide range of soils. The use of any sort of mulch applied during wetter, cooler months can prove invaluable at this time by reducing surface evaporation.

Lessons to be learned

It is obvious from this discourse that the underlying nature of the soil and its drainage play a major part in the range of plants that can be grown successfully. Adventurous gardeners will not restrict their activities to growing only the "easy" subjects but will try ornamentals that are at the edge of their growing parameters. In some seasons they may be successful, in others they will meet with dismal failure. There is no doubt that with increasingly mild winters, gardeners have experimented with more tender plants and been able to keep them alive from one season to the next. If, as predicted, this last winter was the coldest for a decade, many of these "tender" plants could perish, allowing gardeners to renew or review the selection of plants they grow. A severe loss of one genre could inspire a new trend in the plants used in gardens. Nature is dynamic and natural selection occurs to maximize the potential of individual species within a given set of parameters. As gardeners, we have the ability and knowledge to use different types of plant material to achieve spectacular combinations and effects. I am always

Cylindrical red burrs on the wiry stems of *Sanguisorba officinalis* contrast well with the large leaves of *Darmera peltata* AGM. Both plants relish moisture-retentive soil.

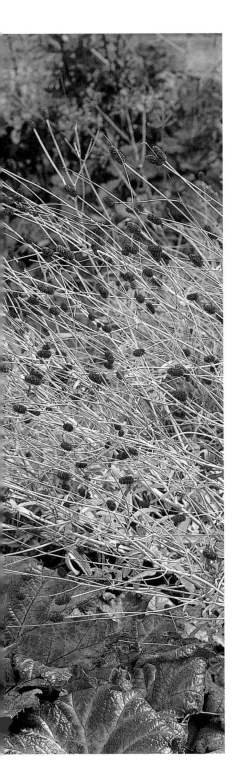

excited by the wealth of new plants that I discover each year and am content in the knowledge that there will always be something interesting that I will be able to experiment with.

My nursery site is an open field so there is no shade for a range of plants that I am very partial to. The most obvious solution would be to plant shrubs or trees to provide shade in future years. I am far too impatient to wait that long so I built a timber building with laths to give 50 per cent shading to the raised beds I had created inside the wooden structure. Not only do I have instant shade beds but the raised areas allow me to gaze at my treasures at waist height, rather than grovelling around at ground level. It also enables me to have some control over the nature and pH of the earth contained within the raised structures. My underlying soil is a sticky, claggy clay with a pH of 6.5–7.0, so it is neutral to slightly acid. Many shade-tolerant plants are most vigorous in an open-structured medium with plenty of leaf mould and humus, tending towards an acid pH. In general, leaf mould is an acidic organic material. When creating my shade beds I formulated a woodland mix, which contained bark, loam, grit and leaf mould, to give me an open, friable soil with an acidity around 6.0–6.5. So far my woodland plants have thrived in this well-drained, moisture-retaining mixture.

As a gardener I would provide dappled shade by planting deciduous trees and shrubs. It is remarkable how quickly they will grow if planted young and provided with optimal conditions of light, good drainage and a well-prepared and humus-rich soil. Within a few years, I would remove the lower growth of the woody plants to leave me space to plant bulbs like aconites, snowdrops and spring squills with herbaceous shade lovers such as hellebores and Solomon's seal. To maximize my success I would introduce organic material in the form of humus and plenty of leaf mould. Deciduous trees and shrubs drop their leaves each autumn, adding to the leaf mould, and, during winter, light and moisture penetrates the undergrowth to give new life to the dormant bulbs and woodlanders lurking in the shadows.

The benefits of raised beds

The term "raised bed" is not restricted to an area with a well

Many herbaceous borders become raised beds in effect, with the annual increment of mulch, enabling a wider range of plants to grow successfully. In this border, a yew hedge acts as a backdrop to interesting foliage clumps such as *Melianthus major* AGM (on right) and the purple-foliaged dahlias. Flower colour and foliage types have been carefully selected to give added texture and interest to this luxuriant border.

defined, formal outline of stone, wood or other material. Many fine herbaceous and mixed borders could be described as raised beds, with the incremental addition of an annual mulch. In time the depth of the soil increases and plant roots penetrate and break up the soil into smaller fragments enabling greater soil porosity and improved drainage. A more extensive range of plants will benefit from these subtle changes over the seasons.

Raised beds are an excellent method of creating different habitats relatively easily and within a tight budget. Wooden sleepers or stone walls can be used to contain the soil. By raising beds, drainage is immediately improved and a wider range of plants will grow successfully. The beds do not have to be all that deep; just raising the earth 10cm (4in) on a clay soil will increase the selection of ornamentals grown. Most of my raised beds are

30–60cm (12–24in) deep over my clay soil. I have not used a membrane between the natural ground level and my infill. Reject stone (5cm/2in in diameter) forms a layer about 10cm (4in deep) and the rest of the infill is based on my specifications for the various types of bed I am trying to create. I have already mentioned my woodland mix but the majority of my raised beds are gritty mixes. I am particularly interested in plants that grow on chalky soils as they encompass many herbs, such as scabious and cornflowers, which are especially attractive to insects. Both these genera are not very tolerant of my wet and sticky clay. My gritty mix is made up of 80 per cent 1–3mm ($^{1}/_{16}$–$^{1}/_{8}$in) grit mixed with 20 per cent loam and has a pH around 7.0 or neutral. As a result, I am able to grow an interesting range of cornflowers and scabious with few or no problems.

Raised beds can be filled with all manner of different mixes to support the growth of plants with vastly different requirements. Using an ericaceous compost, which is open-structured and acidic, many calcifuge (lime-hating) genera could be grown such as *Calluna*, *Gentiana*, *Gaultheria* and *Vaccinium*. If the bed was large enough small specimens of *Azalea* and *Rhododendron* could be cultivated. I have found that most perennial plants will survive favourably in raised beds of 30–45cm (12–18in) and do not require a greater depth. I am sure that there are bound to be exceptions to this rule but I have not come across any so far.

Scree and alpine beds can be constructed and are usually raised beds without the boundaries of sleepers or stone. Embedded rocks of various sizes are positioned in such a manner to provide a maximum of crevices and cracks for alpine plants. Loose grit, gravel and sand on sloping areas provide habitats for plants needing exceptionally good drainage.

Vertical elements

Walled or partially walled gardens create a different environment where plants that would fail in more exposed situations can thrive. A dense hedge may have a similar effect and although it will extract some of the available moisture it will at least give some shelter. Sunny walls create unique habitats and allow many tender plants to burgeon. Not only do they provide shelter from wind, but heat from the sun is absorbed, radiated and reflected to varying degrees, depending on the colour and material of the structure. Pale walls reflect heat, enabling very tender specimens to survive and thrive. Dark walls absorb more heat, which radiates slowly, and help to give a plant an early spurt of growth. Walls, fences, trees and any other structure providing height open up a habitat for clinging and climbing plants. Not all climbing plants are self-clinging and may need some support

Hedges and walls can provide a sheltered environment so that it is possible to experiment with less hardy subjects and large specimens, like *Macleaya cordata* AGM, *Vernonia crinita* 'Mammuth' and *Eupatorium purpureum*, here benefitting from the warmth reflected off the light walls. In this planting, large groupings of grasses interweave with monardas, lythrums, astrantias, sedums and achilleas.

from the gardener in the form of trellis, ties, netting or obelisks. Others require no help, using tendrils or twining and twisting their growth upwards towards the light. Roses, clematis, morning glory and sweet peas are all familiar species that appropriate verticals to flaunt their aerial splendour.

Water features

Ponds, pools and lakes can be created to add a static watery dimension to gardens, whereas rills, streams and waterfalls will add a mobile aspect. Durable butyl liners are the most flexible means of building small- to medium-sized ponds and pools to the specification of the owner. There is a large range of semi-rigid structures for small ponds, but these often have minimal shallow marginal areas for plants or for wildlife and birds to wash and drink. Butyl liners allow the flexibility of changing the shape or depth of a pool once excavations have started.

My first experience of building a pond was a case in point. I had painstakingly mapped out the dimensions, margins and depths of my dream pond only to find that the deepest part was on the site of an old external water closet and outbuildings. After excavating several tons of bricks, the shape of my pond altered significantly on one side to allow the area over the bricks to be an extended marginal area and the deepest part of the pool to be sited in easily dug earth. Lakes and extensive pools are usually excavated by machine and lined with concrete or puddled clay.

Bog gardens and extensive marginal areas can be made by removing earth, laying down a membrane and backfilling with the excavated soil. The subterranean membrane inhibits normal drainage and a boggy, waterlogged environment quickly ensues. This is a suitable habitat for many large structural plants such as *Gunnera manicata* AGM, *Rheum* sp., *Ligularia* sp., *Iris ensata* and *Iris sibirica*. Ponds and lakes are suitable for many aquatic plants including water lilies *Nymphaea* and *Nuphar*. Running water is essential for water plants requiring high concentrations of oxygen, such as some of the aquatic *Ranunculus* sp.

The dramatic seed-heads and dark mahogany stems of *Ligularia* show up well against a backdrop of bamboo and *Miscanthus* foliage. The brilliant fall colour of the shrubs and trees uplifts this lakeside planting.

The Dynamic Garden

Nature is capricious and one season is never totally similar to another. Each season there are plants that excel themselves in growth, quantities of flower and autumn foliage colour, and so on, while others sulk or die. A garden represents a small patch of more or less controlled nature, depending on the activities of the gardener, but the major factor will be the seasonal conditions. For me, it is the seasonal variations that are the lifeblood of my interest in my garden. I may wait all year for the bud on a tree peony to unfold in all its glory, just to have it snapped off by a vicious gale or a marauding flock of birds intent on stripping plants of all their juicy buds! Yes, it is a disappointment, but there will always be some other plant that will surpass all expectations and invoke admiration and elation in its observers. After all, there is always another year and I feel that it is the element of surprise – that there is always something to look forward to – that keeps many gardeners so smitten with their own piece of Paradise.

As plants mature in a garden there will be some that become too dominant and, either insidiously or by sheer thuggery, start to take over while others dwindle. It is down to the skill of the gardener to observe this phenomenon and rectify the problem before plants are lost altogether. Taking periodic photographic records can serve as a reminder of plants that have passed by without their loss being noticed until it is too late. As gardeners, we all make mistakes and it is the process of learning from these errors that tends to produce the most satisfying relationships with the garden.

In the depths of winter, browsing through nursery catalogues it is all too easy, as an armchair gardener, to plan out perfect beds and borders with aesthetically pleasing colour schemes. Naturally you place the plants the correct distance apart and their eventual heights and widths will all meld into a flawless picture. In reality, the pink phlox you chose as companion to the stately purplish-blue delphinium has too much orange in its hue and clashes appallingly with its neighbour. The grass you placed at the front of the border with the delicate ferny cow parsley behind insists on growing 2m (6ft 6in) high whilst the umbellifer

Strong verticals and horizontals: towering verticals, represented by *Macleaya*, *Verbascum*, *Aconitum* and *Atriplex*, are tempered by the flat horizontal plates of achillea flowers and the spherical heads of globe thistles.

sulks at a miserable 30cm (12in) behind it. It happens to us all and there is only one thing to do; move the offending plant to a more suitable position, compost it or give it to an unsuspecting acquaintance. Otherwise, cut it back so that it flowers at a different time to its neighbour. Many of my plants could write interesting travelogues on "my journey around the garden".

Moving plants

To move herbaceous perennials successfully, a little preparation will increase the chances of survival and reduce the "shock" of the transfer. Give the travelling subject a good healthy soaking, preferably with rain water, which is far more organic than the chemical concoction from the tap. Try to take at least a spit's depth of soil and root with your plant, as well as some soil around it, depending on how close together you have planted its companions. I prefer to use a spade as it gives a clean cut and severs roots rather than tearing them. The new planting hole should be well excavated, slightly deeper and wider than the transplant, with a good layer of worked soil and compost at the base. Gently lower the plant into the hole and add compost until it is at the same level as its previous home. Half-fill the hole with soil and then water copiously until the water does not drain immediately; then leave the plant to settle. When it has eventually drained, fill the rest of the hole with compost.

Perennials are accommodating plants and, with enough soil around their roots and plenty of water on replanting, they usually grow away quickly after a move. If the weather is very warm and dry, it may be necessary to cut the plant back hard so it is not losing too much water through transpiration and allows the roots to take up sufficient moisture to satisfy the remaining foliage. Perennials that have been cut back severely often bounce back with renewed health and vigour. In natural drought years many plants lose their lower leaves and weak stems shrivel; in severe dry spells the whole of the emergent growth may die back to be reinvigorated as soon as they have a good soak, either from rain or as the result of watering.

It is probably more useful to move a plant which disrupts the preferred colour scheme when it is in flower, so it can be seen against other potential neighbours. If it is more suitable in

Opposite: Intense fall colours, with orange-red heleniums taking centre stage, a magnificent *Miscanthus sinensis* cultivar in the background and what looks like hazy pink *Panicum* in the foreground. Minor players include *Sanguisorba tenuifolia* and *Persicaria amplexicaulis*, adding soft pink tassels and fiery red tapers respectively.

Below: A drift of *Monarda* 'Cherokee' – a first-class cafeteria for bees and hoverflies.

another position, it can then be cut back and replanted with plenty of water, but at least its colour is not an unknown. If it turns out to be too tall or too diminutive, or does not thrive in its new position, it will begin its journey once more.

Transplanting errors in the placing or sowing of annuals are not a viable option, as most annuals do not respond well to being moved unless they are very small plants, in which case they may not have reached flowering maturity. It would be better to dig out the offending plant and sow again with a more suitable candidate. As annuals grow so fast, a later sowing would probably give good results but with a delay of a few weeks, thus extending interest into the later season.

There are some plants that do not respond well to moving, and it would be best to start off with a new plant if you wish to retain it somewhere in the garden. Alstroemerias are a good case in point. With their long, brittle white roots, they are difficult to move at the best of times and deeply resent disturbance. The roots are so long and tenacious, ending in a swollen storage organ, that it is rare to succeed in digging up the entire root ball.

In the northern and southern hemispheres, as the late summer and autumn progresses, the morning and evening shadows grow longer as the light reaches the earth at an ever-decreasing angle. This can be harnessed to create magical effects in the garden as the angled golden light passes through suitable diaphanous plants. If areas of the garden which receive this light are not utilized fully, this is surely the time to lift and reposition plants that could enhance this wondrous phenomenon. Slanting evening sunbeams passing through a clump of *Stipa gigantea* AGM or early morning tendrils of the dawn light enhancing the vertical variegation of *Miscanthus* 'Morning Light' AGM can be breathtaking and uplifting. The cones of *Echinacea* or the arching stems of *Crocosmia* can appear to be on fire as the sunlight catches them in silhouette.

Some perennials grow too delicately to compete with more vigorous neighbours and once identified should be removed to an area where plants with similar growth rates will not suffocate them within a season. There are also those plants that defy all the rules in the gardening manuals and sulk in areas that should be congenial to their existence. They obviously have not read the books. I usually will try a plant three times and if it still does not thrive with me I choose something else. I have always admired *Romneya coulteri* AGM, but it sulked with me on clay, and did so again when I gardened on a heavy moisture-retaining loam. I built a special gritty bed for it (80 per cent grit) with added loam and bark, and it now behaves like a thug. It now runs in all directions, pokes its stems out of the retaining timbers of its customized home and ousts other precious plants, which I thought would also enjoy the gritty conditions. Similarly *Convolvulus althaeoides,* which resented my ordinary garden soil, has become an invasive pest in a smaller raised gritty bed.

Opposite: *Deschampsia cespitosa* 'Goldtau' – magical when backlit by evening sun.

Below: *Calamagrostis* x a*cutiflora*, *Miscanthus sinensis* and *Stipa gigantea* AGM seen in low sunlight behind a swathe of purple sedum in the foreground.

Strutting their Stuff

Once planted, a border can be left to its own devices and will respond primarily to soil and weather conditions. There are, however, many different techniques and applications that will improve the performance and well-being of the plant communities in the garden.

In *Creating the Habitat* (see page 38), I touched on the influence that the underlying soil type and structure have on plant growth. To maximize the potential success and growth of particular plants there must be some understanding of the conditions that the plant requires or will tolerate. This can be understood more easily if you know something of the conditions

in which the plant originated and then do your best to mirror these factors as closely as possible in the garden environment. Most soils can be improved by a variety of methods, which does not necessarily always mean enriching the basic soil structure. The ultimate requirement for all plants is to have water and the ability of a particular plant to obtain it. Taking the opposite extremes of drought-tolerant plants on the one hand and bog plants on the other, there are distinct differences in plant physiology in allowing water uptake. Many bog plants will have shallow root systems, large leaves – often with margins displaying guttation (which means they secrete water droplets from) – and high growth rates. Drought-tolerant plants, conversely, may have reduced leaves, an extensive and deep root system or a taproot, which enables it to extract water from a

Flowering grasses, seedheads and late-flowering perennials combine to create interesting textures and colours in autumn. Fiery tapers of *Persicaria amplexicaulis* 'Firedance' blend with flowering grasses such as *Calamagrostis brachytricha* and *Miscanthus*, while muted brown seedheads of *Monarda* and *Veronicastrum* add shape and form.

wide area in width and depth respectively. It has always interested me that in container-grown plants, drought-tolerant species, such as many lavenders, salvias and *Cistus*, require far more water than plants which cannot tolerate drought. One explanation is that the root system of these plants is insufficient to take up as much water as they require when container grown. Indeed, the term "drought tolerant" is a bit of a misnomer as these plants appear to need large supplies of water which they are able to acquire when planted by using their extensive root system. This theory is also supported by the fact that growers and nurserymen adapt to their own specific composts and conditions by the amount of irrigation they supply to the plant material. A plant can grow quite happily in media as diverse as rock wool, water (hydroponics), sand, peat, coir and other substrates, as long as they receive water and the correct balance of nutrients. In most cases the soil acts as an anchor for plants in gardens and it is the ability of the plant to marshall the uptake of nutrients and water that is the determining factor in whether it thrives.

This may well sound like heresy to those gardeners who spend long hours improving, enriching and conditioning their soil for the welfare of their plants. There is no doubt that working a soil will aid a plant to produce a better root system and therefore eventually increase the efficiency of water uptake. I have never been entirely sure that feeding a soil is a necessary factor in the welfare of all plants, however, as many natural habitats are relatively nutrient-poor. Plants growing in well-fed soil are often larger specimens but sometimes more lush in growth and therefore increasingly susceptible to pests and diseases. As with all living organisms, there is a wide variation between different plants and a healthy garden is often a collection of plants that will grow and thrive in the particular conditions your garden provides. Finding plants that suit your specific conditions is the secret of a healthy garden community.

In nature there is a large natural wastage of potential material and only the strongest and fittest survive. Of course, some plants will grow in more favoured positions and have a head start on

Deep purple and pink spikes of *Stachys officinalis*, with a massed planting of *Echinacea purpurea*, form an arresting sight in late summer.

others. In a garden situation we often expect every plant to live and thrive without accounting for natural wastage. There are a number of means to maximize the success of these plants including soil improvement and mulching, and staking.

SOIL IMPROVEMENT

This can refer to a number of different treatments of the basic earth on your site and the plants you may wish to cultivate.

If you have waterlogged soil and do not want to grow bog plants, soil improvement may include laying land drains. In a heavily compacted soil, soil improvement would include opening the soil structure up by digging or rotovating.

Chalk soils are often only a few inches deep before solid chalk is encountered and require huge amounts of humus-rich material and/or grit to give a good depth of soil for the majority of plants to thrive. However, chalkland plant communities are some of the richest in species, albeit that these plant species are often small and ground-hugging. It depends on whether you wish to garden with your soil type habitat or provide the conditions to grow a wider range of plant material. Many chalk soils are neutral or alkaline, which will reduce the range of plants that can be grown.

Clay soils are often cold, sticky and difficult to work, and can be conditioned with grit, open humus-rich material, such as mushroom compost, hop waste, leaf mould and bark. Gypsum is useful in breaking up clay soils into a more friable, easily worked soil, whereas manure on clay soils, and the inclusion of sand, can make this type of soil even more sticky and difficult to work. It is better to use a material with a more open structure.

Sandy soils can be difficult to condition. They are warm and easily worked, but usually very well drained and prone to drought. Many sandy soils are also quite acidic which will reduce the range of plants that will grow successfully to those which are acid-tolerant. In dry years plants grown on sandy soils may show many symptoms of nutrient deficiencies, with yellowing leaves and poor growth. These soils require large amounts of organic matter to help retain some nutrients in the topsoil, and annual conditioning is the most successful method of combating this

Below: Bold foliage can look impressive without the need for abundant flowers, providing a green tapestry for small bursts of colour. Many large-foliaged plants, including the gunnera and ligularia in this border, require plenty of moisture. Beds heavily mulched with organic material can increase the water holding capacity of the soil, enabling a more luscious "jungly" foliage effect to be created.

loss. Again, there is a wide range of plants which tolerate, and thrive in, these conditions, especially ericaceous perennials and shrubs. The amount of soil conditioning you require will depend on the range of plants which you wish to grow.

Mulching and soil conditioning are sometimes lumped together as one operation. Many mulches do improve soil quality but not all of them. They are usually used as a thick top-dressing over the soil, which acts as a blanket to reduce moisture loss from the soil and insulates it from cold and frost. A further valuable feature is that many mulches help to reduce weeds or make it easier for weeds to be removed. It is better to apply a mulch on a border after substantial irrigation, preferably from rain water, which contains fewer chemicals than mains water. If the soil is dry when mulch is applied, some of the organic mulch materials can soak up available moisture from the soil, and also from further rain or artificial irrigation, preventing moisture reaching the plant roots.

There is a wide range of materials used as mulches. Landscapers often use textile mulches as a weed suppressant, then cover the material with bark or grit. Plants are placed in position by cutting a hole in the textile and digging a hole in the soil beneath. It is a useful method for amenity planting but I feel it is unsatisfactory for many small gardens where plants may need to be moved around regularly (see *The Dynamic Garden*, page 55) and opportunist plants can seed around with impunity. Unless a good depth of bark or grit is used over a membrane, you can often catch a glimpse of the membrane at surface level, which I find very jarring in an otherwise natural environment.

Recently I saw an advert for mulch made out of recycled tyres. As with textile mulches this will persist rather than break down with time, which I feel is not a good idea in the garden. I prefer natural and organic mulches for use in my own garden and top them up annually, or when the need arises. For me, the resultant reduction in weeding on my heavy clay soil is a real bonus and I am able to work the soil all year round instead of for a few months in spring and then in late summer and autumn. I prefer mushroom compost as it is bulky, sterile and I can throw it over my borders with impunity. I attempt to leave an area around my perennial clumps clear, as a thick layer of moist organic material may result in fungal diseases and rotting of perennial stems and shoots. Mushroom compost is not satisfactory for all gardens and all plants, as there is a tendency for it to release calcium carbonate (soluble chalk), which can increase the alkalinity of the soil with annual treatments. As I prefer chalk flora, I am not averse to a slight increase in alkalinity which may enable me to be more successful with plants such as various *Scabiosa, Centaurea* and *Knautia,* which thrive best on an alkaline soil.

I also use substantial quantities of grit and gravel as a mulch. Incorporating grit and gravel into a soil creates an anomaly. Not only does the soil become better drained, it also becomes more moisture-retentive. The surface area of the grit and gravel holds moisture in the surface tension around each granule. This can be easily accessed by a good plant root system. I enjoy growing many Mediterranean and Mexican plants which do not thrive on my sticky, heavy clay. However, by creating gritty raised beds, I am successful with these plants and have never watered the beds

Below: *Molinia caerulea* 'Variegata' AGM requires a moisture-retentive, slightly acid soil. A mulch of grit, as seen here, can reduce the water lost from the soil surface, creating moister conditions for the plant to utilise. In the background a pennisetum can be seen, with its arching caterpillar-like flowers; this is a grass that is equally at home with a gritty mulch but requires far less moisture to succeed. The root systems of these two plants will adapt to take up the amount of water needed to thrive.

Above: Attractive to bees, the long spires of small, slightly fragrant white flowers of *Veronicastrum virginicum* 'Album' provide strong vertical accents in late summer.

Opposite: Staking with a difference. Exuberant perennial planting is supported with split posts and woven hurdling to make an interesting structural feature. Note the continuation of the woven wood around the tree trunk in the background.

once the plants were established. In 2003 I experienced a 14-week drought with high temperatures and the plants survived without additional water, albeit becoming a little distressed. Also, although I am in a frost pocket, plants that are considered to be tender have survived through cold winters. My gritty mulch provides an insulating blanket through the coldest months but keeps the plants dry at the neck enabling them to survive. Winter cold is not the greatest killer of my drought-tolerant plants, it is winter wet that is the main enemy.

Mulch is important to late-summer and autumn flowering plants in that many of the species, which flower at this time, require moisture to keep in growth the entire season. Mildew is a major problem for late-flowering plants and is usually a symptom of water stress, especially after a summer drought. Bulky organic mulch is infinitely more preferable to me than resorting to a fortnightly fungicidal spray to reduce the incidence of mildew. Some of the most susceptible plants of the late summer and autumn are *Aster novi-belgii* cultivars, monardas and phloxes. Organic mulches are beneficial for soil conditioning as earthworms pull the organic material down through the soil profile, opening up the porosity of the soil. Many North American native plants, which flower in the late summer and beyond, are large prairie plants such as *Silphium, Vernonia* and *Echinacea*. In prairie habitat, the wealth of plant biomass, grass and thatch, act as an organic mulch over the root systems of these late-flowering perennials.

STAKING

Many herbaceous perennials will flop if they are not supported in some way. A well-stocked border may be self-supporting but this is the exception rather than the rule. Using a strict regime of pruning, plants can be grown shorter than their usual height but this can sometimes detract from their natural elegance and grace. There is no doubt that feeding and cosseting plants will ensure increased vigour but staking will be more necessary. Growing perennials hard (without extra feeding) produces stronger, leaner material, which may escape the necessity for artificial support.

Many gardeners with conventional herbaceous borders automatically stake the young growth when it attains a third to a half of its eventual height. This can be achieved by using a wide range of plant supports from hazel twigs to metal hoops, string and wire. Whatever the method, it is preferable that the support is discreet and does not become the overwhelming visual appearance in a planting. In many naturalistic borders, plants are only staked if and when necessary.

In recent years, gales and gusty winds occur at all times of the year. These capricious breezes can have a devastating effect in a voluptuous planting. I would recommend spending the time and effort to ensure the plants have the best conditions to grow well with efficient staking. My preference is to use hazel twigs or some other organic material for support as at the end of the season everything can be cut down and disposed of – secateurs and other cutting devices can be severely damaged when trying to cut through metal plant supports!

There are many attractive supports, such as obelisks and arches, which add another visual dimension to a planting and can often add strong verticals. I have some elegant obelisks which are attractive in their own right, and during the winter months I will often move them around the garden as points of interest. In a dynamic garden plants are not alone in being moved around! I also have some zany, rusted, metal supports with a spiral twist and wooden finials that are great *objets d'art* as well as being excellent temporary supports to recalcitrant plants. During the growing season they are seldom obvious but as foliage dies down during the autumn and winter their structure is revealed.

Plant supports can be temporary or permanent features. Strong metal arches add interesting structure to this bed, as well as supporting the growth of a vine. Mass planting of annual *Cosmos bipinnatus* fills the foreground.

Manipulating the Seasons

The title of this chapter may lead the reader to believe a certain amount of alchemy is afoot. However, there are many different ways that a gardener can extend the flowering season, alter the time of flowering, and even the height and spread of the typical plant growth. Once the basic concepts of plant growth are understood it is easy to see how plants can be manipulated to suit the grower. Many nurserymen automatically treat their plants so that they are able to produce them at a time when there is optimum chance of selling. Without considering their actions as such, they are indeed manipulating the seasons.

The plants cultivated in gardens hail from all over the world and in temperate climates will flower at a particular season. Plants from tropical areas may also have specific times of flowering but, once brought into another climate and time zone, may alter their flowering periods. For instance, diascias native to South Africa have a short flowering period before they face drought conditions, and therefore flower and set seed in a relatively short time span. In more temperate climates, such as the United Kingdom, diascias will flower for many weeks or months and indeed may bloom throughout the British growing season. Therefore, by growing plants away from their native habitats, their flowering seasons can be altered substantially.

Annuals can be described as plants that complete their life cycle within a single season. Seeds germinate, a young plant grows to maturity, flowers, sets seed and perishes, leaving its seed to be dispersed for future generations. This growth habit may also be termed monocarpic in that the plant will only flower once, producing viable seed and then perishing. Monocarpic refers to "one seed" or, in easier terms, "one seed

Orange and purple flowers combine for a sumptuous display late in the season. Asters, *Perovskia*, catmint and verbena provide the purple tones, while dahlias, *Lobelia tupa*, *Leonotis leonurus* and *Eschscholzia* supply the orange highlights. *Melianthus major* AGM adds architectural foliage effects.

set" before dying. Annual plants are all monocarpic but monocarpic plants are not all annuals. Some species may take several years to mature sufficiently to produce a flower spike and mature seed after which the original plant will succumb. This feature is evident in many of the *Apiaceae* and is indeed used by gardener and horticulturist alike to alter growth patterns. Many *Angelica* species are biennial, in that they grow foliage only for one season and produce flowers and mature seed the next, followed by death of the original plant. It is occasionally possible to prolong the life of these "biennials" by removing the flower stems before the seed has matured. This will often fool the plant into producing an offshoot at its base, which will persist and flower the following year. The control of growth and differentiation in plants, as in animals, is usually regulated by chemicals which, in the case of plants, are usually called plant hormones. It is likely that the mature seeds produce hormones which provide a signal to the parent plant, resulting in its death. The fact that removing immature flowering stems usually promotes renewed basal growth suggests that the chemical message to cease active growth has been prevented. Yet again, it is all down to hormones!

Deadheading

The knowledge that removing flowers before seed has matured will alter plant growth has far-reaching effects for the gardener and nurseryman. Deadheading has been used as a method of prolonging flowering for centuries. In reality, it is a delay in the chemical message sent by the maturing seeds that plant growth and flower production can cease as the new generation (in the form of mature seeds) has already been formed. Therefore flowering can be prolonged for many days, weeks, and sometimes months, by regular deadheading. Many plants which normally flower during early summer can have their flowering prolonged into the autumn with this method, which is equally successful with annual, biennial and perennial plants.

Successional sowing

However, in the case of annuals, there are alternative methods for producing flowering at different times. By the very nature of an annual, successive sowings will produce crops at regular intervals throughout the season. It is by experience that one can get to know how late a particular plant can be sown to produce reasonable results. At Great Dixter, in Sussex, the successional sowing of both annuals and perennials for annual displays has been honed to perfection.

Perennials as annuals

Prolonging the flowering season of perennials can also be tweaked in a number of ways. As with annuals, some perennials are suitable for sowing as annual crops, in fact as you would employ bedding. Plants such as *Gaura lindheimeri* AGM and many *Gazania* hybrids, as well as many of the *Lamiaceae,* such as *Nepeta, Salvia, Dracocephalum* and *Origanum,* will flower in the first year and flowering time will depend on the time of sowing. Thus a plant that usually blooms in spring can be fooled into creating a good display during the autumn. This, however, will adjust back to the normal flowering period during the following year, so to achieve similar effects the perennial would have to be sown annually. Beware of complacency – many useful tips are gleaned and gathered by error and chance, along with the vagaries of seasons. It may work to perfection one season and be a complete failure the next, which is one of the reasons why gardening is so challenging and refreshing. The performance of altering sowing regimes is time-consuming and an imperfect art as the weather conditions have a large bearing on the results. Cool, wet summers with low light levels may delay blooming altogether whereas hot, dry seasons can shrivel a potential masterpiece in minutes.

Selective pruning

Another method for altering flowering times and heights of perennial plants, which can often be more reliable than sowing regimes, is selective pruning. This requires experimentation by the gardener to suit their particular area and conditions, and will alter seasonally due to the prevailing weather conditions. Tracey DiSabato-Aust has written extensively on methods of pruning, disbudding and pinching out perennial material (see page 201).

Above: *Gaura lindheimeri* AGM will flower in the same year from an early season sowing and can be used for annual displays, as seen here with penstemons.

Opposite: Umbellifers such as *Angelica archangelica*, which normally grow as biennials, may produce new basal growth if the spent flowerheads are removed. However, as they seed around profusely, it would seem a shame to remove a good source of seed for the birds.

Again, those hormones are to blame. Apical dominance, the means by which a plant usually grows with a strong vertical leader, is controlled by plant hormones, which are present in the apex or growing point of a shoot. Amputating the tip of a shoot will eliminate the hormone that prevents the development of side branches. The terminal shoot will always be the first to flower as it is best developed. Therefore removing the tip, with the subsequent development of side shoots, will cause a delay in flowering time as the plant puts on the new growth necessary for bud and flower production. Taking this one step further, if more than the tip of the shoot is removed, the plant will require longer to recover and develop the necessary material for reproduction. A delay of several weeks before flowering could be achieved with a little experimentation. Selective pruning by removing apical shoots alters the number and size of flowers and the height at which blooming occurs. In general, the flowers will be more profuse and slightly smaller and the eventual height of the plant will be reduced. This may be a feature that the gardener may wish to encourage with very tall plants such as *Helianthus* 'Lemon Queen' AGM, which usually flowers at over 2m (6ft 6in) in autumn. By cutting it hard (by about a third of its growth) in early summer, this sunflower can be encouraged to bloom at a height of 90cm–1.2m (36in–4ft), which may be more suitable. Cutting perennial giants back severely does not always produce the desired effect and I have seen specimens that look stunted and unsuitable in their surroundings from suffering too drastic a removal of shoots too late in the season. Another positive reason to cut back perennials so that they flower shorter is that it creates less work with staking, especially if you happen to be gardening on a windy site.

The effect you wish to achieve will require experimentation or a good dose of luck but it is labour intensive and not for everyone. It is really about the degree of control you wish to assume in your patch of land and the amount of time you have to spend on it. Selective pruning on clumps of perennials can

Giant perennials such as *Helianthus* 'Lemon Queen' AGM and *Eupatorium purpureum* subsp. *maculatum* 'Atropurpureum' AGM could be pruned judiciously during the growing season to reduce their final height.

give an extended flowering time by treating various parts of the plant in slightly different ways. For instance a well-established clump of *Phlox paniculata* could be pruned more extensively at the front of the patch, more lightly in the middle and least, if at all, at the back. This would enable flowering to start at the back, followed by the middle and then the front, by which time the back could be deadheaded, then the middle and lastly the front to allow a second flowering in a similar order. Pruning in this way would prolong the flowering season by several weeks and for many perennials that naturally bloom during mid- to late summer this could encourage flowering well into autumn. Not every perennial will respond in the same way to this treatment and other factors such as day length and temperature play a part.

Disbudding

There are a small number of perennials which flower so late in the season that they may not have started blooming before the first severe frosts of the autumn. *Chrysanthemum* 'Emperor of China' is one example of a perennial that often blooms well into autumn. There are also many examples in the *Aster* clan and for these individuals, which are regularly frosted before flowering, there is a method that could bring them into flower prematurely. Those of you who have bought or received flowers from the florist will be aware of the huge blooms of plants such as *Chrysanthemum* that have been raised under constant glasshouse conditions. The size has been achieved by disbudding – the removal of some or all subsidiary buds on a flowering stem, allowing the terminal flower bud to develop without competition for food or light. This results in a much larger flower head than if the plant grew without interference and will usually hasten flowering time. If late-flowering perennials were disbudded to some extent, there would be a chance to get some earlier but larger flowers before imminent frosts.

Selective pruning and staggered sowing regimes offer the basis for extending the flowering season by judicial manipulation. However, each garden will respond differently and seasonal variations in weather patterns will be the major factor in the success or failure of tweaking nature. It would be a mistake to lay down immutable rules because no season mirrors another.

The Bountiful Border

As a general rule the most successful and relaxing plantings are those that contain large drifts of the same plant – in effect a limited palette but with increased numbers. Planting a new border or any area can be expensive at the start, and if there is a limited budget it can be useful to create a new bed in stages. It is a good idea to create a theme that runs through a planting – maybe a repeating grass – to tie it together into a cohesive whole. So it may be wise to spend a large proportion of the available budget on the backbone of the border and simply infill with fast growers and annuals for the first season. There are many suitable annuals that are both subtle and elegant, do not immediately strike one as "bedding plants" and can be useful tools until other main components of the planting are mature enough to divide, take cuttings from or produce seed. But the beauty of a predominantly perennial bed, as opposed to, say, one with shrubs, is that a large amount of growth can be produced within a single year of planting, often yielding material for propagation within weeks or a few months.

Propagating from your own plants can be a most satisfying experience and there are many weighty tomes that will explain exactly how, when, and why to produce new plants. I have to admit to being rather daunted by these worthy volumes as, being a natural rule-breaker, there appear to be far too many rules and regulations for my liking. If, after following all the instructions to the letter, you are unsuccessful, it is easy to feel a failure and be unwilling to try again. I was fortunate to follow a scientific subject at university and spent much of my mis-spent youth experimenting, and often failing to get the results I was trying to achieve. It taught me many important lessons, which I try to convey in my propagation courses that I give at my nursery.

Leaving seed-heads such as those of salvias (in the foreground) can add to the rich textures and variety of a late-summer border. In this combination, plants have been allowed to mingle and merge so that swathes of monardas and heleniums meld with eupatoriums and filipendulas, with several small-flowered members of the pea family scrambling through the whole.

- There are many methods to propagate successfully. If you find a way which works for you, stick with it.
- Experiment – never be afraid to try. If it doesn't work, all you have lost is a bit of time…and who knows, you may find an easy technique which isn't in any of the text books.
- Observe your plants. Often their habit of growth will inform you how to propagate them. For instance, an iris or similar material will split easily if you follow the line of growth.
- Ask experienced gardeners what they do – they often have useful tips and will show you what works for them. A practical demonstration from a friend can often teach you far more and far quicker than anything you can learn from a book.
- Show the plant who is master. If you approach plant division in a timid fashion you are more likely to spend more time touching the plant, bruising stems and leaves, and generally abusing it. Think of it as though you were making scones: the faster you prepare the mixture, the better the end result. Plant division is similar but it will take time for you to gain the confidence to divide your perennials with impunity. Ask a friendly nurseryman what they do when they divide plants – it may come as a bit of a shock!

There are three main methods of propagation: seed sowing, cuttings and division. I will try to give a resumé of the basic techniques that I use but do remember there are many equally successful methods.

SEED COLLECTION AND SOWING

I have always found that gathering the harvest is one of the most pleasurable activities of the gardening year. Picking fruit warmed by the sun, digging up a clump of fresh potatoes, picking some leaves off a culinary herb or shaking fat, ripe seed into a glass bowl all fall into the same enjoyable category. When stocking a garden with plants, the expense involved in purchasing ready grown specimens can be prohibitive, so collecting and growing from seed is a cost-effective alternative, which is both satisfying and very rewarding.

Opposite: *Papaver somniferum* – seed-pods of the opium poppy with its bluish-green surface bloom make ornamental and interesting shapes for late summer while its tiny seeds are dispersed from small holes, like a pepper pot.

Seed sources

Your own garden can be the source of large quantities of seed that you can then sow to increase numbers of plants you already have. Friends' and neighbours' gardens and other places you visit may also provide the origin of new material, but please always ask permission to beg a pinch of seed. Gardeners are a generous bunch and are usually pleased to share plants with others, but so often have I heard of, and seen, the devastation left by acquisitive and greedy visitors who have removed seed-heads from rare and wonderful specimens which were unripe and therefore lost to everybody.

In autumn and early winter there are numerous mail-order seed catalogues that drop onto the front door mats of keen gardeners. Full of mouth-watering descriptions, enhanced colour photographs and copious instructions for achieving the best results, these lists keep me entertained for hours during the dark winter evenings. I always scour the lists for new plants that I have not grown before, highlighting those I would like to try, and writing lists before realizing I am way over budget, at which point I pare them down to a manageable size.

Meanwhile, in a cool, dry room are the seeds I gathered from my own harvest waiting to be sown. It is often daunting to read manuals about anything; collecting and sowing seed is no exception. Pages of dos and don'ts may easily deter the faint-hearted from ever trying something new. It is important to dispel the myth that you need to be an expert to achieve success so here are a few basic concepts that will aid a favourable outcome.

Collecting your own seed

There are so many ways that this can be achieved; running a small specialist nursery as a commercial enterprise is a time-consuming business so I have little of that precious commodity to waste. I have evolved methods to make my seed collection efficient for my needs. The majority of plants produce seed that is surplus to the requirements of even the most prolific nurseryman so it is totally unnecessary to remove every last seed. Many seed-heads are elegant and architectural, providing late-summer interest, as well as a food source for birds, and a template for the gossamer webs of spiders. The seeds of most

Opposite: Lily seed-pods – these ripen from green to brown as water is reabsorbed into the parent plant, and they eventually split longitudinally to scatter the light, winged seeds.

Seed collection

Collecting seed of *Verbena bonariensis* AGM by tapping it into a glass bowl **(below)**.

After blowing away the chaff, clean seed is decanted into a labelled paper envelope **(bottom)**.

late-summer flowering plants are not ripe until early autumn and it becomes a race to harvest the germ before the wet, windy and frosty weather sets in. Hence seed collection should be limited to dry days, preferably late in the afternoon when any dew will have evaporated and the evening moisture has not begun to settle. When setting off on a seed-collecting mission I gather the following items together in a large cardboard box:

one or more glass bowls

kitchen towel

pen or pencil

paper envelopes (recycled), various sizes

fine tweezers

scissors or secateurs

What are my tools used for? In general I try to clean my seeds while I am on site. This means that I am not taking vast quantities of plant material into the shed, garage or house with their attendant wildlife. Many plants will yield enough ripe seed if you simply vigorously shake the seed-heads over a glass bowl. This also means that once the seed has been collected the seed-heads remain intact on the plants and can provide autumn interest. I like to use a 15cm- (5–6in-) diameter round Pyrex bowl with a small flat base. I do not use plastic because many seeds become static and stick to the sides of the bowl. I tend not to use metal bowls either because, although they do not suffer from static, they are not transparent and it is not always possible to see whether all the seeds have been cleaned out before collecting material from other plants. The kitchen towel is used to clean out my bowls before collecting from other plants; the pen or pencil is essential for labelling the seeds as they are being collected, preferably with name, date and year of collection. All the collected seed is placed in paper envelopes: the cleaner the seed, the smaller the envelope required. It is important to keep paper seed envelopes in a dry place before use as the glue holding the seams together will unstick and valuable seed will be lost through the base of the envelope. I also use fine tweezers for extricating certain seed that will not shake out easily. A good example of this is *Eryngium* where the seed is held fast in a prickly head. The tweezers are used to gently comb the seed out of the head in a stroking action.

Scissors or secateurs are occasionally required if I do have to remove a whole flower stem with its attendant seed-heads and place them upside down in a large envelope.

Which is the seed?

This is a question I am asked frequently and some botanical knowledge is useful in this context. In nature seed is dispersed by water or air, or by birds and animals including insects, either as passengers on fur or feathers or via the alimentary tract after being consumed. Hence some seeds are winged or have parachutes such as those of *Acer* and *Centaurea* respectively, which are disseminated by air currents. Others have waterproof or buoyancy mechanisms in the seed coat (or *testa*) and are dispersed by water. These plants are mainly outside the scope of this book as they are usually aquatic. Some seeds are surrounded by hooks, barbs, thorns or burrs which catch in the coats and feathers of wandering wildlife, such as those of *Eryngium* (barbs) and *Cynoglossum* (burrs). Many trees and shrubs have large seeds encased in an edible coat, such as those of *Malus* and *Taxus*. Once ingested these seeds pass through the alimentary tracts of various fauna, the digestive enzymes often releasing the seeds from dormancy. Defecated seeds have a moist, fertile substrate to germinate in. Thus there is an infinite variety of shapes and sizes of seeds to be collected.

As a general rule seeds and seed-heads or capsules begin to turn from green to brown as they ripen. Some plant families such as the *Ranunculaceae* require prompt sowing as they are not long-lived. These can be collected while still green although I tend to do so as they are just turning colour. Seed capsules with small seed often open at the top when the seed is ready and air currents are sufficient to provide a pepper-pot effect. A good example of this is the opium poppy (*Papaver somniferum)* but others include *Penstemon, Verbascum* and *Lychnis*. These are a pleasure to collect; just hold the bowl under a ripened stem, give it a shake and the seeds pour out into the waiting vessel. So do weevils, spiders, chaff and other creepy-crawlies – it is amazing how much insect life is present in ripening seed-heads! When you have sufficient quantity of seed for your requirements the fun begins – swirling the bowl gently in your hands (rather like

Collecting seed of *Eryngium* with tweezers **(above),** gently stroking the seed out of the spiny seed head without pain!

Types of seed
Different types of seed **(top)**.
Packaged and labelled **(above)**.

a fine glass of wine) with the leading edge slightly lower than the one closest to you, blow steadily but gently into the wind. This, in theory should allow the chaff to fly out of your bowl, leaving you with clean seed (in the majority of cases the chaff is lighter than the seed itself). Don't sneeze, don't cough, else no seed. Blow too gently, too much chaff. Hold the bowl at the wrong angle and you get chaff all over your face and in your hair. It's like flipping pancakes; you need plenty of practice and confidence. Once your seed is relatively clean (you can always finish the cleaning process inside at a later date), pour it into an envelope keeping the flap open. This will allow creepy-crawlies to escape before you take them into your house or shed.

I usually store my collected seeds in their paper envelopes in a cardboard box in a cool, well-aerated room or shed, out of direct sunlight. Using paper and cardboard allows absorption of excess moisture. However, it is important not to dry the seed too much; it tends to inhibit germination or even kill the seed. I believe that many seed firms do dry their seed excessively and I am often disappointed with the low germination rate I get when using bought-in seed. In a quiet moment, during the autumn, take out the box of seed and transfer the seeds to small grip-seal bags or glassine envelopes (used for stamps). Both grip-seal bags and glassine envelopes can usually be obtained from a good stationery supplier. Always label the packets with the plant name and preferably the year of collection, and carry out additional cleaning if necessary. Although placing seeds in plastic bags is not usually recommended I find that it adds to the longevity of the material as long as it is placed somewhere cool, dry and out of the light. I find unfinished pine drawers (such as those you can obtain from furniture stores like Ikea) fit the bill. Many seed firms recommend placing clean seed in the fridge – it is something I have never done and, with the quantities of seed I collect, would certainly preclude me from storing any food!

Autumn is the time that most plants yield their fruit and especially so with late-flowering plants which we are considering here. Therefore, it is the natural time for a seed to be shed onto warm, moist soil and left to survive the winter either in its hard coat or as a young seedling. Germination at this time can be very good although the vagaries of the winter season can take their toll on small plants. As an insurance against winter loss I tend to sow both in autumn and late winter/early spring. Many seeds require cold stratification and allowing them to receive frost often breaks any germination inhibitors and allows the seedlings to grow. This is particularly the case for members of the *Apiaceae* family which seldom germinate until they have been frosted.

I sow my seed in square plant pots (10 x 10 x 10cm/4 x 4 x 4in) using a home-made sowing mix. I have never found a proprietary seed-sowing compost that I liked so I created my own. Different materials work for different people but the mix I make works for my method of seed sowing and germination. I mix equal parts of a sterilized peat-based seed compost with a soil-based John Innes formula (it really doesn't matter if it is grade 1, 2 or 3) and a 1–3mm (1/16–1/8in) washed grit. This is all passed through a large mesh sieve (approx. 1sq cm/1/2sq in holes) to remove the largest particles. Mix it all up in a large clean wheelbarrow and you get a heavy, gritty, open compost which will be free-draining but moisture-retentive. I loosely fill my pots with this mix, then tap them on the potting bench and use a tamper or, in my case, a "professional pot plonker" which fits the size of the pot. This is just a bit of flat wood with a handle, which allows me to lightly pack the compost down to an even smooth surface.

I like to prepare my seeds and labels inside the house where it is clean so everything is ready for sowing. Writing labels and mixing compost usually ends in tears. Before I sow, I place a label in the pot of tamped compost, then gently sow the seeds directly and evenly from the envelope into the pot. I rarely touch the seed I sow; there seems no need to handle it more than necessary and maybe inhibit germination from the oils from one's skin. I then place about 0.5cm (1/4in) of my fine grit over the seed and tamp again to get the seed in direct contact with both seed compost and grit. Despite most books describing a multitude of ways to germinate different seeds I use the same method for all, with a good success rate.

Why cover with grit?

- The interface layer will hold a thin film of moisture, which allows germination to occur without the seeds drying out at any time, which is the main reason for germination failure.

Seed sowing preparation
Fill pots with sowing mix of a third each sterile John Innes soil-based mix, sterile peat-based sowing compost and fine grit **(below)**.

Tamp the surface for an even surface for sowing **(bottom)**.

Sowing seed

Label the pot and sow seeds evenly across the surface of the compost **(below)**.

Cover with a fine layer of grit and tamp again to ensure seed and seed mix are in contact **(bottom)**.

- There are several seeds that require light to germinate and instructions are given to leave them uncovered. A covering of 0.5cm (¼in) of grit allows enough light in to enable germination.
- The grit also helps to reduce the amount of moss (or liverwort), which often invades seed pots.
- It helps to make the young plant stems strong as they push up through the grit.
- In general, there is less problem with botrytis and fungal disease as well.

Once the seeds are sown I place the pot in a container of rainwater (another departure from most instructions about seeds) and allow the water to rise by capillary action. Once there are signs that the water has reached the layer of grit I take the pot out of the water and place it in a cold frame outside, out of direct sunlight. I will only cover the frames with lights if there is excessive rain or snow and will only water again if there is a long period of drought. Otherwise the seeds are left to get on with it. Most perennials will germinate within a season but some of the grasses and most of the shrubs will take longer, possibly up to three seasons. It is important not to be too hasty in throwing away seed pots which have not germinated within a few weeks.

When the seeds have germinated they are ready to pot or prick out when you feel able to handle them. I tend to move my seedlings on, while very young, into root trainers (small deep pots) and they grow on quickly in a cold polytunnel. If you do not have root trainers it is best to pot up the plants you require into small pots. I use 10 x 10 x 10cm (4 x 4 x 4in) pots to sow seed as this enables the seedling roots to grow unchecked for a longer time than is possible in a conventional seed tray and it also uses up less space, so a greater selection of seeds can be sown. Young plants grow best if there is little check to their growth from drought, overwatering or root disturbance. When handling seedlings I always hold them by the leaves; it is only too easy to bruise stems and shoots, which leads to secondary problems such as bacterial or fungal disease. If you should damage a leaf, a young seedling can always grow another but it cannot replace a stem.

Pricking out or potting on seedlings

Once germinated, seedlings can be pricked out or potted on. Here some have their first true leaves **(below left)**.

Gently ease the seedlings out of their pot **(below centre)**.

When pricking out into plug trays, slice through the compost and roots, leaving enough root to prick out the seedlings without bending the tap root in the process **(below right)**.

What to grow from seed?

If you like to grow native plants and are content with filling the late-summer border with straight species or seed-raised selections, there is no real need to propagate by any other method. However, there are many plants available that have been selectively bred to give certain characteristics, such as larger flowers, different colours or more resistance from disease. Some of these are selected as improved seed strains and can be grown from seed whereas others have to be propagated vegetatively as they may be sterile or do not come true from seed. It is a veritable minefield to find out which plants come true from seed and which must be grown by vegetative means. Marketing plants has involved many straight species being given colourful names in the seed catalogues to enable them to sell well. Unscrupulous or just ignorant seedsmen have offered seed for sale from cultivars that can only be propagated vegetatively (in other words, by cuttings) to remain true to name. Thus, if you see a plant you would particularly like to grow it is best to know the rudimentary methods of taking cuttings so you can ensure you get a true replica.

Hold seedlings by the leaf when potting up into small pots. It avoids damage to the delicate stem **(above)**.

SOFTWOOD CUTTINGS

The simplest and easiest way to take a cutting of hardy herbaceous perennials is to take a small non-flowering shoot, preferably in the early part of the year when growth is rapid. This should consist of the growing point and two to three leaf nodes (the knobbly point on the stem from which the leaf grows) below it. When obtaining cuttings material I like to use small sharp scissors or clips which will cause the least damage to the parent plant. I always take a cutting just above a leaf node without leaving a stub that will die back and possibly introduce a fungal infection into the stem; the cuttings will be prepared later so it doesn't matter if there is excess material on them. By taking cuttings like this you leave the original plant looking smart, with the added bonus of gently pruning the plant so more branching will occur and eventually more flowers will be produced. Most late-flowering perennials apart from bulbs and grasses can be increased by taking soft cuttings (which is material that has not yet gone woody). Like the name, they are soft and should root rapidly, generally within a couple of weeks at peak growing season. Gather a few cuttings of each plant you wish to increase and place them in a plastic bag. In general, it is better to take more than one cutting from a plant – for some reason they do seem to root more easily when there are several. This may be due to a soluble hormonal chemical released into the cuttings mix which stimulates the formation of roots, but the scientific evidence is rather thin on the ground. I find grip-seal plastic bags very useful as they can be closed to keep the moisture in. Always label cuttings, and if you are unable to deal with the material immediately it may be a good idea to give it a burst of mist from a hand-held sprayer so as to keep the material turgid. I am often unable to process the cuttings till much later, perhaps even the next day, and I find they are happy left in a fridge. Do not always select the fattest terminal shoots; quite often the more slender side-shoots will root faster than the main stem.

When you are ready to deal with your cuttings (I often deal with mine on the kitchen table, on a chopping board kept specifically for them!), you need to find enough space so that you can work easily without getting covered with compost or

Softwood cuttings

Collect cuttings in the cool of day, preferably in a plastic grip-seal bag, and mist gently to keep them turgid **(below)**.

other debris. I tip out my cuttings and cut them up one by one, discarding the waste material as I go. I use single-sided razor blades as they are very sharp, economical and easy to use with soft cuttings. They can usually be obtained from a chemist or from a hardware store for interior decorating. The blades produced by the American Safety Razor Company are packaged in tens in a convenient safety dispenser so that used razors can be disposed of safely. Otherwise use a screw-top glass jar for old blades. By changing blades frequently there is less chance of infecting other plant material with any pathogens. Most cuttings are taken by slicing horizontally through the swelling at the node and disposing of the leaves that emerge from this point. I usually remove the leaves from the next node as well, leaving a piece of bare stem. If the plant material has large leaves I reduce most of the remaining leaves with sharp scissors so that the cutting is much diminished from the material I originally collected. To succeed, a soft cutting needs to have a reasonably moist environment and the amount of transpiration needs to be less than the moisture available or the cutting will wilt. By reducing the leaves, the transpiration is similarly reduced and turgidity can be maintained. The less stress the cutting receives, the more likely it will put out root initials from the node where it was cut. (At the nodes there is meristematic tissue which allows root initials to form.) When you have completed your batch of cuttings either "stick" them immediately or replace them in a sealed plastic bag to do sooner rather than later.

My cuttings mix is very gritty; I use 70 per cent of my fine 1–3mm (^{1}/$_{16}$–^{1}/$_8$in) grit with 30 per cent peat, which just binds it together. I fill a small seed tray or pot if the cutting has long internodes so that the cut end is at least 1cm (^{1}/$_2$in) from the base of the container when it has been "stuck". There are all sorts of rooting hormone powders on the market and some liquid-based ones, which are reputed to hasten the rooting process. I find with soft cuttings that hormone rooting powder or liquid is just not necessary and I do not use it. However, if you feel more comfortable using one of these compounds it will certainly not do any harm and could dry the end of the cutting (if you are using powder) so there is less risk of fungal infection. As my mix is so free-draining there is less likelihood of getting botrytis and

Preparing softwood tip cuttings
Slice horizontally through a node, removing the leaves at this node and above, to reduce transpiration and prevent wilting **(above)**.

Sticking prepared cuttings
Push rigid cuttings (or use a nail for soft ones) into a tray of cuttings mix. Do not let them touch **(below)**.

To check for rooting, gently tug a leaf **(bottom)**.

other fungal infections although it does mean that watering is slightly more frequent.

Once the cuttings mix is in the tray I tamp it down with a "professional pot plonker" made to size, and label my container. I then use a dibber (I like the yellow plastic ones made by "Jiffy") or a nail to make a small hole to "stick" the cutting, taking care not to push it in too deeply. If the cutting does reach the bottom of the container any developing root will damage itself against the base of the tray. If the cuttings are relatively stiff, I "stick" them without the use of dibber or nail. The abrading action as the cutting is pushed into the mix seems to speed up the production of root initials. Often, if a cutting makes a basal callous instead of a root initial I will turn them out of the tray and gently nick the callous, which will often stimulate root growth, before "resticking" the cuttings in another tray of cuttings compost.

Once stuck, the cuttings need to be watered well, then placed somewhere out of direct sun, preferably in an area with a high humidity to maintain the turgidity of the plant. On the nursery, I have created a unit, with a heated cable under sand and grit, on which I place the trays. Eventually, I will call in the electrician to fit an electric system for an automatic mist unit with electronic leaf sensor but, for the moment, I am Mrs Mister and I check the cuttings several times a day to see if they require a quick spray. There are several types of misting nozzle, which can be purchased to go on the lance at the end of a hosepipe, and the method has proved satisfactory for me.

There is no doubt that using bottom heat either by a cable or a special cuttings blanket will speed up the time it takes a plant to root. However, all is not lost if you are unable to purchase one or there is no electrical source where you keep your cuttings. In the peak of the cuttings season, usually around April and May, when it is not too hot, a cold frame can be almost as efficient. I have never been particularly competent with small enclosed propagator units or with pots covered with plastic bags. I find that although the humidity is higher there is a much increased rate of fungal disease, especially botrytis, which is the scourge of any would-be propagator. Any cutting succumbing to botrytal infection (blackening of stems and soggy brown leaves) needs to be removed from the tray as soon as possible because the disease will spread rapidly by droplet infection. Occasionally, weather conditions that are humid, hot and damp can lead to a higher incidence of botrytis but the quicker plants can be encouraged to root and moved on while growing fast, the less disease is prevalent. I still find it a miracle to see roots appearing out of the bottom of a tray when all I inserted were a few soft green shoots.

The cuttings are ready to pot when roots appear out of the bottom of the tray or you may get to "feel" when a cutting has rooted by a gentle tugging of a shoot by its leaf. This does come with practice!

Removing cuttings from the tray can be a daunting experience; the general idea is to get them out with as little disturbance to the delicate roots as possible. I rock the tray from end to end, loosening the grit. Then, with a deft flip, I toss the entire contents of the tray onto my potting table so it lands in the same position as it was, minus the tray. Then I gently disentangle the cuttings and pot them up individually. One of the advantages of propagating from cuttings rather than seed is that it speeds up the process to a flowering size.

One important tip for producing healthy and stocky young plants is to take the tip out of rooted cuttings. In the apex of a shoot there is a hormone which inhibits the lateral shoots from developing. By taking out the very tip of a growing shoot the apical dominance is lost and side-shoots will start to develop immediately, making a well-branched, sturdy new plant. It takes little time to remove the tips of the cuttings before flipping them out but the difference in the standard of plant produced is incomparable. More side-shoots ultimately means more flowers and a better display for the garden. This basic understanding of growth mechanisms in plant development has far-reaching effects for the gardener, who can manipulate the number of blooms produced and the longevity of the flowering season as seen in earlier chapters. It is a fundamental concept of plant biology.

Preparing cuttings for potting up
Remove cuttings from the tray by rocking compost and then flipping out to land right side up **(below)**.

Extract rooted cuttings from the mix and pot up individually **(bottom)**. For bushier plants, nip out the growing tip.

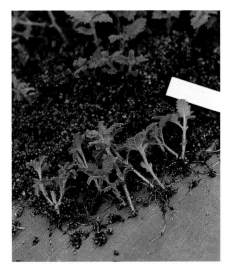

Root cuttings

Remove roots from the stock plant, leaving 5cm (2in) of root intact **(below)**. Replant mother plant.

Wash soil off cuttings and, keeping the right way up, cut into sections 5cm (2in) long **(bottom)**.

ROOT CUTTINGS

One other method which is pertinent to late- summer perennials is the use of root cuttings, which is an effective method of propagating some plants that are difficult to increase by other methods. I am sure you have all experienced the bright red or orange oriental poppy that has turned up in your most subtle and discreet pastel border, and have dug it out in fury, only to find that it is back again the following year, bolder and more brassy. Oriental poppies are one of the most familiar of the plants that will increase by root cuttings, but as their season of growth is earlier in the year they do not really enter into this treatise. However, there are a number of late-flowering plants that are also best propagated by small lengths of root, for instance many eryngiums, acanthus and verbascums as well as some of the smaller plants for raised beds such as *Crepis incana*, many erodiums and some geraniums. The least time-consuming method is to dig out a plant which shoots from the roots, leaving a large quantity of root behind and replanting the top half with its attendant roots in another part of the garden where you want to increase your stock.

When taking root cuttings, you need to lift the plant concerned to get at the roots or excavate a hole alongside the plant in situ until you can trace the course of one or more roots. Excise with a sharp knife, leaving about 5cm (2in) of root on the parent plant and retain the rest of the root material. Either wash or brush the roots free of soil keeping them the right way up. Prepare the plant material by cutting the root sections into short lengths roughly 5cm (2in) long with a very sharp knife or razor. Insert roots vertically the correct way up in a pot of gritty compost (I use the same sterile mix as that used for softwood cuttings) until the top is level with the compost. I cover with a layer of grit about 0.5cm (¼in) and water well. The pots are then left unwatered, out of direct sunlight until green shoots emerge through the grit. Verbascum root cuttings may take as little as 10 days while eryngium roots may only appear after a couple of months. Do not forget to label your pots. If you do place a root cutting upside down it will often shoot but will take longer to reach the surface. On the Continent, I believe that roots are often inserted at an angle of 45 degrees, which may prevent them rotting.

Sticking root cuttings
Stick root cuttings in a tray or pot so the upper surface is level with the top of the compost and space them so that they do not touch **(right)**. Cover with a thin layer of fine grit and water well. Leave out of direct sun. When leaves and roots are growing well they can be pricked out into plug trays or potted up individually.

Young verbascum plants ready to pot up individually or to be planted out **(below right)**.

Finer roots, such as those found on Japanese anemones and phlox, are best cut off the parent plant, washed, and then laid on a tray of gritty cuttings mix and covered with grit. New plants will be ready to pot up when roots appear at the base of the pot or tray. They do take longer than softwood cuttings.

DIVISION

You can propagate many clump-forming perennials, by simply dividing the clumps. In fact, many perennials benefit from being divided, as this serves to invigorate the plant.

Many clumps of perennials die out in the centre as they get older, leaving an unsightly gap in the middle. By lifting and dividing plants every two to three years this can be avoided and the vigour restored. Dig up the clump and split it into smaller pieces, discarding dying or dead material. Trim the roots with a sharp knife, secateurs or scissors, which will stimulate renewed root growth. Replant the pieces making sure they are placed at the same depth as they were originally. As with the planting instructions on page 55, make sure the material is well-watered before and after its transplant operation to improve the chances of success.

As a nurseryman wishing to make as many plants as possible from a single perennial clump, a sharp kitchen knife is my most important tool but for general garden divisions a sharp spade may be fine. Two garden forks back to back are also a useful method of dividing some plants but there will always be more damage to the clump than with a sharp knife. It all depends on how many plants you require to fill the late-summer border.

PLANT DIRECTORY

This directory consists of plants that I have grown and found effective for the late summer and autumn season. It is by no means a comprehensive list but I hope it will enable you to grow some plants that you may not be familiar with.

My own garden and nursery is in Hampshire, in the south of England, and although it is a frost pocket, some of the plants mentioned may not be hardy in more exposed and colder areas. I have tried to indicate their general hardiness but it is always difficult to predict what will survive in any given environment. I grow many plants that hail from the Mediterranean, Mexico and desert conditions. I find that many of these can tolerate severe dry cold but will succumb at a sniff of moisture around their roots in winter. Thus they are cold-hardy but not wet-hardy during the dormant season. As my soil is sticky clay, I grow many of my plants on raised beds with 80 per cent grit, which enables rapid drainage throughout the winter months. The majority survive to give pleasure the following season.

Gardening is dynamic: ideas, trends and techniques change through the seasons – not necessarily an improvement but never standing still. It is the same with one's choice of plant material – over the years my tastes have changed, not only in colour range but also in the shape of flowers and foliage selected. I certainly have bolder hues in my colour range than I would have dreamed of a decade ago. I find them vibrant and uplifting compared to quieter more subtle shades in the border. Sometimes when garden visiting, I espy a tasteful pastel confection and long to insert a clump of pillarbox-red oriental poppy or other such delight. I prefer the understated tones with just a hint of the outrageous and vulgar to give that bit of interest. A riot of colour can be tiring and busy to the eye. Green, in the form of a backdrop such as a yew hedge or a grass lawn, can set off plant combinations well and is restful to gaze at.

I am aware that my choice of plants is often dictated by their ability to attract beneficial insects, birds and mammals. Probably, this is a result of laziness on my part – why spend time spraying a concoction of noxious chemicals at regular intervals against pests and diseases when you could be enjoying the scents and sounds of the garden as hoverflies and birds seek out and ingest

Previous pages: Green-tipped spires of *Veronica longifolia* cv (page 92); steely-blue bracts and flower of an eryngium (page 93).

Above: *Acanthus* cv.

swarms of aphids? Hedgehogs and frogs greedily gobble the surfeit of slugs while blackbirds and thrushes take care of the wrapped versions by smashing them open on a piece of stone, even if it is your patio.

I accept that as I am fortunate enough to have a large area to garden, I do not need to be so precious about losing a few flowers and foliage in the great scheme of things. In a smaller area it is more important that every plant is used to best effect and more draconian methods may be required to achieve that end.

Note: Plants marked AGM have received an Award of Garden Merit from the RHS (Royal Horticultural Society).

Acanthus (ACANTHACEAE)

Handsome, glossy dark green foliage erupts from furled leaf buds, providing an excellent foil for contrasting foliage and flowers. Many of the more familiar species such as *A. mollis* will tolerate some shade and their bold and substantial leaves create points of focal interest in areas that could be lacklustre and dull.

A. mollis 'Hollards Gold' is a cultivar with golden leaves and can be used for its vibrant foliage effect. Some species such as *A. spinosus* Spinosissimus Group and *A. hirsutus* require full sun and good drainage. There are some members of this genus that hail from Africa and require rich, moisture-retaining soil. One such is *A. sennii* from Ethiopia, which flowers during late summer and autumn.

Chosen with care, there are *Acanthus* that will provide interest either with foliage or flowers in the later part of the season. In general there are few problems with pests and diseases, although powdery mildew can be a nuisance in some years. I tend to cut down unsightly foliage, water well and mulch. The resulting new growth can look spectacular and fresh during the autumn. Occasionally there may be an outbreak of aphids but the most common complaint is a lack of flower production. *Acanthus* tend to be vigorous plants, which benefit from division every few years. This appears to rejuvenate the ability to flower, maybe

because it enables the sun to reach the base of the plant. It seems that many *Acanthus* flower well after a hot summer the previous season. The seed-heads and stems provide striking autumn and winter silhouettes, standing clear of the architectural foliage.

A. hungaricus (syn. A. balcanicus) This useful foliage plant from the Balkans and Romania grows in dappled shade in scrub and woodland, and is not as tall as *A. mollis* at 1.5m (5ft), making dense clumps with attractive flower spikes with purple bracts and a white corolla. In gardens it grows best in full sun with good drainage. **Z6–10.**

A. mollis (Latifolius Group) 'Rue Ledan' Hailing from my nursery colleague, Jean-Pierre Jolivot, at Les Jardins d'en Face, this familiar plant differs from the norm by producing pure white bracts and flowers, as a result of the attentions of a "petit chien" over several years! A shaggy dog story indeed! This plant is occasionally seen under the name of *A. mollis* 'Jefalba'. 1.8m (6ft). **Z6–10.**

A. sennii Roy Lancaster wrote about this Ethiopian plant in *The Garden* (January 2001). This handsome spiny *Acanthus* has mid-green leaves with a ghostly white mid-vein and terminal vermilion to orange bracts around its flowers in late summer. A mature specimen can be seen at the Chelsea Physic Garden, London, from where my material was originally sourced. 60–90cm (24–36in). **Z9–10.**

A. spinosus Spinosissimus Group

Spiny, lethal and vicious – ideal for keeping unwanted visitors and livestock away. Almost variegated with handsome prickly foliage with striking white mid-veins; great for a hot spot with good drainage. Shy to flower with me. Combines well with Mediterranean herbs and perennials. 45cm (18in). **Z7–10.**

Achillea (ASTERACEAE)

The flat plates of flowers in a wide range of colours make achilleas useful horizontal components of the herbaceous border. They look particularly good with grasses and herbaceous plants with vertical flower spires. However, with the recent succession of mild, wet winters many cultivars are short-lived especially the most popular colour forms in reds, pinks and terracotta. Given superb winter drainage, achilleas are indeed long-lived perennials but, from my experience, these may have to be replaced on an annual basis for a good display. Even in suitable conditions, the plants rapidly lose their vigour, which can easily be restored by dividing them regularly.

Achilleas are native to northern temperate regions, growing in pasture and scrubby conditions, usually in full sun. There are many different species, mostly with attractive pinnate foliage that may be green or silvery grey. The flower colour range is large, the more perennial types usually white, cream or yellow. In garden conditions achilleas may reach 1.5m (5ft) or more, such as *A. filipendulina* 'Gold Plate' AGM. The taller varieties are a strong architectural component of the perennial border. Pink, red, orange and burgundy hues can be found in the large range of achilleas currently available with new varieties appearing on the market every year. In general, the coloured range are smaller plants, seldom exceeding 90cm (36in) with many less than this. One of the drawbacks of many of the reddish varieties is their propensity to fade to a mustard-coloured tone, whatever their original flower colour. My choice of achilleas favours those varieties that fade less badly. There are many attractive cultivars of *Achillea millefolium* and these can be used very successfully in wilder areas. They have a predisposition to self-seed everywhere and flowerheads should be removed assiduously if the colour palette is not to be diluted.

Pests and diseases are not often troublesome although there may occasionally be an aphid problem and I have experienced an infestation with a fly, which appeared to lay its eggs in the hollow flower stem, leading to collapse. This is not usually a problem unless a garden is adjacent to pasture containing livestock.

With regular deadheading, achilleas can remain in flower until the first frosts. The faded seed-heads can be a striking feature during autumn and winter, providing a structural template for hoar frost. **Z4–8.**

A. 'Belle Epoque' AGM Large heads of rosy buff, raised by Brian Kabbes. Flowers early. 75cm (30in).

A. 'Credo' AGM Pale creamy yellow, raised by Ernst Pagels in Germany. 1.2m (4ft).

A. 'Hella Glashoff' AGM Quite similar to *A.* 'Credo' but shorter and paler. 75cm (30in). Also raised by Ernst Pagels.

A. 'Inca Gold' Short at 60cm (24in), this has a flowering peak through July and August with branched heads of a warm golden apricot and burnt orange, with slightly greyish foliage.

A. 'Marie Ann' Pale lemon-yellow and diminutive at 40cm (16in).

A. 'McVities' Rich biscuit colour, bleaching with age. Robust and more perennial than many. 90cm (36in).

***A. millefolium* 'Lansdorferglut' AGM** Rich salmon-pink flowers fade to rose-flushed ivory. 90cm (36in).

***A. m.* 'Sammetriese'** Strong magenta-red, fading with age. 75cm (30in). Long lived but self-seeds.

A. 'Mondpagode' AGM Also by Ernst Pagels, with large heads of ivory cream in elegant layers. 90cm (36in).

Opposite: *Achillea* 'Credo' AGM
Below: *Achillea millefolium* 'Lansdorferglut' AGM

A. ptarmica 'The Pearl' AGM Larger flowers than *A. millefolium* with pure white double flowers over robust dark green foliage. 75–90cm (30–36in).

A. 'Summerwine' AGM Raised by Piet Oudolf, this has tight clumps of green leaves under multitudes of small claret flower umbels. 60cm (24in).

A. 'Terracotta' A rich rusty orange-brown with grey foliage. 90cm (36in).

A. 'Walther Funcke' Vibrant brick red ageing to a dusky orange. 90cm (36in).

Aconitum (RANUNCULACEAE)

A personal favourite, along with *Eryngium, Sanguisorba* and *Thalictrum*, aconites are under represented in gardens. *Aconitum* is a diverse genus in colour, flowering times and habit. Fortunately through the efforts and collections of plant hunters Bleddyn and Sue Wynn-Jones (Crûg Farm Plants, North Wales) and Dan Hinkley (Heronswood Nursery, Seattle) more species are being introduced into gardens.

Most aconites prefer a moisture-retentive soil and dappled shade. They are native to temperate regions of the northern hemisphere and are hardy and long-lived. They are poisonous in all their parts, although many of them produce a sweet nectar much beloved by bees. They have hooded flowers rather like a monk's cowl, which gives rise to the other familiar name of monkshood. Many have dark purple, bluish-purple or blue flowers, which can look sombre if not combined with lighter tones. There are white, cream and pale yellow forms, usually with corresponding paler foliage. Pink-flowered cultivars are available although many of these have proved to be short lived and rather weak in growth. Several perennial species have tuberous roots starting into growth early in the season. Species such as *A. hemsleyanum* are scrambling climbers and often flower in late summer. The dark green lobed foliage with a glossy sheen provides a good foil to other plants.

This large range of form and flower colour ensures plenty of choice in gardens as long as the soil is not too dry. Pests and diseases are minimal in this genus. They flower from mid to late summer or early autumn. Aconites that flower during late summer have a tendency to shed their basal leaves, which turn an unattractive yellow, then brown, and tend to remain attached to the stem. Where possible, I try to place them further back in the border so their untidy legs can be disguised by more vigorous foliage.

A. **'Bressingham Spire' AGM** Very dark blue flowers in July–August on narrow, erect spikes. 1.2m (4ft). **Z5–8.**

A. carmichaelii **Wilsonii Group** A master of the late-summer border, with deep blue flowers at their peak in August and September when other perennials are on the wane. 1.8m (6ft). **Z3–8.**

A. c. **Wilsonii Group 'Spätlese'** Large pale violet-blue flowers from glossy green buds in late summer. 1.5m (5ft). **Z3–8.**

A. hemsleyanum A vigorous climber with showers of small purplish-blue monkshoods in late August and September. There are many inferior light-flowered plants so it is best to see this species in flower before purchasing. There are climbing aconites, collected in the region of Mount Omei, which may be forms of *A. hemsleyanum* with large, waxy, reddish-purple blooms. They are spectacular and eminently collectable. 2.4m (8ft). **Z4.**

A. heterophyllum The form I have grown has the most understated flowers possible. Green-veined hoods with a wash of pinkish purple ensure that only the most observant garden visitor ever sees it. Unfortunately it is not vigorous. Late summer. 60–90cm (24–36in). Western Himalayas. **Z5–8.**

A. lycoctonum Many small, pale yellow flowers atop glossy dark green foliage in summer. 90cm (36in). **Z4–8.**

A. **'Spark's Variety' AGM** This only just scrapes in as a late-summer flower, as it peaks during July. However, the strongly branched flower stems and seedpods provide an elegant architectural feature through late summer. 1.5m (5ft). **Z5–8.**

A. **'Stainless Steel'** Silvery slate blue flowers in July on this recent Continental selection. 1.5m (5ft). **Z5–8.**

Actaea (RANUNCULACEAE)

A genus unaccountably underused as garden plants, it comprises fine trouble-free perennials that are hardy, well behaved and with a peak flowering period in late August and September. *Actaea* and *Cimicifuga* (recently reclassified as *Actaea* in a doctoral thesis by Dr. James Compton) thrive in a moisture-retentive rich soil in partial shade, out of the ravaging force of the wind. In their native habitats in northern temperate regions they tend to grow in the dappled light of deciduous woodland. A notable exception are the dark-leaved forms of *A. simplex* Atropurpurea Group which requires full sun to develop the most intense bronze-purple foliage.

Left: *Aconitum carmichaelii* Wilsonii Group
Opposite: *Actaea simplex* Atropurpurea Group
'James Compton'

Actaea produce vigorous mounds of glossy dissected foliage and vary in flower height from 90cm–2.4m (36in–8ft) with white, often fragrant, flower spikes that are usually erect or curved in cultivars such as *A. simplex* 'Scimitar'. They continue to provide a strong vertical component late into autumn with their ripening seed-heads in tones of buff and tan. In more exposed areas *A. arizonica* appears to be the most able to contend with adverse conditions. Currently there is a Floral Trial of *Actaea* at RHS Wisley. **Z4–8.**

A. *arizonica* Growing to 1.5m (5ft) with light yellowish-green leaves. Withstands exposure to wind better than other species.

A. *europaea* Up to 1.8m (6ft) tall, this bugbane originates from East Asia and is extremely hardy. Short arching flower stems in late summer. Less than pleasant odour.

A. *matsumurae* 'Elstead Variety' AGM and 'White Pearl'. Similar in height at 2m (6ft 6in) these cultivars have deeply dissected mounds of foliage; in 'White Pearl' it is a bright fresh green whereas 'Elstead Variety' has striking black stems and flowers later into September.

A. *pachypoda* AGM. Native to eastern North America, this has striking fruits in late summer. Sometimes likened to doll's eyes, it has clusters of white berries and a terminal black "eye".

A. *racemosa* AGM The Black Cohosh of North America growing to 1.8m (6ft) or more.

A. *simplex* Atropurpurea Group This refers to purple-leaved forms of *A. simplex*. There is quite a variation in leaf colour from seed and some of the better leaf forms have been selected and given cultivar names. 'Brunette' AGM has very dark purple-black foliage, which is an outstanding foil for the sweetly scented white spikes in later summer. 'Hillside Black Beauty' has even darker foliage and appears to perform better even in drier conditions. Another good dark-leaved form is 'James Compton'.

'Pink Spike' has dark foliage with pink-tinged flowers. All of these are excellent late-summer

flowering plants. 1.5–2.1m (5–8ft). 'Prichard's Giant' is a giant indeed at 2.4m (8ft) with towering, erect, sweetly scented white flowers. 'Scimitar' differs from the above with long, curved, sickle-shaped flowers giving the concept of movement in the late-summer border.

Agapanthus (ALLIACEAE)

South African in origin, this useful genus is a familiar garden plant with its strap-shaped leaves and umbels of blue, purplish blue or white tubular flowers raised on strong round stems. The flowering period is late summer, through July and August, with interesting architectural skeletons and black pendulous seeds continuing into autumn and beyond. They are useful for containers or in the garden if they are hardy. Variegated forms exist although none of these are hardy except for *A.* 'Golden Rule', which needs to settle in the ground before the variegation shows at its best. Size ranges from the diminutive – little above 45cm (18in) – to giants of 1.5m (5ft) or more in flower. They can be used most effectively in gravel gardens with enough moisture and in borders among mid-sized grasses and other herbaceous plants that will not swamp their growth. The Headbourne Hybrids bred by Lewis Palmer have proved hardy in most garden situations in Britain and one of the named Headbournes, 'Castle of Mey', is very floriferous and a good mid-blue.

For container gardening there is no such restriction on the selection of hardy cultivars as long as there is a frost-free site for the containers during the winter months. *Agapanthus* suffer from few pests and diseases, the main criticism being that they do not flower consistently well each year. I have found that flowering is limited when the clumps get too large in a border and improves if the clump is split into smaller pieces. (Possibly when the clump gets very large, the sun is unable to warm the roots to initiate flower formation.) In containers *Agapanthus* prefer not to be over-potted and flower best when they have filled their container with roots. When potting a plant into a larger container I am always surprised how the thick white fleshy roots have completely filled the pot, leaving no sign of the original compost! Plants in containers are automatically subjected to greater extremes of heat, cold, wet and dry than those in the ground and may therefore flower better in these circumstances.

In recent years there has been much breeding work with *Agapanthus* and an exciting new hardy range has been produced. (A good collection can be seen at the NCCPG Collection Holder of *Agapanthus* at Pine Cottage Plants in Devon.) There have been so many introductions that I have not had a chance to assess them so I have limited my choice to a diverse range of flower colour and size, many of them old favourites.

A. **Ardernei Hybrid** A hardy specimen with white flowers opening from purple-tinged buds and purple-washed stems. 1.2m (4ft). **Z6–9.**

A. **'Back in Black'** A new introduction with the darkest purple-black flowers emerging from ebony buds. Inky black stems contrast well with bright green foliage. 70cm (28in). **Z6–9.**

A. **'Blue Moon'** Palest milky blue trumpets in dense umbels. Slightly tender. **Z8–9.**

A. inapertus This species is tall and elegant at 1.5m (5ft) with slim pendulous trumpets. There are some wonderful colour forms, some almost blue-black with dark stems or pristine white. Not too hardy but *inapertus* blood has been bred into many of the new hybrids and hardier hybrids have resulted. **Z7–10.**

A. **'Windsor Grey'** Pale slate-blue flowers in large umbels. Ghostly but enchanting. 1.2m (4ft). **Z7–9.**

Agastache (LAMIACEAE)

As I try more of these aromatic foliaged herbs, I become fonder of them. The colours run through white, burnt orange, red, pink, purple and blue, and they are irresistible to pollinating insects – a steady hum is ever-present around their long-lived flower spikes. The red and orange species originate in Mexico and the southern states of the USA and are pollinated by hummingbirds. The Mexican species and their hybrids such as *A.* 'Firebird', *A.* 'Painted Lady' and *A.* 'Tangerine Dreams' are not particularly hardy unless they are superbly drained so try them on a gritty raised bed or in a pot. The blue-, purple- and occasionally white-flowered species appear to be pollinated primarily by bees. In areas where hummingbirds are absent, bees fulfil the pollinating role. All agastaches have scented leaves, ranging from aniseed, mint to bubble gum, and on hot summer days this aroma is released as volatile oils.

There are few problems with pests and diseases although there is occasionally an aphid outbreak. Hoverflies are highly attracted to the flowers and consume any aphids with ease, so I have never

Left: *Agapanthus* 'Castle of Mey'
Top right: *Agastache rugosa* 'Liquorice Blue'
Right: *Agastache* 'Painted Lady'

resorted to chemical deterrents. Flowers are produced from the end of May onwards, continuing until the first frosts. I do not deadhead because I wish to collect seed from my plants but I could probably obtain a superior display if I deadheaded on a regular basis. In winter, I leave the top growth, especially on the Mexican species, as I believe it offers some frost protection for the basal growth. If you have a windy site, I would reduce the top growth by a third in autumn to prevent wind rock.

A. aurantiaca Grey-green foliage with burnt orange flowers. 45cm (18in). **Z6.**

A. **'Blue Fortune'** AGM Similar to *A. foeniculum* but with blue flowers set in a dark calyx. It is a sterile hybrid so it continues to flower for longer. 90cm–1.2m (36in–4ft). **Z4.**

A. cana Once described by seed company Rocky Mountain Rare Plants as smelling of double bubble gum! It has grey-green scented foliage and deep rose-pink flowers. 45–60cm (18–24in). **Z6.**

A. **'Firebird'** Stiff spikes of orange-pink flowers throughout later summer and intensely aromatic foliage. 60–90cm (24–36in). **Z6.**

A. foeniculum A good border plant for full sun with deep lavender blue flower spikes all summer. Caviar for bees. 90cm–1.2m (36in–4ft). 'Alabaster' is the white form of the above with persistent green seed-heads when the flowers are over. **Z4.**

A. **'Painted Lady'** A pinker sport from *A.* 'Firebird' with coral and pink flowers, originally obtained from Cotswold Garden Flowers. Proved hardy here through 2002 when *A.* 'Tangerine Dreams' AGM succumbed to winter wet and cold temperatures. *A.* 'Painted Lady' was the star of the summer drought in 2003 on a gritty raised bed in the nursery, covered with fragrant foliage and flowers each day, when lesser plants shrivelled in the continuous heat. It was also the main cafeteria for the influx of Hummingbird hawkmoths from the continent. **Z6.**

A. pallida Very showy broad spikes of warm purple-pink over aromatic leaves. 60cm (24in). **Z6.**

A. rugosa I collected this delightful "Korean mint" on

a plant expedition to Korea in September 1993. It has nettle-shaped leaves, green on top and purple suffused beneath, and bluish-purple spears with a strong minty scent. 60cm (24in). Best in sun with good drainage. **Z6.**

A. r. **'Liquorice Blue'** Shorter than *A. foeniculum* at 60cm (24in) but a similar colour. **Z6.**

A. rupestris More muted orange than *A.* 'Firebird' with greyer foliage and a different aroma. 45cm (18in). **Z5.**

A. **'Serpentine'** A tall, 1.2–1.5m (4–5ft) cultivar from Holland with long narrow spikes of bluish-purple flowers. **Z4.**

Allium (ALLIACEAE)

The ornamental and culinary onions have a diverse range of colour and sizes, and are found throughout the northern hemisphere. Many of them do not qualify for inclusion in the late-summer garden as they flower in late spring and early summer. Leaves are strap-shaped and often die back as the flowering stem is produced. In a garden situation this can look untidy, so it is best to site alliums among other herbaceous plants, where the flowering stems can arise majestically above the surrounding greenery.

A number of the smaller species flower throughout summer, depending on the season. I have included a few that bloom into late summer, with a range of colours. Others I have chosen for architectural merit, the dead stems and ripening seed-heads providing interesting features through the autumn. Impressive seed-heads are usually found on the drumstick type of ornamental onion. These include *A. nigrum* (syn. *A. multibulbosum*), *A. hollandicum* AGM, *A. giganteum* AGM, *A. stipitatum* and many hybrids such as 'Mount Everest, 'White Giant', 'Purple Pride', 'Gladiator' AGM, 'Firmament' and 'Globemaster' AGM. Seed-heads fade to buff and biscuit hues and appear suspended in space, but on closer inspection the flower stem can be espied.

A. carinatum subsp. *pulchellum* AGM Starbursts of rosy purple flowers explode from papery bracts in

July. Relishes starved soil in sun and gently self-sows. *A. c.* subsp. *p.* f. album is pure white. 45cm (18in). **Z6–9.**

A. cernuum **'Major' AGM** A nodding onion from North America with large rosy pink umbels. 'Major' has larger flowers than the type. 40cm (16in). **Z3–8.**

A. cristophii **AGM** Large heads of violet-purple star-like flowers appear in late spring and early summer. The value to the late summer garden is the spectacular seed-heads which persist well into autumn, a bare, buff skeleton with black seeds. This, along with *A. schubertii* – which looks like a ball of shooting stars – disperses its seeds by losing its head! The flower stem snaps at the apex and the ripe seed-heads roll away. 60cm (24in). **Z4–10.**

A. cyaneum **AGM** and *A. sikkimense* These are both dwarf blue ornamental onions hailing from China and the Himalayas. They have pendent, bell-shaped flowers in umbels ranging in size from 15–20cm (6–8in) for the former and 30–40cm (12–16in) in the latter. They grow best in soil which is well drained but not too dry. **Z6–10.**

A. flavum **subsp.** *tauricum* I have included this pale lemon-yellow nodding onion for its outstanding sweet scent. Similar to *A. carinatum* subsp. *pulchellum* in resembling a starburst, it too relishes sun and well drained soil. 45cm (18in). **Z6–10.**

A. sphaerocephalon Deep rosy-purple and green egg-shaped flowerheads are ambrosia to bees in mid- to late summer. Swaying on delicate stems, this onion thrives in sun or dappled shade, mixing well with grasses such as *Deschampsia cespitosa.* 60cm (24in). **Z4–10.**

A. unifolium **AGM** Clear pink upward facing flowers on this 30cm (12in) species for sun. **Z4–10.**

Right: *Allium cristophii* AGM with *Eryngium bourgatii*

Amaryllis belladonna AGM (AMARYLLIDACEAE)

Native to South Africa, this is only hardy in parts of southern Britain in a warm and sheltered spot, preferably at the base of a south-facing wall which can reflect the sun's heat. They can also be used successfully as a container plant (a very large, deep container required), which can be moved into a warmer environment during winter months. Blowsy sweetly scented trumpets in varying shades of pink emerge over robust flower stems, which erupt from the bare earth in early autumn. 60cm (24in). There are a number of hybrids between *Amaryllis* and *Brunsvigia* (x *Amarygia*) and also *Amaryllis* and *Nerine* (x *Amarine*). These also flaunt spectacular pink flowers. **Z8–9.**

Ammi majus (APIACEAE)

An invaluable annual cow parsley that can be sown successively through the year. Seed germinated in autumn will provide the largest plants, to 1.5m (5ft), for the following season and the earliest flowering period. To obtain specimens that will bloom through late summer and into the autumn a late sowing is required, probably in late May and early June. Height and spread will be reduced, but the hazy, diaphanous effect of filigree green foliage covered by a fine mist of delicate white umbels will not be lost. Even in maturity the architectural quality remains and the seeds attract finches and other passerines. **Z6.**

Amsonia (APOCYNACEAE)

Starbursts of milky blue flowers are borne in late spring and early summer over erect clumps of stiff stems with linear leaves. Several species originate from North America and are hardy, long-lived and trouble-free perennials. 60–90cm (24–36in). In the fall clusters of linear seedpods appear at the apex of the flowering stems. Easy and effective species for the garden include *A. ciliata*, *A. hubrichtii*, *A. orientalis* (syn. *Rhazya orientalis)* and *A. tabernaemontana* var. *salicifolia.* **Z5–8.**

Anemanthele lessoniana (POACEAE)

Until recently classified as a *Stipa (*syn. *Stipa arundinacea and* known as pheasant grass), it prefers moisture during the growing season. This New Zealand grass is evergreen with broad green blades, coloured with brown and orange streaks during dry summers and russet hues in the autumn. Arching purple-black flowerheads are produced in late summer and autumn. If happy, this grass can seed invasively. 90cm (36in). **Z8.**

Anemone hupehensis and *A.* x *hybrida* (RANUNCULACEAE)

The 'Japanese Anemones' are an indispensable component of the autumn garden, flowering through August until the first frosts. Indefatigable colonisers when happy in a well-drained, open-textured soil, they can be difficult to establish on heavier ground. In recent years leaf eelworm has caused disfigurement to the foliage with ensuing dark brown to black blotching of the leaves. Propagating Japanese anemones by root cuttings should clean up plants infected in this way.

The colour range is white, through pink to deep pinkish-red and there are single, semi-double and

double varieties as well as diversity in size. They thrive in dappled shade and can tolerate full sun if the soil is not too dry. I have selected a few to illustrate the variety available. **Z5–9.**

A. hupehensis 'Hadspen Abundance' AGM This is an old variety that has withstood the test of time. Single flowers with alternating petals of pink and a darker rosy tone. 1.2–1.5cm (4–5ft).

A. h. var. japonica 'Pamina' AGM A relatively recent introduction by Hans Simon, with intense deep pink semi-double flowers on compact plants. 75cm (30in).

A. x hybrida 'Elegans' AGM (syn. A. x h. 'Max Vogel') A blowsy large-flowered pale pink form with overlapping petals. 1.2m (4ft). **'Geante des Blanches'** has immense, flat-faced, semi-double white flowers on softly downy stems to 1.2m (4ft). **'Honorine Jobert' AGM**: simple elegance with pure single white flowers and a golden eye. 1.5m (5ft).

Angelica (APIACEAE)

I have always been interested in umbellifers, which include such diverse plants as *Astrantia*, *Bupleurum* and *Eryngium* as well as the more conventional cow parsleys. Many are useful to man as food, cut flowers, dyes and medicines. They are also of great importance

to insect ecology with many moths and butterflies breeding exclusively on them. In autumn and winter, they are striking as architectural silhouettes, covered with dew-laden cobwebs or stiff with hoarfrost on a bright winter's day. Many cow parsleys are monocarpic, which means they die after flowering leaving prodigious quantities of seed for future generations. Producing an inflorescence may be within a season (annual), two seasons (biennial) or three or more. In *Angelica* it is usually a two-year cycle. Angelicas can sometimes be fooled into behaving like a short-lived perennial by removing the spent flowerhead before seed is formed. Somehow, this detracts from the excellent winter silhouette and deprives the birds of a good source of food. Experimenting with one or two plants may produce good results. Most of the angelicas listed below have

Left: *Anemone x hybrida* 'Honorine Jobert' AGM and *A. hupehensis* 'Hadspen Abundance' AGM
Above: *Angelica sylvestris* 'Vicar's Mead'

finished flowering before late summer and are useful architecturally. *Angelica gigas* produces its sinister purple blooms into August.

A. archangelica Majestic as a single specimen, this is a familiar herb with bright green foliage and domed flowerheads, seeding freely in fertile soil. Adventurous cooks may wish to crystallize young stems and leaves for decorating cakes and puddings. Dappled shade or sun with moisture-retentive soil. 1.8m (6ft). **Z4–9.**

A. gigas A plant I collected in Korea, where it is used as an aphrodisiac. Large fields were dedicated to this single 1.2–1.8m (4–6ft) biennial. Fairly rich, moisture-retentive soil seems to suit it best in sun or semi-shade. Dark purple flowerheads erupt from leafy bracts attracting vast quantities of insects, especially bees and wasps. **Z4–9.**

A. sylvestris 'Vicar's Mead' Deep purple-brown dissected foliage in spring and umbels of pink flowers in late summer contrast well with the burnished ebony stems. It is biennial or a short-lived perennial. 1.2–1.5m (4–5ft). **Z4–9.**

Anthemis (ASTERACEAE)

Cream, yellow and white daisies over attractive mounds of dissected foliage are the main characteristics of this genus. They prefer sun and good drainage to thrive. I do not give them a rich diet as I find it makes them grow too lush and thus prone to aphid attack. A lean diet will help to compact the growth to manageable neat buns with a profusion of blooms. Cut it back hard after the first flush of flowers to encourage a second flowering, which will last late into the summer and beyond into early autumn.

A. punctata subsp. *cupaniana* **AGM** Silvery grey-green clumps of foliage with pure white daisies with a yellow eye. 45cm (18in). **Z6–10.**

A. tinctoria 'Alba' Not white but cream flowers over low mounds of green foliage. 30cm (12in). **Z6.**

'Dwarf Form' Bright yellow daisies on low-growing green mats. 20cm (8in). **Z6.**

A. t. 'E. C. Buxton' Pale yellow blooms on 60cm (24in)

stems. In my experience this is short-lived and only perennial in favourable conditions. **Z6.**

A. t. 'Grallagh Gold' Brassy golden flowers which remind me of summer in the Mediterranean. I love it! 90cm (36in). **Z6.**

A. t. 'Sauce Hollandaise' Pale cream daisies hover over dark green dissected foliage all summer. 60–75cm (24–30in). **Z6.**

A. t. 'Wargrave' A taller, 1.2m (4ft) version of *A. t.* 'E. C. Buxton' which is more perennial but tends to flop and therefore needs staking. **Z4–8.**

Antirrhinum majus 'Black Prince' (SCROPHULARIACEAE)

This sumptuous "snapdragon" has proved easy and perennial with me in well-drained soil in sun. Chosen for its deep-purple-suffused foliage and velvety dark red flowers, which will continue in flower well into late summer with judicious deadheading. 45cm (18in). **Z7.**

Aralia (ARALIACEAE)

These make useful, vigorous herbaceous components to the late-summer and autumn border. From a large fleshy rootstock, new growth emerges to 3m (10ft) or more in a single season. Its value in late summer lies in the architectural qualities of the plant, providing a good foil for other late-flowering plants and autumn colour in buttery yellow hues. Berries are often produced in profusion, varying from black to red, depending on the species used. Rich, moisture-retentive soil suits them best.

A. cachemirica From Kashmir, this sports clusters of purple fruits with reddish tints in autumn foliage. **Z7.**

A. californica Originating from Oregon and California with arching clumps of pinnate leaves with creamy white umbels, followed by glossy purple-black berries. **Z8–10.**

A. cordata A native of Japan and Korea with black, fleshy fruits. **Z6.**

A. racemosa Another North American native from the East coast which is smaller, growing to 1m (39in) or more and rhizomatous in habit. **Z5–9.**

Arctotis (ASTERACEAE)

First-rate subjects for containers or for bedding out in a sunny border or gravel bed. They are not particularly hardy, originating in South Africa, and will survive the winter only if in a warm, favourable position. It is best to take early spring cuttings for a good display in late summer, as those taken in autumn can often get leggy and make untidy plants. In the moist British winters, plants can easily succumb to fungal diseases so it is best to cut back stock plants hard in autumn and keep overwintered in a free-draining soil (under cover with good air movement). Young spring cuttings will form good flowering plants throughout the later season. 20cm (8in). **Z10–11.**

Opposite, top: *Anthemis punctata* subsp. *cupaniana* AGM
Opposite bottom: *A. tinctoria* 'E. C. Buxton'
Left: *Antirrhinum majus* 'Black Prince'

***A. x hybrida* 'Flame' AGM** Brilliant mandarin orange with a contrasting grey-washed green eye.
***A. x h.* 'Wine'** The dark eye contrasts with petals the colour of raspberry coulis.

Artemisia (ASTERACEAE)

A diverse genus which includes many garden-worthy plants. I have selected a small number of *Artemisia* which display widely varying characteristics.
***A. caucasica* AGM** Finely divided tufts of silky silvery foliage require full sun and sharp drainage to give of their best. 8cm (3in). A star in drought-ridden summers. **Z6–10.**
***A. lactiflora* Guizhou Group** Quite different in its requirements to the two examples above, this thrives in a moisture-retentive soil in sun or dappled shade. Purple-suffused young foliage and stems will keep their colour best in full sun but with adequate moisture. Airy creamy white flowers froth above tall stems in late spring and early summer but the foliage

effect persists into the autumn. 1.8m (6ft). **Z4–9.**
***A. stelleriana* 'Boughton Silver'** Selected for its flat silvery grey mats of pinnate foliage, which burst from small swollen buds in spring to cover an area as much as 60cm (24in) in diameter. This ground cover can provide an excellent foil for autumn bulbs such as *Crocus speciosus* or colchicums. **Z6–10.**

Aster (ASTERACEAE)

These colourful daisies come into their own in late summer and through the autumn producing an excellent partnership with many grasses and tall herbaceous perennials such as *Eupatorium* and *Aconitum*. The earliest begin to flower in July and continue until the first frosts.

A large number of asters originate in North America and it is these that are the parents of the majority of garden hybrids. *Aster novae-angliae* originate in eastern North America and are often referred to as the "New England Asters" while *A. novi-belgii* are the "New York Asters".

Aster novi-belgii have the greatest range of colour and the largest blooms but are prone to mildew. *Aster novae-angliae* have a reduced colour and size range but have a characteristic smell which I associate with my years cutting Michaelmas daisies for the cut-flower trade at the original Covent Garden market in London. They are not prone to fungal disfigurement. Many species *Aster* are also mildew-free with elegant and graceful stems of small flowers. Several herbaceous plants, which flower late in the season, require sufficient moisture to keep them in good heart for a colourful display. Additional irrigation as the flower buds swell will repay dividends for the autumn pageant. There are large numbers of garden-worthy asters to choose from but I have selected a few to exhibit the wide range and diversity to be found in this useful genus.
***A. amellus* 'Sonora'** Similar in colour to the deservedly popular *A. a.* 'Veilchenkönigin' AGM, my stock of this more recent cultivar appeared to have broader petals and therefore a fuller flower.

My observations, however, are not borne out by the photograph in *The Gardener's Guide to Growing Asters* by Paul Picton, but it is still one of my favourite early asters, flowering in August and onwards. *A. amellus* is a native of the Caucasus and Asia Minor, growing to 45cm (18in). **Z4–9.**

A. 'Chieftain' AGM is a gem with a haze of pale lavender-blue flowers on tall strong stems, adding an ethereal touch to the late summer border. 1.8m (6ft). **Z3–9**.

A. cordifolius A North American species with countless small flowers on airy stems. **Z3–9**.

A. divaricatus Another North American species with a sprawling habit, wiry ebony stems, fine leaves and countless white starry flowers with a yellow eye fading to brown. This will tolerate dappled shade and looks best in an informal planting. 45cm (18in). **Z4**.

A. laevis Sturdy dark stems to 2m (6ft 6in) with thick glossy foliage and sprays of violet-blue flowers with a yellow eye. One of the most popular named forms is 'Calliope', which was raised in London. *Aster laevis* is not prone to mildew. **Z4–8.**

A. lateriflorus (Some of its cultivars are mentioned in the front of this book). This small-flowered aster characteristically supports a profusion of starry white blooms on the upper side of the wiry, almost horizontal, flower stems in late August and September. As the daisies age, the central disc florets fade from yellow, through pink, to a rosy, reddish hue, a pleasing contrast to the white ray florets. Additionally, spring foliage is often suffused with purple, a welcome distinction from green-leaved perennials. Many good cultivars have been named var. *horizontalis* AGM, which has been grown for a century and has proved itself a superb garden plant with stiffly erect stems to 105cm (42in) that require no staking. 'Prince' is a dwarf form with deep purple foliage raised by Eric Smith, at 60cm (24in), and the more recently introduced 'Lady in Black' has good

dark foliage but is more open and graceful at 1.5m (5ft). There are many other named forms, such as 'Buck's Fizz' and 'Bleke Bet' –all are good garden-worthy perennials. **Z4**.

A. 'Little Carlow' AGM One of my favourites, with its myriad of tiny deep-lavender-blue flowers in early autumn. 1.2m (4ft). **Z3–9**.

A. novae-angliae The foliage of "New England asters" has a distinctive aroma; white-flowered or pale pink forms often have light green leaves. They are usually tall and form strong woody clumps to 2m (6ft 6in). Among my favourites are 'Rosa Sieger', a lovely strong pink selection, 'Violetta,' a deep purple with a yellow eye, and 'Andenken an Alma Pötschke' with vivid pink flowers. There is a white-flowered form, 'Herbstschnee', but I find it looks anaemic. **Z2**.

A. novi-belgii The most familiar of the autumn-flowering asters with a wide diversity of colour and size. Recent introductions include many dwarf forms, which present well in a pot. I sometimes wonder

Opposite: *Artemisia lactiflora* Guizhou Group
Right: *Aster* 'Little Carlow' AGM

whether these have been bred entirely for the nursery trade and not for the gardener as they look stunted and out of place in a garden. Mildew can seriously disfigure this group of asters in unfavourable years but the range of colour is unsurpassed for the late season. Asters combine well with many late-flowering plants such as perennial *Helianthus*, grasses such as *Molinia* and *Miscanthus*, *Aconitum* and *Actaea*. The bluest "Michaelmas daisy" I have grown is 'Blue Eyes' with its 1.2m (4ft) stems of single flowers. 'Fellowship' is a pure pale pink double and 'Lawrence Chiswell' a rich purple-pink the colour of *Lobelia* 'Tania'. 'Thundercloud' is the darkest purple I have cultivated. **Z3**.

The large numbers of asters available do not allow me to do them justice in the confines of this directory. It is far better to see them growing in a garden situation and assess which colours and forms will suit your parameters best. In Britain we are fortunate to have Paul Picton with the National Collection of Asters at Old Court Nurseries, Colwall, Worcestershire, where they are displayed in the garden in their full glory. If you can, visit during the aster season and make your selection.

Astrantia (APIACEAE)

A genus which has now deservedly hit the limelight with many improvements to flower colour, shape and size with the propensity for reblooming throughout the season. The majority of the new generation of named *Astrantia* are propagated by division; few consistent selections come from seed strains although this will soon change with more selective breeding regimes. At present to produce a homogeneous group of *Astrantia* in the garden it is best to buy vegetatively propagated material so there is no variation.

The advent of reliable remontant selections enables this genus to be included in a directory of late summer flowers. Indeed, the autumn flush can be impressive when cooler conditions prevail late in the season. Most astrantias prefer rich moisture-

retentive soil, which does not dry out. The rich red astrantias such as *A. major* 'Ruby Wedding' and *A. m.* 'Hadspen Blood' are always much in demand compared to the pink and white flowered forms. In my experience, the darker flowered plants are not so vigorous and perform poorly in a pot. Astrantias do not suffer unduly from pests and diseases although aphid attack occurs in some years. Cut back the flowering stems as soon as the first flush is over to encourage further blooms. Many astrantias set prolific seed, which may produce inferior offspring – removing flowers before the seed ripens will prevent this from happening. All astrantias selected will rebloom into autumn. **Z4**.

A. 'Buckland' This was discovered by Keith and Ros Wiley at the Garden House in Buckland Monachorum between *A. major* and *A. maxima*. This plant exhibits characteristics of both parents with flowers of subtle pale pink with green bracts. A quiet beauty and not to be placed next to one of the more flamboyant reds. 60cm (24in).

Opposite: *Astrantia major* 'Roma'
Above: *Baptisia australis* AGM

A. major subsp. *involucrata* **'Canneman'** A seed strain which has large flowers in variations of green and pink, some with reddish overtones. 60–75cm (24–30in).

A. m. 'Roma' A sterile seedling from the progeny of *A.* 'Ruby Wedding' selected by Piet Oudolf, with large mid-pink flowers and a vigorous habit. An excellent garden-worthy plant for a moisture-retentive soil. 60–75 cm (24–30in).

A. m. 'Ruby Wedding' One of the most popular astrantias with dark red flowers. Not as vigorous as some it has a quality presence in the border if it has adequate moisture. Stems and leaves are often suffused with reddish-black, especially in good sunlight. 60cm (24in).

A. m. 'Washfield' Named by Piet Oudolf after the exceptional specialist nursery of that name. This has large, muted pink flowers and needs to be seen to appreciate it fully. 75cm (30in).

Atriplex hortensis var. *rubra* (CHENOPODIACEAE)

This is a majestic annual attaining 2m (6ft 6in) or more within a season. Deep beetroot-coloured foliage creates a strong focal point throughout the season and acts as an admirable foil for other plants. It seeds prolifically and is a good food source for finches. Seedlings are obvious as they are also deep purple and are easy to remove if unwanted. In a sunny position the colour is more intense. **Z6–10.**

Baptisia australis AGM (PAPILIONACEAE)

The false indigo is native to eastern North America and is a long-lived herbaceous perennial, which improves with age. It grows to 1.5m (5ft) with blue-grey rounded pinnate leaves typical of the pea family. The spikes of indigo flowers are superseded by light green inflated seed-pods that persist into the autumn. **Z3–9.**

Bidens aurea (syn. *B. heterophylla*) (ASTERACEAE)

This Mexican native flowers for months with a succession of small, pale yellow daisies. It has proved relatively hardy and, where happy, spreads rapidly by runners. 1.2–1.5m (4–5ft). It looks good with purple asters and *Vernonia crinita,* as well as many of the taller grasses. **Z3–9.**

Bouteloua gracilis (POACEAE)

A charming ornamental grass from Mexico and the south and west of the United States. Known locally as mosquito grass, it has almost horizontal flower spikes like small brushes, opening with a strong reddish tint that fades to straw as the flowers mature. Best in full sun and poor, well-drained soil in a position where it can be appreciated. 30–40cm (12–16in). **Z3–8.**

Briza (POACEAE)

Another grass, but one of my favourites from childhood. In Britain *Briza media* is a native grass, which tolerates a wide range of moisture and soil pH, although it prefers slightly alkaline ground. Its tiny lockets move in the slightest breeze.

B. maxima An annual from the Mediterranean with large green lockets (which turn to a warm tan when the flowers have faded) and bright green foliage. 60cm (24in). This is a first-rate grass for drying for inclusion in dried flower arrangements. It can seed profusely. **Z8–10**.

***B. media* 'Limouzi'** This form was selected by Trevor Scott for its larger flowers with purple tints and its height. 45cm (18in). Flowers all summer. **Z5**.

Bupleurum (APIACEAE)

An understated genus from the umbellifer family, it contains many charming and attractive species, which blend well with naturalistic planting. The flowers are often muted greens and bronzes with flowers reminiscent of an astrantia, and much loved by flower arrangers. I have chosen examples that show diverse features. A succession of flowers continues from midsummer to early autumn. **Z3–9**.

B. angulosum This choice diminutive species 15–30cm (6–12in) tall, has subtle greeny-brown flowerheads and requires good drainage but can tolerate some shade.

B. longifolium* subsp. *aureum Glaucous grey leaves encase stout stems with astrantia-like inflorescences but in bronze and copper. Prefers a moisture-retentive soil in sun or dappled shade and will flower in summer and sporadically throughout the autumn if it is deadheaded. 45–60cm (18–24in).

Calamagrostis (POACEAE)

These are most useful grasses to give a strong vertical accent throughout the growing season. 1.5–2.4m (5–8ft). They flower in midsummer and persist well into the autumn without collapsing. They provide a useful foil and support for tall late-flowering perennials such as *Helianthus*, *Echinacea* and *Rudbeckia*. **Z5–9**.

***C. x acutiflora* 'Karl Foerster'** Named after the great German nurseryman, Karl Foerster. His ideas have been a major influence in the "naturalistic planting" designs so popular today. Erect, upright growth to 1.8m (6ft) with soft tawny brown flower plumes that fade to straw later in the season. Well-drained soil but not too dry. **'Overdam'**: A cream and green variegated form of the above. 1.2m (4ft).

Calamintha (LAMIACEAE)

These aromatic herbs have small leaves with a minty aroma and spikes of little flowers that are very attractive to pollinating insects, especially bees and hoverflies. Poor soil with good drainage and full sun are requisites for this genus. They do not appreciate winter wet. **Z5–9**.

C. nepeta This has neat mounds of aromatic glossy foliage and pale lavender flowers for months until the frosts. Beloved by bees. 15cm (6in). It makes a good frontal plant or will combine well with other low-growing plants in gravel or a raised gritty bed. Try it with one of the filigree umbellifers such as *Seseli hippomarathrum* (30–45cm/12–18in) or *Athamanta turbith* (45–60cm/18–24in).

***C. n.* subsp. *glandulosa* 'White Cloud'** This has small white flowers appearing like a haze over the tiny bushlets. The flowers fade to buff with time. 15cm (6in).

***C. n.* subsp. *nepeta* 'Blue Cloud'** In this form the leaves are softly hairy and the flowers a deeper blue. 15cm (6in).

***C. n.* 'Weisse Riese'** A recent introduction which has lovely pale yellow buds before they open to white flowers. Its growth can be rather rangy so is best grown on poor soil to prevent it from flopping. 15–20cm (6–8in).

Carlina acaulis subsp. *simplex bronze* (ASTERACEAE)

I am always on the lookout for plants that are attractive to beneficial insects, as I am an inherently lazy gardener and would prefer my insect minions to gobble up aphids and other pests rather than do anything myself. It helps if the nectar sources I provide are also interesting and attractive to my eye. This stemless thistle thrives in full sun in poor soil and is a good subject for my raised gravel bed. The foliage is prickly, coppery bronze, heavily overlaid with purple, and the flowers are large, flat silvery-white thistles. 45cm (18in). They also make an unusual contribution to dried flower arrangements. **Z5**.

Centaurea (ASTERACEAE)

This group of plants, flowering throughout the summer months without a pause, is caviar to bees and hoverflies. In 2004, several of my plants continued blooming, with no deadheading, until the first severe frosts of November. Seed-heads are ornamental in winter and the seeds themselves are invaluable to seed-eating birds through the winter months. There are a number of species with no real garden merit but a few species and cultivars are first-

rate garden plants, which sit well in naturalistic plantings, requiring little more than full sun, poor soil and reasonable drainage.

C. bella and **C. simplicicaulis** These are both small mound-forming plants to 45cm (18in) and most suited to a raised gritty bed or gravel border although they can be used as frontal plants. They have silvery grey-green pinnate foliage and cornflowers of lavender pink. *C. simplicicaulis* has more refined, dissected foliage than *C. bella*. **Z5**.

C. benoistii In flower reaches 1.5m (5ft) with deepest claret-maroon cornflowers. A good companion to other tall herbaceous plants and grasses. **Z5**.

C. orientalis Yellow flowers on 1.2m (4ft) stems over fine silvery grey pinnate foliage. **Z7**.

C. 'Phoenix Bronze' I grow many species of *Centaurea* to attract insects and a couple of years ago I noticed a bronze-coloured cornflower between a clump of *C. benoistii* and *C. orientalis*. It is reasonable to suppose that this is a hybrid between the two, showing an intermediate colour to the parent plants. I have also seen bronze hybrids between *C. benoistii* and *C. rupestris* but they do not appear so robust or vigorous. This bronze hybrid is an excellent garden plant, 1.5m (5ft) tall, and flowers from the end of May until the frosts. When the flower has finished it produces fertile seed, which is ejected forcefully when the sun warms the seed-head. It opens like a silver star and loose seed drops out. Even when the seed has gone, the spent seed-heads open and close with the sunshine. Buds, flowers and starry seed-heads make a spectacular display for many months. The only problem is that it is slow to propagate vegetatively but I am eagerly awaiting the flowering of the first seed progeny. **Z6**.

C. rupestris A golden scabious with filigree foliage reaching 90cm (36in) in height. **Z6**.

C. ruthenica A pale straw-yellow species with thick, waxy deep green leaves. Although it originates from

Left: *Centaurea* 'Phoenix Bronze'

southern Russia and Romania, I find this more difficult to overwinter. Perhaps it is winter wet that is the problem rather than cold. 1.2m (4ft). **Z3.**

Centranthus (VALERIANACEAE)

These are familiar plants on waste ground and walls, and along motorway corridors. There are white, pink and red forms (known by the vernacular name of red valerian). It flowers in late spring and early summer, but if it is cut back hard after its first flush it will rebloom into autumn. Enticing insects for its nectar, it is a useful plant to provide sustenance for pollinating insects before winter. **Z5–9.**

C. lecoqii Originally I grew this as *C. ruber* 'Mauve Form', but I have now been reliably informed that this is its correct moniker. A native of France and southern Spain, it is a most unusual pale lilac-mauve and has been a good nectar supply for migrant Hummingbird hawkmoths. 60cm (24in).

C. ruber **'Albus'** Pure white with light green foliage. 'Coccineus' is a deep red form, but an inveterate seeder. 60cm (24in).

Cephalaria (DIPSACACEAE)

These giants of the scabious kingdom are distinct with cream to pale yellow flowers. The most familiar species used in gardens is *C. gigantea* which grows to 1.8m (6ft) or more. I find it has rather coarse foliage so is best placed at the back of the border. Butterflies and bees adore the flowers, which set prolific seed and it self-sows. Prefers sun and good drainage although tolerates light shade. It combines well with other tall perennials.

C. dipsacoides This attains 2m (6ft 6in) or more with a strong wiry framework and pale yellow flowers in July. The seed-heads persist to give an elegant skeleton throughout the winter months, as well as providing food for a charm of goldfinches. **Z3–8.**

C. **sp. HWJ695** Collected by Sue and Bleddyn Wynn-

Top left: *Centranthus ruber*
Left: *Colchicum* 'Rosy Dawn' AGM

Jones, this *Cephalaria* has coarse foliage but it flowers late in the season during August to October. The pale yellow flowers have distinct black stamens with purple anthers. 1.2m (4ft). **Z3–8**.

Chrysanthemum (ASTERACEAE)

A genus that has unaccountably changed its name so often that it is difficult to know where the botanists will place it next! At present, I believe the hardy chrysanthemums are included within *Chrysanthemum*. These autumn-flowering daisies are probably the most loved and familiar of the entire composite family, for use as a cut flower. They can also be used with some success in the garden, although they do not tolerate winter wet. It is best to grow them on free-draining soil and, if this is not available, lift them and containerize the plants as stock over winter. Divisions or early spring cuttings will encourage vigour for the new season. The two main groups used as perennials in the garden are the 'Rubellum' and 'Korean' group. The former are derived from *C. zawadskii*, a hardy species found in Korea, China and Japan while the latter arose in the United States from a breeding programme involving *C. coreanum* and a florist's chrysanthemum. **Z5–9**.

C. **'Duchess of Edinburgh'** Semi-double, rich wine-red. 75cm (30in).

C. **'Emperor of China'** Late flowering into October with quilled pale pink petals and foliage suffused with red and maroon. 1.2m (4ft).

C. **'Innocence'** Sugar-pink single flowers. 75cm (30in).

C. **'Paul Boissier'** Double flowers of coppery bronze. Late flowering. 75cm (30in).

C. **'Ruby Mound'** A rich semi-double burgundy red. 60cm (24in).

C. **'Uri'** A recent introduction with deep pink flowers with a yellow eye. This appears to be more perennial than most. 90cm (36in).

Cirsium (ASTERACEAE)

This is another family of thistles providing nectar for pollinating insects and seed for the birds throughout autumn and winter. Flowering starts in summer and can persist until September. They look well in a naturalistic planting especially among grasses and umbellifers. The few I have chosen have stature, growing to 1.2m (4ft) or more. They prefer a sunny position but not too dry. **Z5**.

C. heterophyllum Deep lilac-purple thistles with dark green spiny foliage. 1.5m (5ft). **Z5**.

C. rivulare **'Atropurpureum'** Burgundy-maroon thistles on 1.5m (5ft) flowering stems from July onwards. This does not set seed so it continues to produce flowers over a long period and is propagated by division. It requires a moisture-retentive soil, unlike many of its relatives, and grows best if it is given sufficient space and does not have to compete with other plants.

C. tuberosum Similar colour flowers to that above but with shiny-toothed, grey-green leaves. It has a habit of seeding around. 1.5m (5ft). **Z4–8**.

Colchicum speciosum AGM (COLCHICACEAE)

Invaluable bulbs for a good autumn display in dappled shade or sun if the soil is not too dry. The flowers arise before the foliage and the weak stems can sometimes be damaged by adverse weather conditions at this time. Growing colchicums through low-growing ground cover can help to alleviate this problem by providing some support at the base. White, pink and pinkish-purple flowered colchicums are available, many of them with delicate tessellated markings. The foliage is rather coarse and succeeds the flowers but it is important that the leaves are left intact until they die naturally, or the bulbs are seriously weakened. They need to be placed where the foliage is not an eyesore or behind other plants which will conceal it. 15cm (6in). **Z6–9**.

Convolvulus (CONVOLVULACEAE)

Considered a rampant pest with its insidious creeping white roots and twining stems, Britain's native *Convolvulus arvensis* has many beautiful relatives that do deserve garden room, flowering from midsummer until the autumn frosts.

C. althaeoides At its worst, an unrestrained thug in well-drained soil in sun with large silvery pink *Convolvulus* flowers. Striking grown up an obelisk or allowed to tumble from a chimney pot container, this native of southern Europe has fine silver-grey foliage. **Z9–10.**

C. sabatius **AGM** (syn. *C. mauretanicus*) Satiny blue flowers are produced all summer and up to the first frosts on sprawling stems. Not hardy except in the warmest counties, this growth habit can be used to great advantage in tall containers or on top of a wall where the stems can tumble earthwards with their shower of silvery blue. I have grown a more compact form with dark blue flowers, which set viable seed, but the majority of plants available have larger and paler blue flowers and are infertile, so they produce flower for a longer period. **Z7–10.**

Coreopsis (ASTERACEAE)

Useful golden daisies for late-summer and autumn displays, with prolific flower production for many weeks. They are excellent as cut blooms and last well in water, combining well with purple flowers and foliage. Pore over seed catalogues to select a good range of size and colour.

C. tripteris This native of North America is tall and rangy with fine green foliage and small light yellow flowers produced on stems to 2.4m (8ft). Staking is rarely necessary despite its height. Judicious pruning before flower buds develop will limit the growth of the flowering stems, which may be more suitable in a smaller garden. However, artificially reducing the height of flower production can sometimes result in stunted-looking plants that do not look natural. An intermediate solution would be to prune some stems and not others so flowers appear at different heights on the same plant. **Z4–9.**

C. verticillata 'Moonbeam' AGM A profusion of luminous pale lemon daisies over a haze of fine filigree green foliage. 45cm (18in). **Z4–9.**

Cosmos (ASTERACEAE)

These colourful daisy relatives, originating in Mexico, are useful for enlivening a late-summer border, with white, pink and red flowers predominant in the annual *Cosmos bipinnatus*. This has green dissected foliage, which acts as a good foil for the flowers. Poor soil and sun are requisites for a good display. Rich well-fed soil tends to promote vegetative growth and little flower. There are a number of different seed mixtures which range in size from 60cm (24in), as in the 'Sonata Series' AGM, to 1.2m (4ft), as in the 'Sensation Series'. Single-coloured seed mixes are sometimes available for inclusion in a colour-themed border.

An altogether more demure member of the genus, *Cosmos atrosanguineus* is best known for its deep velvety maroon-black flowers, which are chocolate scented. This plant has similarities to a dahlia with a tuberous perennial rootstock. It is only hardy in the

Above: *Cosmos bipinnatus*
Right: *Crambe cordifolia* AGM

warmest areas and well-drained, warm light soil. In colder areas it can be successfully grown in containers and overwintered inside. Spring cuttings will produce flowering plants through late summer and into the autumn, until the first frosts. 60cm (24in). **Z8.**

Crambe (BRASSICACEAE)

This genus is in the cabbage family but provides us with a couple of ornamental plants, which add a great architectural presence in the border.

C. cordifolia **AGM** A giant which can grow 3m (10ft) tall with great billowing masses of small white flowers, and seen at its best against a dark background, such as a yew hedge. The skeleton persists into late summer and autumn. Flea beetle can disfigure the foliage by eating holes in the leaves, but as this plant is usually placed towards the back of the border this may not be a problem. Proprietary insecticides should alleviate the problem. **Z6–9.**

C. maritima **AGM** The sea kale is a British native growing on poor stony ground on the coast. This is a fine plant for coastal gardens as it can tolerate sea spray. Some forms of this plant have deep purple buds and foliage, turning greener during the season. For ornamental purposes the more purple varieties are the most desirable. Succulent, undulating, broad-leaved foliage persists from late spring to autumn. Large and Small White butterflies (the Cabbage whites) can be a serious pest, laying eggs on the undersides of the leaves. The larvae consume vast amounts of the fleshy foliage disfiguring them badly. If you garden organically, these caterpillars must be removed rapidly, either by hand picking or with a non-chemical spray. An infusion of garlic in boiling water, cooled and filtered, works well but it is important to remember to lift up all the leaves to spray the undersides where the eggs are laid. I tend to scrape off the eggs before they hatch. 60cm (24in). **Z6–9.**

Crocosmia add flashes of colour and interest. There are many beautiful cultivars to choose from, all with graceful arching stems bedecked with flowers. A few have attractive bronzed foliage, which combines well with the blossoms. Crocosmias originate in South Africa and are adapted to summer moisture. If they are too dry during the warmer months they can succumb to attacks by red spider mite, which disfigures the foliage. They range in size from 45–90cm (18–36in), flowering from midsummer to early autumn. **Z5–6.**

Crocus (IRIDACEAE)

*Autumn-flowering crocus are wonderful naturalized in woodland or under shrubs and trees. They are better in a sheltered position, as bad weather can damage their delicate petals, and growing through low ground cover or in grass to support the slender stems. They are seldom taller than 10cm (4in) and best grown in generous swathes. **Z6–10.**

C. sativus This is the saffron crocus with large open purple flowers with darker veins and distinctive deep orange stigmas, which are the source of saffron. A Mediterranean plant, it thrives with summer drought in a well-drained alkaline soil.

C. speciosus AGM The most familiar autumn-flowering crocus with cool bluish-violet flowers with darker stencilled veins. Good forms such as 'Oxonian', which is deep blue, and 'Albus', a pure white, are available from bulb suppliers.

Crinum x *powellii* AGM (AMARYLLIDACEAE)

For massed planting and a superb autumn display, *Crinum* x *powellii* is unrivalled. It is the most hardy of these tropical plants but still requires a warm sheltered spot and copious amounts of moisture in summer for the large bulbs to thrive and produce their giant funnel-shaped flowers. 1.5m (5ft). In cooler climes they could be used successfully in big containers but require a good depth of soil to accommodate the bulbs. If they are left in the ground, mulch around the bulbs with straw, leaves or bracken. *C.* x *powellii* AGM has soft pink flowers, *C.* x *p.* 'Album' AGM a lovely white. **Z7–10.**

Cyclamen hederifolium AGM (PRIMULACEAE)

A harbinger of autumn, this cyclamen flowers before its leaves appear. It naturalizes well under trees and shrubs or the base of hedges in well-drained soil. It can also thrive under conifers, which are notorious for drying out the soil. Cyclamen will only flourish in these conditions if they receive enough winter

Crocosmia x *crocosmiiflora* (IRIDACEAE)

With lively colours in red, mandarin, soft orange and yellow, these are not candidates for the pastel garden but look best in a hot border or among naturalistic plantings with abundant grasses. As herbaceous plants and grasses fade to browns and tans during early autumn, the numerous forms of

moisture. Some forms of *C. hederifolium* are scented but by no means all and they vary in colour from deep rose-pink to almost purple through pink, pale blush and white. 15cm (6in). Foliage is also very variable; there are some with fine leaf markings, others with silvered or pewter-washed leaves. **Z5–10.**

Cynara (ASTERACEAE)

A thistle relative with deep rosy pink flowers and ornamental scaly bracts that are good for providing nectar for pollinating insects. They are strong architectural components in the border. Sun and good drainage are prerequisites to thrive.

C. baetica subsp. *maroccana* Not too easy to flower, this requires poor soil, sharp drainage and full sun. It has very spiny, narrow grey-green leaves and stems, with fabulous flowers of luminous reddish-purple and a hint of blue in mid- to late summer. 75cm (30in). **Z8–10.**

C. cardunculus AGM A giant in the herbaceous border at 2m (6ft 6in) or more with vast silvery grey mounds of foliage and tall stems with large rosy pink thistle-flowers. **Z6.**

C. c. Scolymus Group This is the edible globe artichoke, growing to a mere 90cm (36in) but a handsome ornamental plant if allowed to flower. As with the above, the seed-heads persist into autumn and contribute to the food supply of many hungry birds. **Z6.**

Cynoglossum amabile AGM (BORAGINACEAE)

An annual or biennial which, if sown successively throughout the season, will continue flowering until the early frosts. It is easy in most soils and has powder-blue forget-me-not flowers. 15cm (6in). Where happy, it will seed gently around. **Z7.**

Dahlia (ASTERACEAE)

This is a genus that I have gradually come to admire. As a child I would watch gardeners on their allotments erecting a concoction of sticks with upturned flowerpots stuffed with paper or straw. On enquiring what these things were for I was told, "That's for them there earywigs". The damage caused to the flowers by earwigs is indeed disfiguring as they eat great notches out of the petals but they do not seem to be as great a problem today as they were in my childhood.

I am fascinated by the pompom dahlias – surely nothing so perfectly formed and symmetrical could possibly be real. I find myself patting them gently; for me gardening is just as much about the tactile senses as the visual. I love the flamboyant quilled varieties, and find them somehow comical. That said, they are excellent as a cut flower because of their longevity in water but there are few that I would want to include in my garden. I always gravitate to single-flowered varieties or species and those that have interesting foliage. If a lush, tropical effect is desired, dahlias work particularly well with pollarded paulownias, bananas (*Musa*), agaves, *Melianthus* and cannas.

Dahlias originate in Mexico and are considered half-hardy. They make substantial storage tubers to survive the winter, when they are dormant. Lifting dahlia tubers after the first frosts once the top growth had died down used to be an annual task but today it

is more likely that the tubers will be left to overwinter in the ground, with a thick layer of open-structured mulch, such as straw, bracken or mushroom compost, to protect them from frost. Dahlias have an extensive colour range and flower late in summer and autumn, prolonging the season.

D. 'Bishop of Llandaff' AGM Introduced in 1926, this is still one of the most popular varieties grown today with its rich semi-double red flowers with a yellow eye. The bronzed purple foliage and stems enhance the flower colour. **Z8**.

D. coccinea A species with small single flowers of orange, red or yellow that combine gracefully with autumn flowering grasses. **Z7.**

D. sherffii Similar to *Dahlia merckii* but more substantial in flower and stronger in growth, this lavender purple species is still uncommon in cultivation. **Z8**.

Datisca cannabina (DATISCACEAE)

Although unrelated, this is the closest look-alike to hemp that you can legally plant in your garden! Used primarily for foliage effect, it has graceful arching stems to 1.5m (5ft) and rather insignificant tassels of greenish-yellow flowers. Male and female flowers are borne on different plants and fruit will form only when both sexes are present – with impressive pendulous fruiting stems in autumn. **Z8–9.**

Delphinium (RANUNCULACEAE)

This is another familiar genus for use in the garden and on the show bench. Delphinium breeding has tended to select for longer and more congested flowering spikes, which require support. Peak flowering is in early summer but removal of the spent flower stems usually results in a second flush when grasses are at their peak in late August and September. My preference is always for the smaller-flowered varieties or those that most closely resemble the species with well-spaced smaller blooms, which can survive the rigours of the elements without the need for staking. *Delphinium*

elatum is very variable and hardy, and a useful breeding parent. Crosses between *D. elatum* and *D. grandiflorum* have produced the *D.* x *belladonna* hybrids with many vivid blue varieties such as 'Atlantis' AGM and 'Volkerfrieden' AGM. The majority of delphiniums range through pink, blue and purple sectors of the spectrum. *Delphinium nudicaule* is a red-flowered species from North America that is pollinated by hummingbirds – these tiny birds appear to be attracted to reds and oranges and are responsible for pollinating agastaches and salvias in that colour range. *Delphinium zalil* (now *D. semibarbatum*) is yellow, and hails from Iran, but neither of these unusual-coloured species appear to be long lived and perennial in our climate. Slugs are the main enemy of delphiniums, eating the succulent new shoots as they emerge from the ground. There are so many good delphiniums to choose from that

Below: *Delphinium elatum*

I will only mention an exciting new introduction.
D. 'Liz Pelling' This fully double cultivar was raised
from seed collected by Ron Watts, who is responsible
for enriching Britain's garden flora with many good
introductions including *Aster* 'Kylie'. To my eye,
'Liz Pelling' is an improvement on 'Alice Artindale',
another powdery blue double variety, in which the
blooms look slightly pinched unless grown in the
best conditions. I hope 'Liz Pelling' will be widely
available in the next few years. 1–5m (5ft). **Z6–9**.

Deschampsia (POACEAE)

These are grasses of low to medium height – 90cm
(36in) – which can tolerate some shade if the soil is
not too dry. They tend to be short-lived and are better
if replaced every two to three years. Inveterate self-
seeders, the seedlings should be removed if a
named variety has been planted. It is all too easy for
variation to creep in. Rust is the main problem for
this grass, especially in dry conditions – it weakens
the plant but does not usually kill it. Most named
varieties flower in June and July producing a
translucent haze of bronze or golden panicles. The
flower stems persist into late summer and autumn,
adding useful brown and tan hues that associate well
with rich autumn colours of reds, russets and
yellows. Good associations with these grasses
include crocosmias, small kniphofias, coreopsis and
many of the reddish orange achilleas. *Deschampsia
cespitosa* 'Goldtau' flowers latest in July and persists
well into winter. The other named forms tend to
disintegrate in late autumn. **Z4–9**.

Dianthus (CARYOPHYLLACEAE)

Many species dianthus have small flowers atop wiry
stems, appearing to be suspended in mid air. Early
breeding regimes attempted to enlarge flower size
and produce more compact plants for the
conventional herbaceous border or as edging plants.
However, with the interest in more naturalistic
planting, small flowers have their place among
grasses and herbaceous foliage.

D. carthusianorum With its bright, magenta-red
blooms, it looks like a shower of fireworks. It grows to
60cm (24in) and prefers sunny, well-drained soil, and
will flower throughout the summer. **Z3–9**.
D. cruentus This is deep pink and has a similar effect.
45cm (18in). **Z7**.
D. knappii Has straw-yellow flowers and is not as
long-lived as the others but seeds around where
happy. I am also experimenting with some of the
smaller species, which could look good with smaller
grasses at the front of the border. 30cm (12in). **Z3**.
D. amurensis This is an unusual mauve (60cm/24in),
while *D. superbus* is frilly, pink and scented
(20cm/8in). **Z4**.

Diascia (SCROPHULARIACEAE)

This is a South African genus that has proved
relatively hardy in the British climate. In its native
country it flowers for a few weeks and then ceases to
do so as the temperature soars. In this country
flowering can continue for many months, well into
autumn. If the plant is cut back hard after the initial
flush, a good second blooming usually occurs. There
are many new hybrids instigated originally by the
successful breeding programmes in Britain carried out
by Hector Harrison, who sadly died recently. His
memory will linger in our gardens with his careful
selection of new colours and forms of diascia. They
are good in containers, including hanging baskets, as
many of them have a sprawling habit. Colours range
from white, through soft pink, apricots, red and
purple. Some of the salmon hues are difficult to place
although they make good companions to blue
flowers, such as calaminthas and nepetas. Most are
small, from 10–30cm (4–12in) in height, but often
make larger mats across. **Z7**.

Dictamnus (RUTACEAE)

This wonderful aromatic herbaceous plant gets better
with age, forming substantial clumps to 1.2m (4ft) in
time. Slugs are the main enemy to young shoots
emerging in spring. Flowers emerge in midsummer,

followed by attractive seed-pods in autumn. It requires a rich, moisture-retentive soil in sun to thrive. **Z3–8.**

D. albus var. albus AGM Spires of pure white starry flowers atop dissected foliage covered in small glands containing citrus scented volatile oils. The seed-heads that follow turn from green through brown and are highly decorative with shiny black seeds within. When ripe, the seedpods explode, catapulting the seed away from the parent plant. *D. a.* var. *purpureus* 'Purpureus' AGM The purple form of the above.

D. caucasicus Rarely seen, this species has larger pink flowers than the above.

Dierama (IRIDACEAE)

Narrow grass-like foliage and great arching wands of flowers make this a good subject to be placed by water, where the reflections can be much admired. Native to South Africa, there are many species that are worthy of inclusion in gardens. The most familiar is *D. pulcherrimum* with a range of colour from pure white to the almost blackcurrant shade of *D.p.* 'Blackbird', raised by the Slieve Donard Nursery in Northern Ireland. Smaller species such as *D. dracomontanum* and *D. pauciflorum* are deep rose-pink and magenta-pink respectively. They prefer a moisture-retentive but well-drained soil in sun. Their contribution to the late summer garden is mainly in the elegant arching seed-heads which, when ripe, open to expose the orange red seeds within. Recent introductions include *D. p.* 'Merlin', *D.* 'Lancelot' and *D.* 'Guinevere' bred by Jim Cave of Fir Tree Farm Nursery in Falmouth, Cornwall, UK. **Z7–9.**

Digitalis (SCROPHULARIACEAE)

Foxgloves create important vertical accents, especially in dappled shade and poor soils. The British native, *Digitalis purpurea,* is a biennial that flowers in late spring and summer, producing copious small seeds for future generations. There are other perennial foxgloves that flower later in the season and contribute to the late summer border with high-rise spikes of seed-heads, turning brown and russet as the season progresses. Indeed, the old flowering stems of *D. ferruginea* AGM persist well into winter, providing a superstructure for cobwebs and hoar-frost. *D. laevigata* is another perennial which blooms later in the season.

D. ferruginea AGM A giant at 1.5m (5ft), this golden-brown-flowered foxglove creates subtle vertical accents in a herbaceous border or among grasses. Perennial and easy to grow in well-drained soil. **Z7–9**.

D. laevigata This unusual foxglove has spires of orange-veined sacs with a protruding white lip on 90cm (36in) stems. Much prettier than its description. **Z5–8**.

Dipsacus (DIPSACACEAE)

The teasel is well known for its spiny leaves and prickly flowerheads and seeds. The spent seed-heads were once used for raising the nap on cloth.

D. strigosus Biennial. A large teasel up to 2.7m (9ft) tall. It is architectural and spiny, with flowers that can be dried for decoration or left for the charms of goldfinches in autumn. Especially good when silhouetted against the sky and rimed with hoarfrost during the winter months. **Z4–9**.

Echinacea (ASTERACEAE)

The magnificent cone flowers of North America are at their best in late summer and early autumn, requiring moist soil and plenty of space. Definitely not for the faint-hearted – their flamboyant blooms in strident shades of deep reddish pink and purple with contrasting orange cones are bold and extravagant but combine well with late-flowering grasses.

Recent breeding work between different species of echinacea at the Chicago Botanic Garden, led by Jim Ault, and at Itsaul Nursery, Atlanta, by Richard Saul

Opposite: *Digitalis ferruginea* AGM seed-head among *Deschampsia cespitosa* 'Goldtau'.
Right: *Echinacea purpurea* 'Rubinglow'

has provided some fabulous colour breaks – rich oranges, mango, sumptuous scarlets, pinks and russets. I predict that the demand for echinaceas has only just begun.

Already on the market are *Echinacea* Art's Pride (Orange meadowbrite), *E.* 'Mango Meadowbrite', *E.* 'Sunrise' and *E.* 'Sunset', the latter pair being sweetly scented. 'Sunlight', 'Twilight' and 'Harvest Moon', to be launched this year, are also reputed to be strongly fragrant. Other recent introductions include *E.* 'Razzmatazz', which looks like a mop-head, *E.* 'Fragrant Angel', a strongly scented white form, *E.* 'Doubledecker' with an absurd second row of petals at the top of the cone and *E. tennesseensis* Rocky Top Group, a more vigorous improvement on the species.

E. pallida This species has narrow drooping pink petals on 90cm (36in) stems. **Z5**.

E. paradoxa Unlike other members of this genus, this has yellow drooping rays. 90cm (36in). **Z3**.

E. purpurea 'Jade' A white-flowered form, selected by Piet Oudolf, with a central green cone rather than orange. E. p. 'Rubinglow' is an improved seed strain selected from E. p. 'Magnus' AGM by Piet Oudolf to give larger flowers and darker stems. **Z3**.

Echinops (ASTERACEAE)

The globe thistles are members of the aster family with spherical flowerheads with masses of starry flowers, which are blue or white. The nectar produced is caviar for bees and butterflies, which are ever present during flowering time through July to September. The orb-shaped seed-heads persist well into winter and are useful for drying or as food for the birds. Echinops require sun and good drainage to thrive.

E. bannaticus 'Taplow Blue' AGM A light blue globe thistle reaching 1.5–1.8m (5–6ft). **Z3–9**.

E. 'Nivalis' A white-flowered form with beautiful silvery-white divided foliage. This is probably a garden hybrid. 1.5–1.8m (5–6ft). **Z3**.

E. ritro 'Veitch's Blue' Deep blue orbs to 1.2m (4ft) over elegant stems clothed in grey jagged foliage. **Z3**.

E. sphaerocephalus A vigorous thistle 1.8–2.1m (6–7ft) with large greyish-white orbs. **Z3**.

Left: *Echinops bannaticus* 'Taplow Blue' AGM

Echium vulgare (BORAGINACEAE)

A British biennial native, known as viper's bugloss, that is found on poor calcareous soils in sun and adored by bees for its tubular blue or purplish-blue flowers, rarely pink or white. It has rather coarse, prickly foliage. Annual seed strains have been developed that will provide colour throughout the summer including shades of pink, rose and white. 60–90cm (24–36in). In Australia this plant has naturalized and I saw fields of viper's bugloss at heights to 1.2m (4ft). **Z3**.

Elymus hispidus (POACEAE)

To my mind still the best silvery blue-green non-running grass. Preferring full sun and sharp drainage it forms tight clumps, to 60cm (2ft), and looks good associated with plants such as *D. carthusianorum*, calaminthas, *Dracocephalum* and origanums. **Z6**.

Epilobium (ONAGRACEAE)

The willowherbs, some now classified as *Chamerion*, include many of our most pernicious weeds but there are some that are good garden plants. I have included two very different members of this genus which are still flowering in late summer.

E. dodonaei (now *Chamerion dodonaei*) Slender linear, pale grey-green leaves on stems tinged with pink give rise to multitudes of cerise pink flowers like hovering butterflies. In 2004 my stock plant was host to two larvae of the Elephant hawkmoth, which feed on *Epilobium* sp. before metamorphosing into a beautiful pink and green confection of a moth. Sun and good drainage suit this plant best. 1m (39in). **Z6**.

E. glabellum This New Zealand willowherb requires a moisture-retentive soil and grows best in dappled shade to 30cm (12in). It blooms continuously with its funnel-shaped creamy white flowers through late spring into autumn. Indeed it will flower itself to death if it is not cut back hard at the beginning of September. This drastic treatment enables the plant to make vegetative growth so it has a chance to overwinter. In 2004, my stock plant was host to a single larva of the Elephant hawkmoth, this time in its green form camouflaging well with the green leaves of the host plant. Most of the larvae are mustard-brown and stay well concealed during the day by aligning themselves with the stems of their host plant. **Z8–10.**

Epimedium (BERBERIDACEAE)

The flowering time of epimediums is in the spring and early summer but they are indispensable ground-cover plants for dry shade with many of them exhibiting brilliant fall colours of yellows, reds and reddish-purple. They are members of the *Berberis* family and have interestingly shaped leaves, often softly spiny on thin wiry stems. For shady sites under deciduous trees and shrubs they provide a point of focal interest late in the season and combine well with hardy cyclamen, colchicums and autumn-flowering crocus. 30–45cm (12–18in). **Z5–8.**

Eragrostis (POACEAE)

These are the "love grasses" of Africa, the Americas and Australia. Many of them seed around rather too freely and can become a nuisance. Keep a vigilant eye out for any unwanted seedlings and remove them before they become established. Most *Eragrostis* live on wasteland with poor soil and good drainage in full sun. Giving them the richer diet of a garden soil can make them lush, with a tendency to flop. A gravel bed and poor nutrients keep the plants more compact.

E. airoides A profusion of minute flowers on slender stems give this grass the impression of a web of gossamer in the dew. Starve in poor soil and full sun, and treat as an annual. 30cm (12in). **Z7.**

E. chloromelas Arching blue-green leaves with spikelets of purple and olive. 90cm (36in). **Z7.**

E. curvula From Africa, like that above, this forms an graceful arching clump, flowering throughout the summer. 60cm (24in). **Z7–10.**

E. spectabilis From North America and Mexico, this grass produces a filmy gauze of small reddish-purple tinged spikelets in late summer and autumn. Tends to be short-lived but easy by seed. 60cm (24in). **Z5.**

E. trichodes Much taller than the above, to 1.2m (4ft), this perennial grass does not colour so vividly as *E. spectabilis* but still has attractive greenish-purple flowers. North America. **Z5.**

Erigeron (ASTERACEAE)

A North American daisy relative, the erigerons have multiple slender-rayed petals with a yellow eye. Many of them are alpine plants but a few are suitable for the border. They prefer a sunny site with good drainage but tend to flop and require support if the soil is too rich.

E. karvinskianus AGM A myriad of small white daisies, fading pink, then purple, adorn this low-growing prostrate herb for several months during summer and into autumn. Seeding into walls and crevices, this delightful plant can soften hard landscaping features. 40cm (16in). **Z7.**

E. 'Quakeress' A rather floppy hybrid which tends to require staking or the support of closely planted neighbours, this 60cm (24in) daisy has slender white, pink-flushed ray petals with a yellow disc. **Z3.**

Erodium (GERANIACEAE)

I enjoy growing these relatives of the hardy geranium family, which flower for an extended period, and have attractive, dissected foliage. They revel in my gritty raised bed with full sun and sharp drainage. There is a tremendous range to choose from – silvery grey or green foliage and colours from white, pink, magenta, purple and yellow, many etched with fine maroon lines and blotches. They flower continuously from the end of May until the first heavy frosts. They are small and compact, rarely more than 30cm (12in) high.

E. 'Ardwick Redeye' A selection by Richard Clifton with clear green leaves and white flowers with a vivid red basal blotch on the upper two petals. A most unusual and distinctive hybrid. 15cm (6in). **Z8.**

E. chrysanthum This has always been a favourite of mine with its soft primrose-yellow flowers and tactile silvery grey ferny foliage. It is shy to flower but there is a vigorous hybrid called 'Arcadia' which blooms more freely. 20cm (8in). **Z6–8.**

E. gruinum An annual species with deeply dissected green leaves with striking crimson-to-burgundy mid-veins, which develop intensely during the colder months. In early spring slender stems arise from the leaf rosette with bluish-purple veined flowers, which remain fleetingly for a day, before a long beaked fruit, to 10cm (4in), emerges. Hails from Sicily and other Aegean islands. 50cm (20in). **Z8–10.**

E. x kolbianum 'Natasha' Pale lilac-pink flowers with a deep basal blotch on the uppermost petals and etched with maroon lines over silvery green foliage. Compact. 15cm (6in). **Z6–8.**

E. 'Merstham Pink' Shell-pink flowers with deeper pink veining and ferny foliage. 20cm (8in). **Z6–8.**

E. 'Robespierre' Selected by nurseryman Pierre Jolivot from Jardins d'en Face, this is somewhat similar to the vigorous *E. manescavii* with lusty mounds of green dissected foliage and large magenta-pink flowers with a maroon basal blotch on the upper petals and fine maroon veining. 30–40cm (12–16in). **Z6–8.**

Eryngium (APIACEAE)

I have always been interested in this genus – the Old World species eryngiums (or sea hollies) with their attractive prickly foliage and steely green, grey, blue or violet flowers and the dissimilar New World ones with their spiny sword-like leaves and green or red thimble-like inflorescences. Over the years I have built up a fine collection and find that many contribute to the late summer and early autumn scene with flowers and spectacular seed-heads.

As a general rule the Old World eryngiums, especially those that colour blue or purple, require good drainage. Sunlight intensifies the coloration. New World eryngiums prefer a richer, moist soil. This could well be because of their physiological differences – the former have long fleshy taproots whereas the latter have a fibrous root system. There are few pests and diseases although aphids can be a problem on lush new growth, especially at the point where flowerbud meets the stem.

Many of the Old World eryngiums flower in early to mid-summer and cannot really be included in a late-summer list. Seed-heads, however, do look architectural till late in the season and contribute to the structure of a border by providing a template for cobwebs or droplets of dew. Those with showy bracts around the flower umbels persist longer: for example, *E. giganteum* AGM and *E. g.* 'Silver Ghost' AGM with their large cones, *E. alpinum* forms with their soft feathery bracts, *E. bourgatii*, *E. x oliverianum* AGM, *E. x zabelii* and *E. amethystinum* with their ruff of sharply spiny bracts. They are all good subjects for drying for indoor decoration.

The New World eryngiums are spectacular for foliage effect throughout most of the year. Their flowers tend to be smaller and not so decorative but flowering time is usually in the late summer and autumn with the skeletal remains of the flower stems persisting into winter.

I have selected a few examples of late-flowering sea hollies.

E. ebracteatum Thin wiry stems with tiny green cylinder-like flowers, resembling small sanguisorba burrs, and narrow sword-shaped grey-green leaves. 1.2m (4ft).

E. e. var. poteroides One of my favourites, flowering through August and September with tiny reddish brown cylinders. 1.2–1.5m (4–5ft). **Z8.**

E. maritimum Our native sea holly with glaucous grey-green prickly leaves and greenish rather globular flowers in August. Needs a strict starvation diet and sun to grow well. 60cm (24in). **Z5.**

OPPOSITE Top left: *Eryngium ebracteatum* var. *poterioides*; top right; *E. giganteum* AGM; bottom left: *E. maritimum*; bottom right: *E. pandanifolium* 'Physic Purple'.

***E. pandanifolium* 'Physic Purple'** This is the form
from the Chelsea Physic Garden, London, which is
particularly robust and makes a fine specimen plant.
In late summer the flowering stems emerge from the
large green rosette of spiny leaves to reach 2.4m
(8ft), covered with small dark red thimble-like
flowers. It blooms so late that the frosts often
prevent seed ripening, hence this eryngium is rarely
available. **Z8.**
***E. planum* 'Blaukappe'** A seed strain of this species
with multitudes of round blue thimbles on branched
stems and a more circular serrated leaf than other
named *E. planum* varieties. **Z5–9**.
E. proteiflorum A New World eryngium with large
prickly basal rosettes and steely green flowers
reminiscent of a *Protea*. This species requires good
fertile soil with good drainage but is not completely
hardy. 45cm (18in). **Z8.**
E. venustum A very distinct South American species
making squat clumps of broad, sharply toothed
leaves under stiff stems carrying multiple green
thimbles. 60cm (24in). **Z7.**

Eucomis (HYACINTHACEAE)
A genus of bulbous perennials from the southern
regions of Africa, often referred to as pineapple lilies
because of their extraordinary topknot of star-shaped
flowers on thick round stems, above a rosette of
strap-shaped fleshy leaves. They make excellent
container subjects, provided they are given a good
depth of well-drained but moisture-retentive
compost. They flower late in August to November and
look best planted in groups. In milder counties, they
will survive over winter in a sheltered position in the
garden but it is best to provide them with a frost-free
environment. 45–75cm (18–30in). **Z8.**

E. bicolor is one of the hardiest species with dark
green foliage, and purple-edged flowers and bracts.
E. comosa often shows a tendency towards purple
foliage and breeders have selected hybrids with good
leaf colour. *E.* 'Zeal Bronze' was selected by Terry
Jones from Zeal Monachorum, Devon, and has

reddish-purple foliage early in the season, fading to a
bronzed-green by midsummer. *E. comosa* 'Sparkling
Burgundy' has burnished reddish-purple leaves and
deep pink flowers darkening to reddish bronze.

Eupatorium (ASTERACEAE)
Tall herbaceous plants, which flower from midsummer until the autumn in shades of pink, purple
and white. These include the Joe pye-weed from
North America that provides the backbone to many
late-summer borders and provides food for late
butterflies on the wing. The native *E. cannabinum*
thrives in moisture-retentive soils, growing naturally
alongside watercourses. They start to bloom in early
summer and often continue for several weeks with
large heads consisting of hundreds of fluffy pink
flowers. I hesitate to mention the pink hue is a touch
muddy in colour. Other forms are available, *E. c.*
'Album', which is white flowered,and *E. c.* 'Flore
Pleno', which is a double. The latter flowers for many
weeks as it is sterile and so not putting energy into
seed production. The real star for late summer is the
American *E. purpureum* and there are many good
cultivars available. **Z3–10.**
***E. capillifolium* 'Elegant Feather'** A foliage plant
totally dissimilar to other members of this genus with
wand-like 1.5m (5ft) stems clothed in filigree bright
green foliage. Insignificant flowers appear in
November.
E. purpureum The trouble with the Joe pye-weeds are
the Latin names – so cumbersome and so long – but
the plants are hardy, long-lived and easy if given
enough moisture through the growing season. They
are giants, often attaining heights of 2.4m (8ft) or
more, with vast heads of rosy-purple scented flowers.
***E. p.* subsp. *maculatum* 'Album'** (See what I mean
about the names!) Towers to as much as 3m (10ft)
with sturdy stems topped by fluffy white flowers.

Top right: *Eupatorium capillifolium* 'Elegant Feather'
Right: *E. purpureum* subsp. *maculatum* 'Atropurpureum'
AGM

E. p. subsp. m. 'Atropurpureum' AGM In good forms this has purple-stained stems and leaves with great reddish-purple plates of flowers. 1.8–2.4m (6–8ft).

E. p. subsp. m. 'Purple Bush' Similar to the above but always 30cm (12in) shorter. Possibly a subject for the smaller garden.

E. p. subsp. m. 'Riesenschirm' Gigantic salvers of reddish-purple blooms and dark purple-stained stems. Outstanding display in the current *Eupatorium* trials at RHS Wisley. 1.8–2.4m (6–8ft).

Euphorbia (EUPHORBIACEAE)

These are valuable architectural or specimen plants for the garden, often with striking foliage and coloured leaf bracts surrounding the unusual flower formation. Several species have lime-green bracts, which combine well with many other colours and are much loved by flower arrangers. It is important to note that the white sap exuded by cut stems or foliage is a skin irritant and must be washed off immediately.

Many euphorbias flower in spring and early summer, the foliage providing interest later in the year. They are not subject to much in the way of pests and diseases although various rusts have been causing a few problems in recent years and powdery mildew can badly disfigure certain species, such as *E. amygdaloides* 'Purpurea'. *E. dulcis* 'Chameleon', a good deep purple-foliaged form, which provides an excellent foil for pink or white flowering plants, was a victim to euphorbia rust several years ago. More recently, *E. griffithii* forms have succumbed to the fungus. Spraying is an option but the chemical used has to be changed frequently to prevent immunity.

The following contribute to the late-summer border but there are many more.

E. cornigera AGM A handsome July-flowering spurge with mahogany red stems contrasting well with the greenish-yellow heads. 1.2m (4ft). In autumn the foliage turns butter yellow and the burnished red stems look wonderful if backlit by the setting sun. **Z7.**

E. nicaeensis A superb foliage plant making clumps of blue-green foliage and jade-green flowers throughout

the summer. The bracts gradually change to terracotta as the autumn progresses. 60cm (24in). **Z6**

E. sarawschanica Stately at 1.5cm (5ft) with wonderful soft yellow autumn coloration and contrasting pink flower stems. Lime-yellow flower heads through summer. **Z7.**

E. schillingii Excellent foliage plant with striking white mid-veins on the linear leaves. It flowers through July with lime-green bracts. 90cm (3ft). **Z7.**

E. stygiana A superior plant to *E. mellifera* in all its attributes – more hardy and robust, larger waxy leaves with a prominent mid-vein and honey-scented flowers in summer. A definable presence for a sunny sheltered spot. From the Azores. 1.2m (4ft). Hybrids between *E. stygiana* and *E. mellifera* (now called *E.* x *pasteurii*) are even more handsome specimen plants growing to 1.8m (6ft) tall, but not so hardy. **Z7.**

Ferula communis (APIACEAE)

A handsome umbellifer with mounds of fine filigree green foliage to 75cm (30in). *F. c.* subsp. *glauca* has grey-green foliage but is not so hardy and is only suitable for a warm sunny position against a wall. In midsummer the flowering spike emerges from the foliage, towering to 3.6m (12ft) in good conditions, with large yellow umbels that persist into the autumn. A fine architectural plant but one that does not flower annually. It occasionally aestivates (has a summer dormant period) while it builds up vim to flower again. **Z8.**

Foeniculum vulgare 'Giant Bronze' (APIACEAE)

A good bronze selection with finely cut foliage that provides a good foil for other plants. Best in sharply drained soil in full sun, with yellow flowers in summer and attractive seed-pods throughout autumn. A template for dew-laden cobwebs. 1.5m (5ft). **Z5.**

Left: *Ferula communis*

Galanthus reginae-olgae (AMARYLLIDACEAE)

Snowdrops are generally considered to be the harbingers of spring but this Greek species flowers in autumn when the summer drought has ended. It is faintly scented and has linear leaves with a distinct pale mid-vein. 15cm (6in). **Z6.**

Galega (PAPILIONACEAE)

These are members of the pea family that flower through the summer months. They have a tendency to produce copious amounts of foliage and a limited amount of flowers but the attractive pinnate leaves are decorative in their own right.

G. x hartlandii 'Alba' AGM Large, leafy herbaceous plants with pure white flowers. 1.5m (5ft). **Z4–8.**

G. orientalis Clear bluish-purple spikes of pea flowers to 1.2m (4ft). Plants have a running habit. **Z5–8.**

Galtonia (HYACINTHACEAE)

These South African bulbs flower in late summer, in late July and into August. They require rich, moisture-retentive soil in sun or dappled shade.

G. candicans AGM White-flowered pendent bells on 90cm (36in) stems. **Z5.**

G. viridiflora A colour much sought after by flower arrangers, this bulb has slender pendulous greenish-white blooms. A cool effect for the heat of August. 90cm (36in). **Z8.**

Gaura lindheimeri AGM (ONAGRACEAE)

These are light, airy perennials with almost continuous flower production from early summer through to the frosts. As they have a tendency to flop, it is best to grow them on a starvation diet in sun with sharp drainage. I find this keeps them more compact although cultivars such as *G. l.* 'Whirling Butterflies' are supposed to be more erect. Clouds of butterfly-like flowers atop wiry flowering stems give an informality that suits a cottage-garden style or naturalistic planting.

Several years ago, a colour break in deep pink from the US became very popular, selling as *G. l.* 'Siskiyou Pink'. Since then several more forms have been introduced and I have lost count of them all and feel that many are not sufficiently distinct to warrant a name. They are sold as patio plants, useful for containers but are generally short-lived. **Z7.**

G. lindheimeri AGM Willow-like leaves and clouds of white pink-tinged butterflies from midsummer onwards. 75cm (30in).

G. l. 'Corrie's Gold' A number of variegated forms have been named but I think this is still the finest with bold and regular gold margins to the leaf. 75cm (30in).

Geranium (GERANIACEAE)

There is a hardy geranium for almost every microclimate that may be found in a garden. Dry shade, full sun, perishing winds – nothing seems to deter this versatile group. Even severe pruning as a result of the ravages of deer and rabbits encourages bushier and vigorous growth after the original setback. Most geraniums flower in late spring and early summer and are not subjects for this book although good autumn red-coloured foliage is common. Cutting back hard after flowering will encourage most to produce a second flush of flowers in late summer. I have chosen a limited selection, usually in flower through July to the first frosts.

G. 'Orion' AGM This deservedly popular recent introduction, a seedling from 'Brookside', was selected by Brian Kabbes, a Dutch nurseryman, and has large bowl-shaped blue flowers. 75cm (30in). **Z4–8.**

G. 'Patricia' AGM A hybrid with *G. psilostemon* in its parentage, it flowers throughout summer with strident magenta-pink flowers etched with purple. 90cm (36in). *G.* 'Ivan' AGM is a similar cross but is shorter at 60cm (24in) with more defined etchings to the underside of the petals. Both are sterile which prolongs flower production. **Both Z4–8.**

G. 'Pink Delight' A plant selected by Juliet Robinson from her garden with soft pink blooms, which appear to be particularly attractive to Small Tortoiseshell butterflies in autumn. For a well-drained site in full sun. 10cm (4in). **Z7–10.**

G. x *riversleaianum* (*G. endressii* x *G. traversii*) These hybrids have attractive tactile, softly hairy foliage and a sprawling habit ending in billowing masses of small flowers. 'Mavis Simpson' AGM has pretty soft-pink blooms and 'Russell Prichard' AGM is a vivid magenta-pink. They flower endlessly as they are sterile and do not produce seeds. 15cm (6in).

G. *sanguineum* There are many good selected forms which flower for months on end. Some of the more vivid pinks and magenta forms are a little acid but the pale pink *G. sanguineum* var. *striatum* AGM with its darker pink etched markings is delightful and charming. 15–30cm (6–12in). **Z4–8.**

G. *traversii* var. *elegans* Not totally hardy, this New Zealand geranium has softly hairy rounded grey-green leaves that feel like velvet. The small, shell-pink flowers are a bonus. 10cm (4in). **Z8–10.**

G. *wallichianum* 'Buxton's Variety' This indispensable geranium starts late into leaf and begins to flower in July, continuing until the first heavy frosts. It prefers a humus-rich soil and partial shade – in sun the flowers will be purple with a white eye instead of blue. Sprawling growth can extend to 90cm (36in) diameter in a season. 20–30cm (8–12in).

Recent introductions using *G. wallichianum* as a parent have produced some outstanding sterile hybrids, which can tolerate sun and remain blue, starting into flower earlier in the season. They also have larger flowers. Rozanne ('Gerwat') and 'Jolly Bee' both have Plant Breeders' Rights but are first-rate garden plants. **Z5.**

Top left: *Geranium* x *riversleaianum* 'Mavis Simpson' AGM
Left: *Geranium* Rozanne ('Gerwat')
Right: *Gillenia trifoliata* AGM

Gillenia trifoliata AGM (ROSACEAE)

A personal favourite and one that exhibits great qualities throughout its growing season. Although a woodlander in its native North America, I have found that it performs best in full sun with a moisture-retentive soil. 90cm (36in). Pink-bronzed shoots emerge in spring, its delicate white flowers are subtended by a showy red calyx, followed by beautiful seed-heads, and the foliage turns crimson in autumn. What more could you ask? **Z4–8.**

A less known relative, *G. stipulata,* has finer foliage and is not so robust but it flowered two to three weeks later than the above, extending the season. According to the books it should flower earlier, so I am confused. Maybe it is confused? **Z4–8.**

Gladiolus papilio (IRIDACEAE)

This has dusky maroon, green and brown hooded blooms over fine bluish-grey foliage. A South African bulb, it prefers a moisture-retentive but well-drained soil in sun and flowers best when physically restricted. 45cm (18in). August to October. **Z8.**

Glaucium corniculatum (PAPAVERACEAE)

Clear orange poppies over crenulate grey foliage – it thrives in lean, stony soil with full sun and sharp drainage. 60cm (24in). July–September. **Z7–10.**

Gypsophila paniculata (CARYOPHYLLACEAE)

Hardy, branched perennial with billowing, translucent clouds of minute flowers, *G. paniculata* grows to 1.5m (5ft) and flowers through July and August. A popular item for the cut-flower trade, its delicate blooms provide a good foil for larger flowers. There are many good named forms in pink or white and several double-flowered forms such as 'Bristol Fairy' AGM (white) and 'Flamingo' (pink) which generally bloom for longer. They are equally at home in a conventional herbaceous border or among a more naturalistic planting alongside grasses and tall perennials. **Z4.**

Hakonechloa macra (POACEAE)

One of the best grasses for winter interest, this is the non-variegated *Hakonechloa* with green foliage and decorative spikelets in August and September. 75cm (30in). A native to Japan, it prefers a cool root-run and not too dry conditions, tolerating some shade. The foliage fades to browns and tans during winter and, when planted en masse, at the slightest breeze resembles a rippling sea. **Z4.**

Helenium (ASTERACEAE)

Invaluable in the late-summer border with rich hues of yellow, brown, gold, rust and red, these daisies work well with later flowering grasses in a sunny position and moisture-retentive soil. Easy and trouble free, these North American daisies are becoming increasingly popular for providing late-season colour. **Z5–8.**

H. **'Butterpat' AGM** Clear butter yellow flowers on stems to 90cm (36in). A selection from Alan Bloom.

H. **'Dunkelpracht'** Rich, rusty red daisies. 1.2m (4ft).

H. **'Flammendes Käthchen'** Coppery orange-brown, fading to yellow. 1.5m (5ft).

H. **'Moerheim Beauty' AGM** An old variety with reddish-brown flowers. 1.2m (4ft).

H. **'Rubinzwerg' AGM** Floriferous with mahogany-red flowers on 90cm (36in) stems.

H. **'Sahin's Early Flowerer' AGM** Earliest to bloom at the end of July with large daisies of varying colours from ochre through yellow, red and brown during its development. 1.2m (4ft).

Helianthus (ASTERACEAE)

I have a sneaking respect for these towering giants of the daisy world, thrusting their flowers well above my head towards the sunlight. Usually yellow (a colour spurned by many experienced gardeners) they are an uplifting addition to the more subdued purples and

Left: *Helenium* cvs
Opposite, top: *Helianthus annuus* cv
Opposite, bottom: *Helianthus* 'Gullick's Variety' AGM

russets of the autumn border. Dare I admit that yellow is one of my favourite colours? But I prefer the primrose end of the spectrum rather than the brassy mustard hues. To add to my enjoyment many sunflowers smell of chocolate (another indulgence) especially *H.* 'Monarch' AGM and *H.* 'Gullick's Variety AGM. Unfortunately many of these perennial sunflowers run, but in a wilder area of the garden, who cares? Staking is often necessary as the flowering stems become top-heavy. **Z4.**

H. **x *kellermanii*** Similar to *H. salicifolius* with a touch more refinement and not so liable to topple among its neighbours. 2.4m (8ft).

H. **'Lemon Queen' AGM** Unusual for its small lemon-coloured daisies, it is often more acceptable to gardeners who despise the more brassy yellows. 2.1m (7ft).

H. **'Monarch' AGM** Large semi-double golden-yellow flowers with a chocolate-scented brown disc. 2.4m (8ft).

H. ***salicifolius*** Willowy green leaves on whippy decumbent stems are topped by small golden daisies late into September. 2.7m (9ft). This plant needs a large space to sprawl through other tall perennials – it can be cut back in summer to provoke it to flower on shorter stems but somehow the distinct lanky character of the sunflower is lost. Combines well with *Vernonia crinita* and *Eupatorium maculatum* ssp. *purpureum* 'Atropurpureum' AGM.

There are many annual sunflowers that can be grown from seed. They are fun and easy to grow, and have a wide colour range including dusky reds, orange, yellow and creamy white. Try a few.

Heliotropium arborescens (BORAGINACEAE)

A good range of colour and form is available providing good subjects for containers and formal plantings, flowering for months into late autumn. I always favour those that are scented; it is rather like choosing petunias or tobacco plants – what is the point without the scent? If colour is the important feature, however, there is far more choice. These are

tender perennials and require a frost-free environment to overwinter successfully. 'Chatsworth' AGM is an old variety, propagated by cuttings, the scent slightly reminiscent of the "play dough" of my-far-too-distant youth. 'Marine' is a seed strain and has a compact and bushy habit with clusters of fragrant deep violet blooms and 'White Lady' is another old variety with scented almost white flowers and vegetatively propagated by cuttings. 45–60cm (18–24in). **Z10–11.**

Hemerocallis (HEMEROCALLIDACEAE)

A genus that has kept the plant breeders occupied for decades. There are so many to choose from in such a wide range of colours and form that it is almost impossible to select a choice few. I have always admired the elegant graceful flowers of some of the species daylilies and prefer the fragrant forms. Daylilies flower for many weeks, often starting in summer and continuing until early autumn.

H. altissima Slender trumpets of pale yellow, which are scented at night. 1.5m (5ft). **Z6–9.**

H. **'Chicago Blackout'** Rich mahogany red – one of the darkest flowers. 75cm (30in). **Z4–9.**

H. **'Corky' AGM** Large numbers of elegant small yellow trumpets flushed with mahogany red. 60cm (24in). **Z4–9.**

H. **'Gentle Shepherd'** Large ruffled ivory-white flowers with a jade-green throat. 75cm (30in). **Z6–9.**

H. **'Whichford' AGM** This offers wonderful scent from its pale greenish-yellow blooms. 90cm (36in). **Z4–9.**

Hordeum jubatum (POACEAE)

This is an annual or short-lived perennial grass from North America and north-east Asia, related to our native wall barley. It has silky, nodding flowerheads of pale green, washed with pink and purple flushes. Great used as a bedding plant, providing a good foil for other taller-growing plants to emerge from. 45cm (18in). **Z4.**

Impatiens glandulifera 'Candida' (BALSAMINACEAE)

This is really a noxious annual weed, found often on waste ground and along riversides, but who can resist pressing the seed pod when ripe so it ejects its seed explosively to start the next generation? This form of the policeman's helmet has white flowers and coarse, lanceolate leaves. 1.2m (4ft). **Z10**.

Inula magnifica 'Sonnenstrahl' AGM (ASTERACEAE)

A veritable giant of the herbaceous world with its massive mounds of leaves beneath the 2.4m (8ft) high heads of large deep-yellow daisy flowers with their drooping rays and a broad golden disc. It starts into flower early, by mid-June, but will usually continue flowering at least into September. **Z4–8.**

Kirengeshoma (HYDRANGEACEAE)

This is a choice woodland perennial for moisture-retentive soil and dappled shade. It is herbaceous with maple-like leaves and thick waxy pale yellow flowers in August and September. **Z5–8.**

K. palmata AGM This is slightly shorter than the form below, growing to 1.2m (4ft), with nodding clusters of waxy bells with overlapping petals.

Opposite left: *Heliotropium arborescens* 'Marine'
Opposite right: *Hemerocallis* 'Corky' AGM
Above: *Hordeum jubatum*

K. p. Koreana Group There is some dispute as to whether this plant is a separate species or a form of the above. Current nomenclature suggests the former, the difference being that this plant is taller at 1.5m (5ft) and has more erect flowering stems with pendent blooms.

Knautia macedonica (DIPSACACEAE)

Crimson-purple scabious flowers on long wiry stems act as a gourmet restaurant for butterflies and pollinating insects. It flowers all summer long. *K. macedonica* thrives in well-drained soil and in full sun.

K. macedonica European Form This plant was obtained from one of the Dutch nurseries and appears to come true from seed. It differs from the

Below: *Kirengeshoma palmata* AGM
Below right: *Knautia macedonica*
Opposite: *Kniphofia* cv

K. macedonica usually offered by British nurseries in that it is more robust, erect and has larger but slightly paler flowers. It grows to 90cm (36in). **Z5–9.**

Kniphofia (ASPHODELACEAE)

The "red-hot pokers" that hail from South Africa, Ethiopia and Tanzania are not all red and orange but can be found in a wide range of colours including greeny-white, lemon-yellow, cream and apricot, often with a contrasting tip to the flower spikes. They were often criticized for the abundance of rather coarse strap-like foliage and shyness to flower but most of the newer cultivars have narrow, grass-like leaves and a profusion of flowering spikes. They mix particularly well with late-summer grasses, adding a strong vertical accent, rather like the candles on a cake.

To thrive, red-hot pokers require a rich well-drained soil in sun and some of the species are rather tender. *K. uvaria* 'Nobilis' AGM has egg-shaped orange flowers from orange buds but untidy evergreen growth

to 1.5m (5ft), while *K. rooperi* is the latest-flowering species, through October and November, with orange-red flowers, fading yellow with age. 1.5m (5ft). 'Percy's Pride' was a selection from Alan Bloom with greenish yellow fat spikes and quite floriferous at 1.2m (4ft) while 'Ice Queen' is a whitish-green but shy to flower. 'Green Jade' is a selection from Beth Chatto with creamy green flowers but again reticent with its blooms. Smaller cultivars with finer grassy leaves include 'Timothy', a coppery salmon taper with gently flared trumpets, 'Little Maid', another selection from Beth Chatto with creamy white spikes, 'Buttercup' AGM, a lovely yellow, starting early in to flower and 'Brimstone' AGM, which is the latest to flower with pale-lemon flowers and green buds. All these have slender grassy foliage and are 90cm (36in) or less.

There are many other cultivars that are equally useful for autumn colour and seedling pokers can also make excellent garden plants.

Kniphofias are good flowers for cutting but I would prefer to leave them in the garden to enjoy, when little else is so exuberant.

Lathyrus (PAPILIONIACEAE)

Annual or perennial climbing peas can be useful vertical components for covering obelisks, trellises and walls during the growing season. Sweet peas are especially good as cut flowers and to add fragrant oases in the garden.

L. odoratus The sweet pea is the best known of all the annual members of this family and has kept breeders busy for over a century. The original sweet pea was small-flowered with purple and blue flowers on short flower stems. Breeding work has increased the size of flower and length of flowering stem so they are more suitable for cutting and has also increased the colour range and shape of the bloom. I favour the old-fashioned, highly scented sweet peas as it is their perfume rather than size of flower that

appeals to me. There is a good range to choose from and a number of nurseries and seedsmen who sell the older varieties. Regular deadheading will keep them in flower until the frosts. Picking large bunches of sweet fragrant blooms for the house and for your friends makes you very popular – in effect this is deadheading at its most pleasurable.

L. latifolius **AGM** Often referred to as the "perennial pea", this has broad grey-green leaflets on vigorous climbing stems, which can easily cover 1.8m (6ft) in a season. The wild species is pink or, rarely, white but selected forms have been named. 'Rosa Perle' AGM is a good mid-pink, 'Albus' AGM a pure white with a satin sheen on the petals, ' Red Pearl' a deep carmine rose and 'Blushing Bride' a white, flushed with pink. Their only fault is that they have no scent. **Z5.**

Left: *Leucanthemum* x *superbum* cv
Right: *Ligularia dentata* 'Desdemona' AGM

Leucanthemella serotina AGM (ASTERACEAE)

Another member of the daisy family that has been subject to a surfeit of name changes. The pure white pristine marguerite daisy flowers on 2.1m (7ft) flowering stems can make a huge impact on an autumn border composed mainly of reds, russets and tan fall colours. It spreads readily forming large clumps in time and is easy and trouble free, tolerating dappled shade. **Z4–9.**

Leucanthemum x *superbum* cultivars (ASTERACEAE)

These shasta daisies are hybrids between *L. maximum* x *L. lacustre* and are some of the most popular "daisies" grown in the garden for cutting and the herbaceous border. Flowering through the summer months and often with a good second flush during early autumn, they are long-lived, easy and indisputably hardy, preferring a moisture-retentive alkaline soil.

There are many named cultivars with single, semi-double or double white flowers. 'Aglaia' AGM is a fringed semi-double form while 'Beauté Nivelloise' has slender double rays. 'Sonnenschein' has creamy yellow ray florets while 'Mount Everest' is a classic white single. **Z5.**

Leymus arenarius (POACEAE)

One of the best glaucous blue-green grasses with broad blades. It is, however, very invasive and will rapidly form large clumps. It is a native to Britain and northern and western Europe where it plays a valuable role stabilizing sand dunes and other light soils, and adds stability to artificially built mounds and banks. The flowers are of little ornamental value reaching 1.2m (4ft) but the foliage is a wonderful foil for purple-suffused foliage, burgundy and pink flowers. *Dianthus carthusianorum* and *Scabiosa tenuis* are good examples of flowers that combine well with *Leymus*. **Z6.**

Ligularia (ASTERACEAE)

Large chunky leaves and vigorous growth give a lush tropical appearance to this genus, especially those with purple-suffused foliage. They originate from temperate Asia and Siberia so are hardy in British gardens. They are large plants and not suitable for all gardens, requiring plenty of space, moisture-retentive humus-rich soil and dappled shade. Swathes of *Ligularia* are most impressive and are best observed in a grand setting. There are several good species with yellow or golden-orange flowers, as spikes or in flat heads, and many differing leaf shapes. As well as handsome foliage, many of them possess brown, almost black, flower stems, contrasting with the bright flowers. *L.* 'The Rocket' AGM grows to 1.8m (6ft) and is thought to be a hybrid between *L. stenocephala* and *L. przewalskii* AGM. It has deeply toothed foliage, dark stems and long spires of golden-yellow flowers. Another excellent hybrid is *L.* x *palmatiloba*, a cross between

L. japonica and *L. dentata,* with glossy toothed foliage and orange daisies bursting from fat jade-green buds. 1.5m (5ft). *L. dentata* is grown more for its dark-leaved foliage forms than its rather coarse orangey- yellow flowers. *L. d.* 'Desdemona' AGM has heart-shaped foliage with purple suffusion on the stems, leaf undersides, stalks and veins while *L. d.* 'Othello' also has a purple-green wash on the top of the leaf. A fine new cultivar, *L. d.* 'Britt-Marie Crawford', has blackish-purple foliage.

All these plants require copious amounts of moisture and dappled shade to ensure the foliage does not burn. They are also martyrs to the depredations of our mollusc friends (or should I say enemies?) in early spring when the foliage is emerging and very succulent. **Z4–8.**

Ligusticum lucidum (APIACEAE)

This is a "cow parsley" relative with fine filigree glossy green foliage with umbels of creamy white flowers. 1m (3ft 3in). It is suitable for the wilder parts of the garden. Grow in either dappled shade or in sun in moisture-retentive soil. Flowers from summer to early autumn. **Z6.**

Lilium (LILIACEAE)

These are good subjects for containers or as cut flowers, or for the border, and there is a vast range of choice to suit every taste. Many are scented, some of them overwhelmingly perfumed and definitely not to be confined in a small space. Several have brightly coloured pollen just waiting for you to shove your nose into the flower, and then covering your face and clothes with a powdery orange, red or yellow stain that is impossible to remove.

Large-flowered lilies are most suited to containers whereas the more refined, smaller species combine well in the border or in dappled shade among shrubs and trees. I will not attempt to list the possibilities available for containers but just mention a couple that I am particularly fond of for use in the garden.

Right: *Linaria purpurea* 'Canon Went'
Opposite: *Liriope muscari* AGM

Lilium x dalhansonii A choice hybrid between *L. martagon* var. *cattaniae* (syn. *L. martagon dalmaticum*) and *L. hansonii* with reflexed petals of dark mahogany. 1.5m (5ft).

L. henryi AGM Be bold with this easy Chinese lily which tolerates dappled shade, neutral or alkaline soil and grows to 2m (6ft 6in). The Turk's-cap flowers are bright orange with dark flecks and prominent orange anthers. **Z5.**

L. martagon AGM This is the beloved Turk's-cap lily that has flower stems with numerous blooms in pink and purple with elegant recurved petals, some spotted. The pristine white form, *L. martagon* var. *album* AGM, can lighten a shady corner. They are useful for naturalizing and prefer leaf mould, dappled shade and a moisture-retentive soil. 1.2m (4ft). Other martagon forms have dark hairy buds or deep coloured flowers. *L. martagon* var. *pilosiusculum* was a form I grew many years ago and would love to grow again, with its furry buds and almost reddish-black waxy blooms. **Z4–8.**

Linaria (SCROPHULARIACEAE)

The slender, vertical flowering stems of the toadflax bloom for many weeks in summer and autumn, preferring sun, good drainage and lean soils. In richer soils the plants often require staking, producing lush growth that is more susceptible to aphid attack. These are useful supporting plants, with fine linear leaves, often glaucous, blue-green and relatively small flowers. They contrast well with the flat flowerheads of achilleas. **Z5.**

L. dalmatica A tall grey-green glaucous-leaved perennial with yellow flowers and a slightly darker orange lip. 1.5m (5ft). **Z6.**

L. purpurea 'Canon Went' Spires of sugar-pink flowers over grey-green foliage. Blends well with grasses and herbaceous perennials and will thrive in most soils with good drainage and sun. This is a

seed strain and some are much better than others. There is a form with a dark pink staining to the stems and leaves that combines well with the flowers. 90cm (36in). **Z6.**

L. p. 'Springside White' The pure white form of our native *L. purpurea*, with pale apple-green foliage. 60cm (24in). **Z6.**

L. 'Toni Aldiss' A lovely dusky pink sterile hybrid originating in the garden of the UK Hardy Plant Society member, Toni Aldiss, it reaches 1.5m (5ft) in sun and well-drained soil. **Z6.**

L. triornithophora This is a large-flowered toadflax with three flowers perched at the top of the stem resembling nothing so much as a triumvirate of parrots. The species is usually purple but there is also a charming shell-pink form. 60–90cm (24–36in). **Z7.**

Linum (LINACEAE)

Fields of linseed are a common sight in recent years with fine linear green foliage and cup-shaped flowers that open during the day, giving a blue haze over acres of land, returning to green in the evening as the flowers close. Commercial linseed is a different species to that usually grown in gardens.

L. narbonense To my eye this is the best blue form to grow in the garden, although not the easiest. It is suited to a gravel border or raised gritty bed in full sun and a starvation diet to keep it compact. It has fine grey-green linear leaves and angled wiry stems with upturned flowers of azure blue. 60cm (24in). I am convinced that most of the plants distributed in the trade are incorrect and are, in fact, forms of *L. perenne*, which have pendent blue flowers in clusters. I am therefore inclined to think that *L. narbonense* 'Heavenly Blue' is a good colour form of *L. perenne*. **Z5.**

Liriope muscari (CONVALLARIACEAE)

An early autumn-flowering stalwart, this member of the lily family has glossy deep green tufts of evergreen leaves with densely clustered purple flower spikes followed by blue-black fruits. It is a good ground cover for dappled shade and acidic soils grown primarily for its foliage. 45cm (18in). There are several different named clones that are available. **Z6.**

Lobelia (CAMPANULACEAE)

This genus belongs to the campanula family and is familiar for the small blue bedding plants, *L. erinus*, as well as the vivid tall red varieties from *L. cardinalis* AGM. A recent trial at the RHS garden at Wisley with seed-raised and clonally produced plants indicated that there was greater vigour from seed generations. There are many good garden plants in this genus that mix equally well in a conventional herbaceous border, cottage garden or naturalistic planting. Tall spikes of red and purple combine well with late-flowering grasses, asters, achilleas, crocosmias and kniphofias.

L. x *speciosa* Fan Series This is a fine group of seed-grown lobelias in shades of deep pink, deep red, burgundy and scarlet. 60cm (2ft). **Z6.**

L. x *s*. 'Hadspen Purple' A recent introduction with sumptuous plum-purple flowers on tall sturdy stems to 1.2m (4ft). **Z6–7**

L. x *s*. Kompliment Series Another group of fine vigorous seed-raised lobelias. Taller than the 'Fan Series' at 90cm (36in) and sparsely branched but flowering well in the first year from seed. 'Kompliment Scharlach' AGM is an eye-searing scarlet. **Z6–7.**

L. x *s*. 'Tania' This cultivar is a strong mauve-purple with dark leaf rosettes. Its colour is similar to several lythrums and they enjoy similar conditions of a moisture-retentive soil in sun or dappled shade. 75cm (30in). **Z7.**

L. *tupa* From large handsome clumps of grey-green leathery foliage arise 1.5m (5ft) stems of fiery burnt orange-red tubular flowers. Not particularly hardy but will survive in a protected well-drained position in moisture-retentive soil. **Z8.**

Lomatium (APIACEAE)

This is an important genus of perennial umbellifers native to North America and inexplicably underused in gardens. They have deep taproots and handsome dissected foliage that is grey-green or green with impressive umbels in white, yellow, yellowish-green, purple or reddish-brown. Germination is rather erratic, which may be a contributory factor to their scarcity; the seeds are best sown on their edge. Young plants often aestivate before they have built up enough vim to flower and need to be kept hot and dry, so a gravel bed in sun is ideal. **Z4–8.**

L. *columbianum* Glaucous grey dissected foliage with deep purple-brown umbels on 60cm (24in) stems.

L. *dissectum* Very finely divided blue-green foliage with large umbels of golden-yellow flowers to 30cm (12in).

L. *grayi* Similar to the above with aromatic bright green filigree foliage and yellow umbels. 30cm (12in).

Far left: *Lobelia x speciosa* Kompliment Series
Left: *Lychnis coronaria*

Lychnis (CARYOPHYLLACEAE)

A genus with many good border and rock plants, the majority in shades of pink, red, magenta and white. Basal rosettes persist over winter and flowers are produced from late spring and through the summer months.

L. chalcedonica **AGM** The Maltese Cross is a vivid orange-red and a good hardy perennial with green hairy leaves. There are more subtle shades: 'Carnea', which is pink, and var. *albiflora*, which is white. A double red form, 'Flore Pleno', is also available. Several other named varieties are on offer. 60cm (24in). Thrives in most soils in sun or light shade. **Z4.**

L. coronaria Eye-catching cerise-purple campion flowers contrast well with softly hairy silver foliage. In the first year the plant produces an attractive grey rosette with flowers produced on branching stems the following season. Usually biennial although sometimes a short-lived perennial, especially if spent flowers are removed. Seeds around. 60cm (24in). Needs sun. As before there are several named seed strains and forms. 'Alba' AGM is white, Oculata Group are white forms with a contrasting deep pink eye and Gardener's World ('Blych') is a sterile, double cerise-purple form, which is propagated by vegetative division. **Z4.**

Lysimachia (PRIMULACEAE)

Useful border perennials, which usually prefer a rich moisture-retentive soil to thrive. Many of them are vigorous and inclined to be invasive although they offer useful ground cover for large areas. They start to flower in early summer and continue for several weeks.

L. ciliata A vigorous colonizer with invasive roots, this is a native of North America. Light yellow pendent flowers are produced in leaf axils on wiry pedicels. 60cm (2ft). A deep purple-leaved form, 'Firecracker' AGM, is a good foliage plant and contrasts well with the yellow blooms. **Z4.**

L. clethroides **AGM** Flower spikes with a marked kink, looking nothing like so much as an elegant swan's neck, with small white flowers. En masse the bent flower stems are very effective and convey the idea of movement. This is further enhanced if the planting is next to moving water. 90cm (36in). **Z4.**

L. ephemerum This hardy perennial shows all the attributes of a perfect border plant. Growing to an erect 90–1.2m (36in–4ft) in a moisture-retentive soil it is clump-forming and requires no staking, with handsome, glaucous grey-green foliage and spires of white flowers in late summer. **Z7.**

Lythrum (LYTHRACEAE)

Like the above these are plants that thrive in moisture-retentive soil in sun or dappled shade. Their native habitat is in marginal sites by streams, rivers, canals, lakes and any other freshwater course. In recent years there has been a surfeit of named cultivars and seed strains but I can see little difference between them. In general they all make good garden plants, flowering throughout the summer with long spires of purple flowers. I have chosen just a few to illustrate the range available. **Z3–4.**

L. salicaria **'Blush'** **AGM** To my knowledge the only pale pink form, on short compact plants to 90cm (36in). *L. s.* 'Morden Pink' is a strong pinkish-purple. 1.2m (4ft). *L. s.* 'Zigeunerblut' has strident spikes of magenta-purple that contrast strongly with *L. s.* 'Blush'. 1.2m (4ft).

L. virgatum Altogether different from the above with graceful willowy foliage and small pinkish-purple flowers on airy, branched stems. It associates well with bulbs and grasses. 90cm (36in).

L. v. **'Dropmore Purple'** This has larger flowers and longer spikes of deep purple than the above and looks rather more like a *L. salicaria* cultivar to me. 1.2m (4ft).

Macleaya (PAPAVERACEAE)

The plume poppies make an imposing statement in the summer herbaceous border with fine, decorative, glaucous grey-green foliage with white undersides. Tapering spires of flowers are produced on upright stems of 2m (6ft 6in) or more, which rarely require staking. They prefer a moisture-retentive soil in sun or dappled shade.

M. cordata AGM Beautiful foliage and long spikes of white flowers bursting from buff-coloured buds. This species is not so invasive as *M. microcarpa*. **Z3**.

M. microcarpa This is probably the best known of the plume poppies with an aggressive running habit but a large stand creates an impressive spectacle. 'Kelway's Coral Plume' AGM is a good cultivar with rich buff and coral tones. 'Spetchley Ruby' is a less familiar sight with lovely reddish buds and fluffy terracotta and buff flowers. **Z4–9**.

Above: *Macleaya microcarpa* 'Spetchley Ruby'
Opposite: *Melianthus major* AGM

Malva (MALVACEAE)

Single cup-shaped, tissue-like flowers with notched petals add simplicity and serenity to a "busy" planting. They are native herbs of waste ground and do not require rich soils, preferring sharp drainage and sun. Mallow rust can be a problem in some areas, which a proprietary fungicide can alleviate; if chemicals are not an option, it may not be possible to grow members of this family, including *Lavatera, Alcea* and *Althaea,* as this rust can seriously disfigure foliage. That apart, it is a genus that is hardy and easy, providing flowers for many weeks over summer and into autumn, especially if regularly deadheaded.

M. moschata f. **alba** AGM The white form of the British native musk mallow with attractive, dissected green adult foliage and round, lobed, juvenile leaves. The pure white mallow flowers have pink tinged stamens. 60cm (24in). Will gently seed around. Short-lived perennial. **Z3**.

M. sylvestris Another native with palmately lobed leaves and a somewhat spreading growth. Named forms are usually offered, such as 'Tournai', a form which is white flowered; 'Brave Heart', with an erect habit with pale purple-blue flowers and a dark eye; and 'Primley Blue', which is an excellent candidate for growing in containers. It has spreading growth and a profusion of small bluish-violet flowers with darker veins. **Z5**.

Malvastrum lateritium (MALVACEAE)

Another mallow relative but in my experience not so prone to rust. It has long spreading stems, which root at the nodes, and can be used as a ground cover in sun or dappled shade as long as there is sufficient moisture. It is covered with apricot-pink, dark-centred mallow flowers for months. At Sissinghurst Gardens in Kent it has been trained up a wall to great effect. **Z6–9**.

Melanoselinum decipiens (APIACEAE)

This unusual umbellifer from Madeira is a large biennial reaching some 1.2m (4ft) in height and

microclimate there but it is the foliage that is sought by gardeners rather than the flowers. 1.5m (5ft). **Z9.**

Miscanthus (POACEAE)

In the past few years there has been great excitement over the ever-increasing selection of these stately autumn-flowering grasses. Combined with late herbaceous perennials or as solitary specimens these rustling giants lend a magical feel to the late season in the garden. (To experience this at first hand it is well worth a visit to Marchants Hardy Plants in Sussex where several cultivars of *Miscanthus* are silhouetted against the Downs to great effect.)

Ernst Pagels, a nurseryman and great plantsman from Leer in north-west Germany, selected over many years some excellent *Miscanthus* cultivars and it is to him that we owe many of our best forms. More recently, breeding work in the USA has produced yet more *Miscanthus* varieties; many of them with bold variegation such as 'Dixieland' and 'Cabaret'. RHS Wisley conducted a trial of *Miscanthus* cultivars, which looked spectacular through early autumn and winter of the trial years. The summary of this trial can be obtained from the society.

Piet Oudolf has been at the forefront of introducing these deservedly popular grasses into large naturalistic plantings. There is such a diversity of size, colour and form that there is a *Miscanthus* suitable for every garden. (For further information see *The Garden*, October 2002, and *The Plantsman*, December 2003.)

In 1987 the first edition of *The Plant Finder* was published in Britain (compiled by Chris Philip) and listed the plants available in British nurseries. There were nine entries for *Miscanthus* in 1987; the eighth edition in 1994 listed 44 entries and in 2000, the fourteenth edition, there were at least 76 species and cultivars. The current P*lant Finder* suggests that 99 different *Miscanthus* are available. In a couple of months the new edition will be published – will there be a similar meteoric leap in the number of cultivars

almost as much in girth. It has stout stems and lilac-pink flowers in its second year. A talking point! In autumn it is bedecked with black seeds from whence it received its name, and for which it is included in this directory. **Z9.**

Melianthus (MELIANTHACEAE)

Not hardy except in warm sheltered positions, where the top growth can be cut down by frost but will reshoot the following year producing the architectural foliage so beloved of gardeners. They can be used successfully as container plants provided they are given sufficient water. **Z9.**

M. comosus Greener foliage than the more familiar *M. major* and smaller at 60–90cm (24-36in).

M. major AGM Choice foliage plant with large, pinnate glaucous grey-green leaves. Terminal brownish-red flowers develop on older growth, which rarely occur in Britain as the foliage gets cut to the ground by frost. A specimen at the Chelsea Physic Garden in London occasionally blooms in the warm

offered? The majority of *Miscanthus* cultivars are derived from *M. sinensis*.

For the average garden, if there is such a thing, a selection of three to five cultivars is likely to be sufficient. Maybe a dwarf variety, an early and a late form and a couple with markedly contrasting flowerheads, possibly one or two with variegated foliage. In the early years when *Miscanthus* became available, I grew, or at least observed, most of the cultivars offered at the time. I confess that with the current rash of new plants I have experience of less than 50 per cent of the *Plant Finder* entries so my recommendations are severely limited in a genus with which I was once reasonably familiar.

Miscanthus are easy to grow and suffer from few pests and diseases. They require a soil that does not dry out completely although they can tolerate drought as long as their root system is sufficient to enable them to extract enough moisture. In wet or particularly dry seasons the foliage and flower colour varies significantly from year to year, with richer, redder hues with more moisture; a dry season will produce more uniformly buff and tan tones. Similarly the same *Miscanthus* planted in dry or moisture-retentive positions in the same garden will show quite different characteristics in the same season. Growth starts in spring, usually around mid-March to April and flowering starts from late July for the earliest varieties, such as 'Vorläufer', to November for 'November Sunset'. The spent flowerheads persist all winter on rustling tan and buff clumps of foliage. In February, this top growth should be cut down to a couple of inches from the ground.

Miscanthus combines well with tall asters, vernonia, helianthus, echinacea and eupatoriums in late summer and autumn when they are in flower. Before flowering starts, these grasses create a strong green canvas for summer plants such as phlox, achilleas and veronicastrums. They vary in height from 'Adagio' and 'Little Kitten' at 60cm–1.2m (24in–4ft)

to *M. sacchariflorus* and *M.* x *giganteus* at 3m (10ft) or more. Most are substantial plants and in time will make large clumps, which can dominate a planting. They do require splitting into smaller clumps every few years, which is easier said than done. Using them as isolated specimens with plenty of growing room around may render splitting unnecessary but good combinations with other late-flowering material would be sacrificed.

Some *Miscanthus* forms are grown primarily for their foliage rather than flower. 'Morning Light' AGM has narrow variegated leaves and when backlit by the rising or setting sun the silver and green foliage has almost magical qualities; it is lovely sited by water. 1.5m (5ft). 'Gracillimus' has a rounded habit with narrow leaves and is an excellent foil for other perennials. Some clones do not flower within the British growing season, which may be beneficial when using it as a canvas to paint with other flowers. 1.5m (5ft). There are several excellent variegated forms: 'Zebrinus' AGM is an old arching form with horizontal stripes; 'Strictus' AGM has a more erect habit and 'Pünktchen' is not so obviously marked. 'Cosmopolitan' AGM has broad foliage with longitudinal cream or white stripes and is the best of this type of variegation. *M. s.* var. *condensatus* 'Cabaret' has its longitudinal variegation in the centre of the blade and is bright green and cream. 2m (6ft 6in). Variegated forms are sometimes subject to leaf burn, which leaves rusty marks in the cream markings.

Small and medium-sized *Miscanthus* are probably more suited to smaller gardens. Already mentioned are 'Little Kitten' and 'Adagio', but 'Yakushima Dwarf' is also reasonably small, but as broad as it is tall, reaching 1.5m (5ft) in time. Some *Miscanthus* are not so vigorous, especially some of the highly coloured foliage forms. *Miscanthus oligostachyus* 'Afrika' and 'Ghana' AGM and

Opposite: *Miscanthus sinensis* 'Kaskade' AGM
Right: *Miscanthus sinensis* 'Strictus' AGM

'Roterpfeil' are good examples of this type with excellent red or burnished bronze coloration in autumn. 'Ghana' has exquisite bronzed reddish foliage whereas the other two are redder. 'Flamingo' AGM has graceful dangling dark purplish-pink flowerheads in autumn before fading to lighter pinkish tones 1.8m (6ft), 'Ferner Osten' AGM has early rich red arching heads and good yellow autumn foliage colour 1.5m (5ft), 'Kaskade' AGM has cascading warm-pink flowerheads to 1.8m (6ft) and 'Kleine Fontäne' AGM is a more delicate grass than the former with similar flowers of pearly rose.

Larger specimens make imposing statements and there is no lack of good candidates in the *Miscanthus* cultivars offered. One of my favourites, with large reddish-purple plumes and excellent autumn colour, is 'Malepartus' 1.8m (6ft). 'Gewitterwolke' AGM has brooding dark flowers emerging early on this substantial clump-forming variety . 1.8m (6ft). 'Roland' is not for the small backyard at 2.4m (8ft) with gracefully arching flowerstems, 'Rotfuchs' has rusty red plumes, 2.1m (7ft), and 'Zwergelefant' has crinkled rose red plumes, which give it a rastafarian hair-do as it unfurls from the flower stem. 1.8m (6ft). **Z4–6.**

Another miscanthus, *M. nepalensis* is not particularly hardy but a gem when grown well. Hailing from the Himalayas and Burma with golden honey-coloured flowerheads to 1.5m (5ft) through August and September. **Z9.**

Molinia (POACEAE)

Another important and versatile group of grasses adding height and movement from summer through to the winter months. *M. caerulea* subsp. *caerulea* cultivars (purple moor grasses) do require slightly acid soils of pH 6.5 or less whereas *M. c.* subsp. *arundinacea* cultivars are more lime-tolerant and withstand drier conditions. As a general rule the first group are shorter with darker stems and flowers to about 1.2m (4ft) whereas the latter forms often reach 2m (6ft 6in) or more. They do not persist so well during winter as *Miscanthus* but their stems are a glowing butter-yellow throughout autumn. They are truly herbaceous and easy to clear up after the winter, as the stems break off at the base (unlike many other grasses, which have to be painstakingly cut down in February). Molinias are wonderful grasses for cutting and drying for indoor decoration and will look good for many years. Cut

them before they open to keep the most solid flowerheads. **Z4–5.**

Molinias start into growth at the end of March with strong new green shoots and are easy to divide at this time. There are a number of variegated cultivars with slender white or cream with green longitudinal striped leaves, which form good clumps. 'Variegata' AGM is the best known with slightly arching growth, but 'Claerwen' and 'Carmarthen' are also good variegated forms. 'Claerwen' is more erect with creamy flowerheads. All these variegated forms belong to the subspecies *caerulea* and are relatively short at around 60cm (24in).

The taller *Arundinacea* forms create imposing vertical accents in late summer. Some are strictly erect to 2m (6ft 6in) or more, such as 'Windspiel', 'Windsaule' and 'Skyracer' while others arch gracefully like 'Transparent', 'Bergfreund' and 'Fontäne'. All have an elegant and diaphanous presence, allowing the eye to travel to subjects beyond the grasses, contrasting strongly with *Miscanthus*, which make dense clumps. 'Transparent' has to be my favourite with its graceful arching stems and darker flower spikes that hold the dew like glittering jewels. 1.8m (6ft). 'Fontäne' is shorter at 1.5m (5ft) with stems that arch out like a fountain. The erect forms are fairly similar with heavier or darker flowerheads distinguishing them. 'Zuneigung' gently arches and the flowerheads intertwine, giving it its name 'affection'. I have grown most of the cultivars available and find that 'Windsaule' has more presence than the others when grown together but I doubt whether I could be confident of identifying them easily when they are used as solitary specimens. I have a few seedling molinias that display burnished bronze stems and I look forward to assessing them over the next few years.

There is a variety of form, colour and shape in the *caerulea* cultivars, which are quite distinct from each other. I have already mentioned the variegated forms

Left: Molinia caerulea *with* Dianthus carthusianum

but 'Heidebraut' is probably the tallest at 1.2m (4ft) with erect stems that fade to tawny orange in autumn. 'Strahlenquelle' is the most arched form, with green foliage and pendent flowers, and 'Edith Dudzsus' makes bold clumps of dark stems with dark flower spikes with hints of purple, black and green. 75cm (30in). 'Moorflamme' has spreading growth with traces of orange, red and gold in the ageing flowerstems while 'Moorhexe' is a dense, stiffly upright clump-forming form with dark purplish green foliage during summer and rusty orange fall colour. 50cm (20in).

Molinias and *Miscanthus* are two of the most important groups of grasses for naturalistic planting. They are good structural, clump-forming, components, long-lived and pest free, tolerating a wide range of conditions.

Molopospermum peloponnesiacum (APIACEAE)

A favourite umbellifer, which is a perennial with incredibly dissected green foliage and large yellow umbels through summer. Although the flowers may be over by late summer, the foliage attains a height of 1.2m (4ft) and almost as much in girth – a dramatic plant for a moisture-retentive soil in sun or dappled shade. **Z4–8.**

Monarda (LAMIACEAE)

The bergamots originate in North America and provide us with a wide range of colour and form for late summer. In less than ideal conditions, especially in the southern counties of Britain, mildew will become rife even in the so-called resistant strains.

The aromatic leaves and flowers are a boon to the summer border and a magnet to pollinating insects; the autumn silhouette is exquisite when covered with dew-laden cobwebs. Bergamots require plenty of moisture through the growing season but do not like wet feet during the winter months. It is a clear case for moisture-retentive well-drained soil and any deviation from this will result in the disfiguring mildew. Fortnightly fungicidal sprays will alleviate the problem but if you garden organically this is not an option. There is an indication that young plants propagated each year do not suffer the ravages of mildew in the same way as older plants. Also, if monardas are not grown on improved soil they do not grow so lush and are less susceptible to fungal attack. Watering with liquid seaweed feed is another recommended treatment. I feel that if I cannot find a way to grow these valuable late-summer perennials successfully, I must find some substitute for them.

A number of resistant cultivars have been raised, the majority of them from the Netherlands by Piet Oudolf, who introduced the Indian range, 'Comanche', 'Cherokee', 'Squaw', 'Pawnee' and so on, and the zodiac bergamots such as 'Fishes', 'Scorpion' et al. They appear to be reasonably resistant in areas where there is a high water-table and less extremes of drying winds. New cultivars are added every year, some with beautiful coloured bracts as well as flowers. Spent blooms drop rapidly leaving the rounded seed-heads to add to the autumn spectacle and structure of the border, and

are a welcome addition for hungry birds. To achieve a longer flowering period, some of the stems could be cut by a third in early summer, which would cause those stems to flower a few weeks later.

Monardas combine well with most other herbaceous plants, ranging in colour from a slightly dirty white, through pale pink, rose, violet, purple and red including scarlet. My list is not exhaustive, and there are plenty of good forms to choose from.

M. **'Balance'** Vivid rose-pink. 1.2m (4ft).

M. **'Beauty of Cobham' AGM** Pale mauve flowers with prominent dark bracts. Outstanding in recent trials at RHS Wisley. 1.2m (4ft).

M. **'Cherokee'** Pale to mid-pink. 1.2–1.5m (4–5ft).

M. **'Comanche'** Mid-pink. At 1.8m (6ft) a good background plant.

M. **'Elsie's Lavender'** This showed well at the recent monarda trial at Wisley showing little signs of mildew. Pale lilac flowers with green calyces. 1.2m (4ft).

M. **'Fishes'** I used privately to nickname this bergamot as fishy wishy-washy as I considered its pale pink flowers too wan against other strong colours. However, in the right position it can look marvellous and I have reassessed my opinion of it. When the petals drop the central boss of green remains to give substance for many months. 90cm (36in).

M. **'Gardenview Scarlet' AGM** This bergamot proved the best scarlet in the recent RHS trials with strong scent and sturdy flowering stems. 1.2cm (4ft).

M. **'Mohawk'** Deep lilac-mauve with dark bracts. 1.5m (5ft).

M. **'Neon'** A recent Piet Oudolf selection with vivid neon lilac-purple flowers. 1.2m (4ft).

M. **'Pink Tourmaline'** Vivid raspberry-pink flowers, similar to the hue of *Phlox paniculata* 'Starfire', with dark bracts. 1.2m (4ft). **Z4–8.**

Left: *Monarda* 'Scorpion'
Opposite: *Nepeta racemosa* 'Walker's Low'

M. punctata A delightful North American species, which is better treated as an annual. It has pale pink and green coloured bracts and subtle straw-yellow flowers with purple spotting. **Z6.**

M. 'Purple Ann' Reddish-purple flowers that bloom for many weeks. 1.2m (4ft).

M. 'Ruby Glow' Compact growth, 90cm (3ft) with deep reddish-purple flowers and dark bracts.

M. 'Scorpion' Violet-purple and long flowering. 1.5m (5ft). **Z4–8.**

Monardella odoratissima (LAMIACEAE)

A charming North American aromatic herb best suited to a raised gritty bed or gravel border in full sun. It has rounded grey-green leaves and globular heads of rose or violet flowers. 15cm (6in). **Z8.**

Morina longifolia (MORINACEAE)

At first glance you may be forgiven for thinking that the rosette of green spiny leaves belongs to a thistle. It is, however, a beautiful Himalayan plant with flowering stems to 60–90cm (24–36in) with congested flower spikes of white and pink, flushing deeper with age. **Z6.**

Nemesia denticulata (SCROPHULARIACEAE)

A useful plant for containers or the front of the border that flowers for months and does not suffer from pests and diseases. *N. denticulata* has proved to be winter-hardy for most British gardens although it would be advisable to take a few cuttings in autumn as an insurance policy. The flowers are a dusky pink with a golden-yellow eye and slightly fragrant. 45cm (18in). **Z9.**

Nepeta (LAMIACEAE)

Aromatic and easy perennials with a range of pastel colours through pink, white, blue, purple and primrose yellow. Many possess silvery grey foliage and require sun with good drainage. A few are definite thugs and should be confined to wilder parts of the garden, while others are nirvana for our feline friends, transporting them to ecstasy as they roll in our favourite plants. I grow *Nepeta cataria* subsp. *citriodora* to please my cats and hope that they will leave the rest alone. Out of all the catmints I have grown, I have only had to cease growing *N. racemosa* 'Snowflake' because of feline attentions.

Catmints are excellent plants for a sunny well-drained site and a lean diet keeps them compact and less floppy. Once the first flush of flower is over, they can be sheared back hard and will rebloom throughout late summer and early autumn. Nectar for bees and butterflies, there is always a constant humming around the plants. The foliage is aromatic, some with a more pleasant fragrance than others. The attractive foliage and clouds of small flowers makes them good supporting actors to more dominant members of the herbaceous clan or for softening hard-landscaped edges.

N. govaniana I was greatly impressed by this plant in the herbaceous border at Waterperry Gardens, Oxfordshire, where it attained 1.8m (6ft) in partial shade with moisture-retentive soil. With its cool lemon flowers and evocative citrus-scented leaves it is an elegant border perennial. **Z5.**

N. grandiflora 'Bramdean' This catmint, found in

Victoria Wakefield's Hampshire garden, has long spires of deep lavender-blue flowers shown off to great effect by the dark-blue-stained flower stems. 90cm (36in). **Z3.**

***N. g.* 'Dawn to Dusk'** Selected by nurseryman Coen Jansen, this 60cm (24in) grey-foliaged nepeta has dark calyces and delicate pale pink flowers with a hint of blue. It needs careful placing near other pinks – it can turn a blue-pink slightly muddy. **Z3.**

***N. racemosa* 'Walker's Low'** An excellent frontal plant with grey foliage and soft powder-blue flowers. Easy and forgiving this benefits from hard pruning to enable a good second flush in early autumn. I grow this on a lean diet of 80 per cent grit/20 per cent loam and it forms a tight mound to 60cm (24in) covered in a haze of blue. In richer conditions it will tumble and grow to 90cm (36in). **Z4.**

***N. sibirica* 'Souvenir d'André Chaudron'** An old favourite with large purplish-blue flowers on spreading clumps of upright green leaved stems. 90cm (36in). **Z3.**

N. subsessilis Short at 45cm (18in) or less, this large-flowered catmint is often mistaken for a penstemon. It is an easy and long-lived perennial provided it does not suffer the depredations of slugs in spring as the shoots emerge. Sun and good drainage. **Z3.**

***N. s.* pink** This is a pink variant of *N. subsessilis*. At first I was rather unimpressed by the rather grey-pink hue to the flowers but it can be strikingly successful if carefully placed. **Z3–9.**

N. tuberosa Congested spikes of purplish-blue flowers are held above densely hirsute grey-green leaves and stems. Not all that hardy, but excellent in a pot. 75cm (30in). **Z8.**

There have been several new nepeta introductions from the Netherlands in the last couple of years under the 'Cat' series and breeding work has been carried out on a number of species. 'Cool Cat', 'Wild Cat', 'Snow Cat' and 'Candy Cat' are some of the new varieties offered but I have not grown them long enough to assess their merits. **Z3–9.**

Nerine (AMARYLLIDACEAE)

This is an important genus of autumn-flowering bulbs from Africa. The majority are not hardy and they are best displayed in containers in frost-free conditions during winter. Nerine breeders have produced an amazing range of beautiful bulbs in white, pale to deep pink, apricot, orange to damson, with every tone in between. Petals may be entire or have wavy edges – why is it that so many of the frilly pink flowers are named after men? As there is such a wide variety it is best to visit a good collection. In Britain we are fortunate to have two excellent collections of nerines, which are available to view during the flowering season in the Isle of Wight and in Worcestershire. Flowering bulbs can be used as interior decoration – they last for weeks in the house as long as they are not too warm.

I have made a small selection of bulbs that are tolerably hardy and have not included any of the cultivars that require frost-free conditions. They need a sheltered position in sun and flower best if their bulbs are proud of the earth.

***N. bowdenii* AGM** This is the best known and most reliably hardy nerine with its vivid pink flowers. 45–60cm (18–24in). **Z8.**

***N. b.* 'Quinton Wells'** Delicate frilly edges on the pale pink petals. 50cm (20in). **Z8.**

***N. flexuosa* 'Alba'** Only hardy in the most favoured position but good in a container, it has pure white crimped petals at 45cm (18in). **Z8–9.**

***N.* 'Hera'** A good deep-pink hardy form. 50cm (20in). **Z8.**

***N.* 'Zeal Giant' AGM** Brazen shocking-pink flowers on this large-flowered variety selected by Terry Jones. 60cm (24in). **Z8–9.**

Nicotiana (SOLANACEAE)

The majority of tobacco plants originate from tropical areas of South America and Australia with rather sticky foliage and long trumpet-shaped flowers, and evening fragrance. This latter characteristic attracts the insect pollinators namely in the form of long-tongued Hawkmoths. On balmy summer nights in the Mediterranean these large moths are a familiar sight visiting tobacco plants and oleanders. Along the south coast of Britain, nicotianas are often used in bedding schemes along promenades and hotel fronts and these are some of the most likely places to encounter these large pollinating moths. Unfortunately the breeding work on nicotianas to make them more weather-resistant, colourful and compact has bred out the strong evocative scent; the slight fragrance remaining is a poor substitute.

As I am so interested in my insect friends I have chosen a selection for scent as well as interesting colour forms. Many flower arrangers adore green flowers and *Nicotiana* offers several, such as *N. langsdorffii* AGM, *N.* 'Hopleys', *N. knightiana*, *N.* 'Lime Green' AGM and *N.* 'Perfume Lime'. Nicotianas are best grown annually apart from a few

exceptions that can be overwintered in a frost-free environment. *N. mutabilis* appears to be able to tolerate some frost and survived temperatures down to −8 degrees C (18 degrees F) in 2003 here. In recent years there has been a problem with tobacco wilt. **Z7.**

***N. alata* (syn. *N. affinis*)** Tender perennial from South America with large, very scented greenish-white flowers. 90cm (36in). A parent of many of the garden hybrids.

***N. langsdorffii* AGM** Slim, tubular, pendent green flowers. 1.2–1.5m (4–5ft).

N. mutabilis In the last couple of years this tobacco plant has withstood several sharp frosts in my garden and in many warmer counties can be relied on as a perennial. It grows to 1.5m (5ft) and is smothered in small white flowers, which fade first to pink, then darker pink with age (contrasting well with a dark eye), throughout summer until the frosts. Its only fault is the lack of scent.

Opposite: *Nerine bowdenii* AGM
Right: *Nicotiana sylvestris* AGM

N. suaveolens Rarely seen, this graceful Australian plant has slender white tubes and a greenish-purple flushed throat. 1.5m (5ft).

N. sylvestris **AGM** Probably the best known of all the tobacco plants with large, clammy pale green foliage and erect stems, to 1.8m (6ft), with cascades of long, highly scented, tubular white flowers.

Nigella damascena (RANUNCULACEAE)

An attractive annual, which happily seeds around the garden, with fine filigree green foliage and single or semi-double flowers in white, pink and blue. To 45–60cm (18–24in). The "petals" are, in fact, coloured bracts with the true petals lying above them holding nectar for insect pollinators. They are winter-hardy annuals and can be sown in autumn for larger plants and early flowering. A spring sowing will extend the flowering season into autumn. There are many good seed strains of this useful infill plant including Persian Jewels Group: double flowers in

white, rose and blue; 'Miss Jekyll': semi-double blue or white; 'Albion Black Pod' and 'Albion Green Pod': with black or green seed-pods; and 'Mulberry Rose': a deep pink selection from the Persian Jewels Group. **Z8–10**.

Oenothera (ONAGRACEAE)

There are many evening primroses that flower through late summer and into early autumn, the majority of them being some shade of yellow. I have chosen just a couple of them that are a little different in character.

O. acaulis Looking rather like a dandelion with its foliage rosette, this Chilean plant sends out long, sprawling, angled branches that flower in every axil over several weeks. The flowers are pure white and open in the evening with a fragrance reminiscent of sweet-scented soap to attract night pollinators. But once the flowers are pollinated, they undergo a colour change and blush to pink. Wouldn't you? It grows to 15cm (6in) tall only but spreads much more, 90cm (36in). Needs sun and good drainage to thrive. **Z5**.

O. macrocarpa **'Greencourt Lemon'** A native of North America, known as Ozark sundrops, this variety has pale lemon-yellow flowers on sprawling stems. The foliage is silvery green with a soft satin sheen created by the silky white hairs covering the leaves. An excellent subject for a hot, sunny position in sharply drained soil or in a pot on a sunny terrace. **Z5**.

Omphalodes linifolia AGM (BORAGINACEAE)

A favourite annual or biennial for hot, dry, poor conditions. A late-spring sowing will continue the display into late summer. White forget-me-nots hover above the glaucous grey foliage, looking like broderie anglaise, with brown seeds resembling small flying saucers. Will seed around gently. 40cm (16in). **Z8**

Left: *Nigella damascena*
Opposite: *Origanum* 'Rosenkuppel'

Onopordum (ASTERACEAE)

Statuesque members of the thistle family, reaching 2.4m (8ft) in flower, for well-drained soil and full sun. If you want to know the origin of the name, it is derived from the Greek *onos* (ass), and *porde* (fart). Luckily, I have not seen these plants grown near donkeys grazing so I have not put it to the test. Usually biennial, a rosette of silvery-grey spiny foliage is produced in the first year, followed by the towering flower stem, covered with silvery white down. The flowers are rosy purple and thistle-like, creating a three-star restaurant for bees and butterflies, while the seeds provide sustenance for birds in late autumn. *Onopordum acanthium*, the Scotch thistle, and *O. nervosum* AGM are the most likely species to be available to gardeners as seeds or plants. **Z6-8.**

Origanum (LAMIACEAE)

A versatile genus for late summer and autumn colour as well as being useful for the kitchen, sweet marjoram (*Origanum majorana*) being one of its number. They are highly decorative, mix well with autumn-flowering asters, phloxes, grasses and sedums and are easy to grow. The range is extensive, from alpine and rock garden subjects to good border perennials. All prefer sun and reasonable drainage and are highly attractive to pollinating insects.

O. 'Barbara Tingey' A lovely hybrid (between *O. calcaratum* and *O. rotundifolium* AGM) which arose in the alpine house of Frank and Barbara Tingey. It is best grown in an alpine house or on a sharply drained raised bed. It has hairy rounded leaves with purple undersides and tubular pink flowerheads from hop-like bracts. 10cm (4in) tall with 30cm (12in) spread. **Z8.**

O. 'Buckland' Raised by Keith and Ros Wiley at the Garden House, Buckland Monachorum, this may be a hybrid between *O. amanum* and *O. calcaratum*. It has grey-green hairy leaves and dislikes winter wet but is fine in an alpine house. Small pink flowers have darker bracts in summer. 15cm (6in). Dislikes overhead watering. **Z8.**

O. 'Kent Beauty' This is a lovely *O. rotundifolium* hybrid from Elizabeth Strangman from the famous Washfield Nursery. It has large hop-like bracts suffused with deep pink. Requires sharply drained soil and full sun. **Z8.**

O. laevigatum 'Herrenhausen' An excellent border perennial with dark purplish bracts and pink flowers with deep reddish-tinged foliage in winter and early spring. 60cm (24in). **Z8.**

O. l. 'Hopleys' This has larger purple flower spikes than the straight species and small rounded leaflets. 75cm (30in). **Z8.**

O. microphyllum For a hot and sunny spot this is a shrublet with diminutive grey leaves and dark lilac-purple terminal flower spikes. 50cm (20in). **Z8.**

O. 'Rosenkuppel' A good recent introduction from Germany with rose-purple flowers and dark bracts with purple-stained rounded foliage in winter and early spring. 60cm (24in). **Z8.**

Orlaya grandiflora (APIACEAE)

One of my favourite annuals or biennials for midsummer, this cow parsley has fine filigree foliage and large flat-headed umbels of white flowers with much enlarged outer petals. Easily grown in a sunny open position in poor soil. 45–75cm (18–30in). Autumn sowing will give early-flowering large plants but a spring sowing will give plants that will flower throughout summer and into early autumn. Associates well with almost everything. **Z8.**

Osteospermum (ASTERACEAE)

These gorgeous, colourful daisies originate from S. Africa and Arabia and continue flowering for months throughout summer and into the autumn. A few are hardy with good drainage and sun while others are more tender so it is advisable to lift the plants for winter or take a few autumn cuttings. In the last two decades there have been large numbers of new introductions from the breeding work of Danish and German nurserymen, and those at Cannington College in Somerset, so there is an excellent range to choose from. This work will continue to find forms that do not close their flowers in dull conditions. They are good in containers and also seen tumbling over a low wall while the prostrate varieties provide useful ground cover. The flowering season is long but will cease or slow down in very hot weather, resuming with cooler conditions. I have selected a meagre number showing a range of characteristics.

O. 'Buttermilk' AGM Pale yellow flowers with a bronzed reverse and a dark mahogany eye. 45cm (18in). Tender. **Z9.**

O. 'Whirlygig' AGM In this form the silvery white ray petals are constricted in the centre resulting in a spoon-shaped petal with a dark blue eye and grey-green leaves. A curiosity but I cannot make up my mind whether I like it or not. 60cm (24in). 'Pink Whirls' is its pink counterpart. **Z9.**

O. 'White Pim' (syn. *O. ecklonis* var. *prostratum*) A hardy perennial, useful as spreading ground cover with pure white daisy flowers with a dark blue eye and bluish-purple reverse. 30cm (12in) and 75cm (30in) spread. **Z8.**

O. jucundum AGM Another hardy species with muted pinkish-purple flowers, a dark eye and bronzed reverse. 20cm (8in). **Z8.**

Paeonia (PAEONIACEAE)

Peonies flower in spring and summer but some of the species are spectacular in autumn with their decorative seed-pods and deserve a mention in the late summer border for this alone. The seed-pods of many species peonies are large – 5cm (2in) – and in terminal clusters, like an upturned bird's claw. When the seeds are ripe, the pods split open longitudinally to expose the shiny, rounded, fertile black seeds and the vivid cerise-pink infertile fruits and seed-pod interior. Good examples are *P. cambessedesii* AGM from Mallorca, *P. mascula* and its many subspecies and *P. mlokosewitschii* AGM, the exquisite pale primrose-yellow peony from the Caucasus. Some species peony have almost matt brown or black seed which is not as rounded, but more ovoid or rectangular in shape. *P. californica* has brown seeds while those of *P. peregrina* are matt black. **Z5–8.**

Panicum (POACEAE)

These are graceful airy prairie grasses from North America, which flower late in the season. They appear to require poor, starved soil in sun to give of their best otherwise they grow too vigorously with a tendency to flop. Many exciting new cultivars are being bred in the USA and gradually becoming available in Britain. Their one fault is that the British growing season is not always long and hot enough for them to reach flowering time before the frosts inhibit further growth. Provided they have been grown lean and mean, the skeleton will persist throughout the winter months with little disintegration and can be cut down to the ground in

Right: *Panicum virgatum*

February before the new season's growth emerges. **All Z4.**

P. miliaceum **'Violaceum'** This is an elegant, tall, annual grass with broad, hairy leaves and broody dark-purple pendent flower spikes in late summer and early autumn. 1.2m (4ft). The seed-pods split open to reveal shiny, spherical, burnished-orange seeds.

P. virgatum **'Blue Tower'** A recent introduction with broad blue-green leaves and flowers to 2.4m (8ft).

P. v. **'Cloud Nine'** Glaucous blue-green leaves with deep golden fall colour. 1.8m (6ft).

P. v. **'Dallas Blues'** Broad leaf blades and the most blue of all the switch grasses. 1.2m (4ft).

P. v. **'Hänse Herms'** Arching stems to 1.2m (4ft) with deep red fall colour.

P. v. **'Heavy Metal'** A good name for this bolt-upright switch grass with its steely blue-grey foliage. 1.2m (4ft).

P. v. **'Northwind'** Dense clumps of glaucous blue

foliage with burnished gold autumn colour. 1.2m (4ft).

P. v. **'Prairie Sky'** Steel blue-green foliage and a vigorous arching habit. 90cm (36in).

P. v. **'Rehbraun'** Good red and gold autumn tints and arching flower stems. 1.2m (4ft).

P. v. **'Shenandoah'** Clumps of dense foliage suffused with deep burgundy in the fall. The best for red autumn colour. 105cm (42in).

P. v. **'Strictum'** Stiffly erect clumps of purple-tipped leaves and reddish flower spikes with yellow, gold and red fall colours. 1.5m (5ft).

Patrinia scabiosifolia (VALERIANACEAE)

Useful among naturalistic plantings, the umbels of small greenish-yellow flowers mix well with grasses and other herbaceous plants such as asters and aconitums. The flowers are useful for cutting where they produce a hazy effect like that of gypsophila. They prefer a moisture-retentive soil in sun or dappled shade. A late-flowering season through July and August makes this a useful herb to plant in swathes to add cohesion to a late-flowering border. 70cm (28in). **Z6–9**.

Pelargonium (GERANIACEAE)

As container plants, this genus is unsurpassed for creating eye-catching displays for the terrace, formal areas around public venues and hanging baskets, which will remain in flower for months on end. Every imaginable combination has been bred to suit every site and personal taste, from compact bush-like growth to trailing types suitable for an aerial container. In most areas these are not hardy and must be overwintered in a frost-free environment or as cuttings taken in the autumn. Botrytis, a fungal disease, can be a problem in humid conditions as the spores spread easily. Good ventilation is important for healthy pelargoniums. Another potentially serious problem for British growers is the introduction of a small blue butterfly from South Africa that lays its eggs inside the stems of pelargoniums. The emerging larvae consume the inner tissues causing eventual collapse of the plants. The butterfly is now common in the Balearic Islands where it is able to overwinter successfully. If global warming increases winter temperatures in the UK, it is only a matter of time before this pest reaches these shores and wreaks havoc on the pelargonium population. The global trade in plants makes this potential danger a plausible reality if material is transported from infected areas.

Enough gloom, the range of pelargoniums available to the consumer is vast and I do not intend to make a personal choice of those offered. I am interested in a few rather subtle species pelargoniums with interesting leaves and small flowers, which make interesting specimen plants. **All Z10.**

P. acetosum Glaucous blue-green fleshy fan-shaped leaves with salmon-pink flowers with long attenuated petals. Sprawling in growth but graceful tumbling out of a container or over a low wall. 45cm (18in).

P. quinquelobatum The height of subtlety, with extraordinary flowers of a yellowish blue-green overlaid with dove grey and hairy bluish-green leaves. A curiosity more than a great beauty, maybe. 30cm (12in).

P. reniforme A tactile, softly hairy, kidney-shaped leaf with a silvery grey-green velvety appearance and vivid pink flowers. It is rather leggy and untidy with small tuberous roots but can be kept in shape by pinching out growth at the tips. The leaves are faintly aromatic. 30cm (12in).

P. sidoides One of my favourite species and the form I grow has almost purple-black velvety blooms above silky grey-green heart-shaped foliage that is a pleasure to touch as I pass by. This makes a handsome container plant, flowering for many months, with a rather lax habit. There are other colour forms ranging from deep reddish-purple to almost black. 30cm (12in).

Pennisetum (POACEAE)

This is another important genus of spectacular autumn-flowering grasses with hairy spikes like fat caterpillars swaying in the breeze. Similarly to some of the switch grasses, the British season is not always long or hot enough to bring them into flower each season. The majority are clump-forming although a few are inveterate colonizers, such as *Pennisetum incomptum* which spreads aggressively by wandering rhizomes. You have been warned. It has prolific straw-coloured pipe-cleaner flowers and there is a purple form with purple spikes. **Z4** A clump-forming species with even longer slender spikes is *P. macrourum* 1.2m (4ft). **Z6**.

A number of recent *Pennisetum* introductions are not particularly hardy and can be lost even in a frost-free environment. These include *P. setaceum* 'Rubrum' and *P. macrostachyum* 'Burgundy Giant'. Both are spectacular foliage plants with rich purple leaves and reddish-purple arching flower spikes. They look wonderful covered with droplets of early morning dew but are not good perennials and best purchased each year as "bedding" plants. **Z9–10.**

P. alopecuroides and its many cultivars are hardier than the above but only in warmer counties will they flower well. They require good drainage and sun. **Z6**.

A few compact, dwarf varieties are offered with the smaller garden in mind. I cannot see any merit in what appears to me to be stunted, distinctly ungraceful subjects but others may see their charms. They include *P.* 'Little Bunny' and *P. a.* 'Little Honey'. Other forms of *P. alopecuroides* have graceful arching growth with swarms of colourful hairy caterpillar-like flower spikes. Particularly effective is 'Cassian's Choice' with its light brown catkins and good golden-red autumn coloration. 75cm (30in). 'Hameln' is a good clump-forming form with pale creamy greenish-white flowers to 60cm (24in) and 'Moudry' has deep purplish spikes over dark green foliage: a wonderful colour but the flowers are sometimes lost within the foliage. 'National Arboretum' is a similar colour but

Opposite, top left: *Pennisetum alopecuroides* 'Moudry'
Opposite, top right: *P. villosum* AGM
Opposite, below: *P. orientale* 'Karley Rose'

its fluffy spikes are held well above the foliage 75cm (30in). *P. a.* var. *purpurascens* grown from seed produces handsome plants with almost black fluffy catkins. A recent introduction, 'Black Beauty', selected from the above has superb dark spikes of great presence.

Pennisetum orientale AGM is reliably hardy in most areas with substantial fluffy white flowers with subtle hints of pink in profusion through July to October. 60cm (2ft). **Z6.**

P. 'Karley Rose' is a selection with rosy pink spikes 90cm (36in) and *P. o.* 'Tall Tails' has erect growth and creamy- white-flushed pink flowers to 1.2m (4ft).

P. villosum AGM is an attractive clump-forming species with large creamy buff fluffy spikes. 60cm (24in). In all but the warmest counties this should be treated as an annual and it makes an excellent container plant. **Z8.**

Penstemon (SCROPHULARIACEAE)

A vast decorative genus with the majority originating in North America. Breeding work has produced many cultivars that are suitable for growing in the British climate and there is a wide choice available. Many species are not suitable for growing in Britain, as they require a dry atmosphere and sharp drainage with full sun. The more humid atmosphere causes unsightly fungal diseases to the foliage and many of the blue-flowered penstemons appear mauve. There are, however, some more tolerant species that grow well in these conditions. They flower for many months from midsummer until the first frosts.

P. barbatus This has linear leaves that are often glaucous and a neat rosette of foliage, topped by slender, tough stems with red tubular flowers, often yellow within. 60cm (24in). There are many named forms of *P. barbatus* with the majority red, scarlet or orange-red flowered although there are pink forms and an extremely attractive pale yellow variety called 'Schooley's Yellow'. I found this short-lived but enjoyed it for a while. **Z3.**

P. glaber The plant available in the nursery trade under this name does not look anything like the plant I grew from wild collected seed. However, it is a good garden plant with rather lax growth, shiny green leaves and prolific bluish-purple flowers. In dry weather the flowers are more blue and in humid conditions they become more purple-blue. A pristine white form was discovered as a sport by John and Sarah Phillips at their Dorset home and named 'Roundway Snowflake'. **Z3.**

P. digitalis A good border plant with rounded rosette leaves suffused with purple staining during winter and early spring and tubular mother of pearl flowers. 60cm (24in). There is a white-flowered form with paler green leaves and a seed selection from Dale Lindgren (Nebraska) which has dark red-purple leaves ('Husker Red') and is worth growing for its foliage rosettes alone. **Z3.**

P. heterophyllus Many different forms are available and are the bluest flowering penstemons generally offered in Britain. Cultivars such as 'Blue Springs' and 'Zuriblau' are good blues. **Z8.**

P. ovatus A personal favourite with rounded green leaves turning crimson-purple with low temperatures and upright 45cm (18in) stems with clusters of brilliant sky-blue flowers in whorls throughout summer. **Z3.**

P. Mexicali Series These were bred by Bruce Meyers from Washington State, who was responsible for extensive breeding work on species penstemons. These hybrids grow well in the British climate. 'Gilchrist' is a fine bushy plant with slender foliage and fairly squat flowers of a strong pink with a hint of blue. 50cm (20in). It is increased by vegetative propagation, mainly cuttings. 'Sunburst Ruby' is a seed strain with ruby-coloured tubular flowers with a white throat and red guidelines. Reliably hardy and easy. 40cm (16in). **Z6.**

P. smallii Seedlings are certainly minute but this is a handsome penstemon with large, toothed leaves which turn reddish-maroon in the cold. 60cm (24in). The pale purple to reddish squat flowers are large for a species. **Z6.**

Persicaria (POLYGONACEAE)

Vigorous, useful ground cover for both spring and autumn, with a long flowering period, makes this ian invaluable genus for linking flowering seasons. In early spring, *Persicaria bistorta* and its allies produce successions of pale pink or red pokers for a sunny position and moist soil, but are no more than a memory when the real stars of the late-summer stage put on their display. The most notable of these are forms of *P. amplexicaulis* with their vigorous production of foliage and then a profusion of elegant taper-like flowers in white, 'Alba', pink 'Rosea' and red, continuing until the first heavy frosts. Several good selections of red-flowered *P. amplexicaulis* have been made: 'Atrosanguinea', with its dark red (with a hint of blue) spires; 'Firetail' AGM, with its matt red flowers; 'Firedance', with vibrant fiery spikes and 'Summer Dance', which is lighter still with its flowers held well above the foliage clumps. They grow quickly to give good ground cover with attractive foliage; flowering starts in midsummer. Most grow to 1.2–1.5m (4–5ft) tall and as much in girth. They will also tolerate light shade as long as there is enough

Below: *Persicaria amplexicaulis* 'Firedance'

moisture in the soil. Annual whittling away of the perimeter growth is necessary to prevent this plant overwhelming less vigorous subjects. **Z5–9.**

There are several other *Persicaria* species that contribute to the border in late summer and autumn. The bistort types with their erect pokers have a few good representatives later in the season. *P. affinis* 'Superba' AGM, a pink form; 'Darjeeling Red' AGM, a deep red, and 'Donald Lowndes' AGM, a salmon pink fading to deep pink, are short, mat-forming perennials to 25–30cm (10–12in) that also flower until the frosts and often display good autumn coloration of reddish-bronze. A neat clump-forming species is *P. milletii* with its crimson spikes of flower for moisture-retentive soil. 25cm (10in). **Z4–8.**

Quite different is *Persicaria polymorpha*, a gentle giant with no bad habits. At 1.8m (6ft) in height and about the same in girth, this has white flowers in summer, which fade to a dusky pink with age, and the foliage takes on autumn tints of red and gold late in the season. **Z4–9.**

An annual, *P. orientale* from China grows vigorously to 1.5m (5ft) with stout, branched stems with pendent spikes of white, pink or rose flowers – seldom seen but a useful infill plant for late season.

There are also many *Persicaria* species that are grown for foliage alone with striking markings on the leaves. *P. microcephala* 'Red Dragon' has green, red and grey markings while *P. virginiana* 'Painter's Palette' is green and cream with maroon blotches. **Z5.**

Peucedanum verticillare (APIACEAE)
Pinkish-purple foliage emerges in spring, turning green as it ages. This monocarpic cow parsley may take several years before it flowers; the longer it takes the taller it grows to a maximum of around 3.3m (11ft) with multibranched flowering stems and greenish yellow umbels. It reliably self seeds. **Z4–8.**

Phacelia (HYDROPHYLLACEAE)
From North America, this genus provides several annuals and short-lived perennials, which can be used to provide late-summer colour. A late-spring sowing will ensure flowering late in the season.
P. campanularia An annual with white or deep blue (with a white eye), cup-shaped flowers to 30cm (12in). It requires sun and good drainage. **Z3.**
P. sericea A short-lived perennial, has silky silvery grey foliage and purplish-blue flowers to 45cm (18in). **Z3.**
P. tanacetifolia Perhaps the most familiar *Phacelia* to be grown in the UK. It is an annual with delicate, *pinnate* grey-green foliage and unusual powder-blue flowers that are ambrosia to bees, butterflies and hoverflies. This plant is used as an organic means of encouraging insect beneficials, such as hoverflies, which will gobble up aphids in adjoining crops. Self seeds freely in sunny positions. 60cm (24in). **Z8.**

Phlomis tuberosa (LAMIACEAE)
Many gardeners are familiar with the shrubby *Phlomis* – not so many with the herbaceous types that can provide an admirable backbone to a naturalistic planting. From clusters of spherical storage tubers arise strong stems and bold, cordate green leaves suffused with purple in spring. Flower stems attain 1.5m (5ft) by midsummer and pinkish-purple flowers

are produced in whorls, contrasting well with the purple stalks. *P. t.* 'Amazone' is a form that stands erect without toppling. As the flowers fade the flowering stems and seed-heads remain, providing a strong architectural shape into the winter months. **Z4–9.**

Phlox (POLEMONIACEAE)

This is another important genus for summer and autumn, originating from N. America and much worked upon by plant breeders to produce a fine selection of form and colour to suit most garden requirements. The two main groups of phlox for the late-summer garden are *P. maculata* and *P. paniculata* and their cultivars, with *P.* x *arendsii* (*P. paniculata* x *P. divaricata* AGM) playing a smaller part. The scent of phlox is so evocative of balmy summer evenings and the saturated luminous colours in the blue and purple spectrum range are seldom found in other herbaceous material.

The popularity of phloxes as garden plants has dwindled in recent years but I am aware of the stirrings of a revival. They are susceptible to mildew, which can be very unsightly, and eelworm in the stems, leaves and flowers is severely disfiguring. However, both these problems can be overcome with good cultural practices. Mildew is prevalent when plants are under stress so a good growing environment with a moisture-retentive soil is essential. There are several recent introductions that are mildew-resistant. Eelworm is only present in aerial parts of the phlox so propagation by root cuttings will keep the stock clean. Where infected plants have been grown it is better to leave the area phlox-free for several years before replanting.

Phlox maculata appears to contend with drier soil conditions than *P. paniculata*. They are shorter – at 75–90cm (30–36in) – and have narrower dark green leaves and spotted stems and are usually more erect in growth. A limited colour range is available, many of them having a contrasting eye. 'Alpha' AGM (Arends) is a soft pink, 'Reine du Jour' is white with a maroon eye, 'Natascha' has pink and white striped flowers and 'Schneelawine' is pure white. The scent is sweet and spicy but not as strong as some of the *paniculata* types. **Z5**

Phlox paniculata has a wide range of colours from white, through pinks, reds, lilac, mauve, blue, indigo and purple. Included in this section are some excellent hybrids bred by Coen Jansen using open pollinated *P.* x *arendsii* with *P. paniculata*. A large clump of pure white phlox such as 'Casablanca' (bred by Jansen), 'David' (Dr Hans Simon) or 'Mount Fuji' AGM is a wonderful, cooling apparition on a hot summer's day. Blue and purple phloxes have complex optical properties and in dry conditions in sun will appear purple. Cool, humid and wet conditions will allow blue overtones to predominate,

Opposite, top: *Phacelia tanacetifolia*
Opposite, bottom: *Phlomis tuberosa* 'Amazone'
Right: *Phlox paniculata* 'Blue Paradise'

especially in the evening and early morning. 'Blue Paradise' (Piet Oudolf), 'Blue Evening' (Piet Oudolf), 'Cool of the Evening' (Symons-Jeune) and 'Toits de Paris' (Symons-Jeune) are particularly good blue-purple phloxes with a delicious fragrance.

There is a marked variation in size with *P. paniculata* cultivars. The species, with its small lilac flowers in terminal pyramidal heads on strong wiry stems to 1.5m (5ft), is all too rarely seen. Breeders have increased flower size and also reduced the height of many named forms. In the pale pink spectrum, 'Rosa Pastell' (Foerster) is a large-flowered salmon pink with a strongly scented sweet fragrance at 90cm (36in); 'Utopia' (Coen Jansen) is a vigorous tall pale pink at 1.5m (5ft) and 'Monica Lynden-Bell' is a soft shell pink at 1.2m (4ft).

Large subtly coloured flowers include 'Violetta Gloriosa' (Foerster), which is similar to 'Prospero' (Foerster), but with substantial blooms of pale lavender and white with a glorious sweet scent; 'Grey Lady' has grey-washed blue flowers and a white eye and 'Lavendelwolke' (Foerster) has almost white, lilac-flushed petals. Some varieties have better foliage than others, retaining the lower leaves, which are unblotched. These include 'Hesperis' (Coen Jansen) with pyramidal heads of small lilac-mauve flowers with a spicy sweet scent; 'Lichtspel' (Piet Oudolf) with small lilac-pink flowers with a darker pink eye at 1.5m (5ft) and 'Luc's Lilac' (Coen Jansen), which is larger than 'Hesperis' at 1.5m (5ft). **Z6.**

Phuopsis stylosa (RUBIACEAE)

This is a ground-covering, mat-forming plant for moisture-retentive but well-drained soil in sun or dappled shade. It has dome-shaped flowerheads of pale pink or deeper purplish-pink and, in the form 'Purpurea', tubular flowers with a starry corolla. The foliage has a pungent foxy scent but it is a useful late-flowering subject through July to September for difficult areas. 20cm (8in). **Z7.**

Left: *Phygelius* x *rectus* 'African Queen' AGM

Phygelius (SCROPHULARIACEAE)

My first introduction to this South African genus was *Phygelius aequalis,* a subshrub that flowers towards the end of summer. I perversely nicknamed its matt flesh-pink coloured tubular flowers as "dead man's fingers" and have never quite got over the image the name conjured up. *Phygelius* are useful late-summer perennials and, fortunately, are found in other colours than flesh pink. Indeed there is *P. a.* 'Yellow Trumpet', which is a pale, luminous cream-yellow, with a bushy habit, to 90cm (36in), and able to tolerate light shade. *P. aequalis* is not reliably hardy in any but the warmest counties. **Z8.**

Phygelius capensis is often called the Cape fuchsia and has more slender tubular flowers in vibrant oranges and reds. It is also a much hardier plant than *P. aequalis*. The hybrids produced between these two species are called *P.* x *rectus* and there have been many good recent introductions with various combinations of the parents and hybrid

forms. 'African Queen' AGM was one of the first hybrids raised by John May in 1969, which combines the hardiness of *P. capensis* and the more compact flowers of *P. aequalis*. 'Moonraker' is a pale lemon, 'Winchester Fanfare' a dusky reddish-orange, 'Salmon Leap' AGM more orange and 'Pink Elf' a dwarf pale pink. **Z6.**

Phytolacca americana (PHYTOLACCACEAE)

This North American perennial bears the unlovely name of pokeweed and contributes to the autumn display with fine purple fall foliage and impressive spikes of berries, which turn from green through red, and finally a shiny purple-black, contrasting well with the red stems. It is a bit of a thug and will seed around freely in moisture-retentive soil but is useful in wilder areas of the garden. 1.5m (5ft). **Z4–9.**

Platycodon grandiflorus (CAMPANULACEAE)

The "balloon flower" enjoys a moisture-retentive but well-drained soil in sun or light shade and makes neat clumps of foliage. In summer the flower buds inflate like small balloons, hence the common name, held together at the tips until they open to reveal a bell-shaped flower at 45cm (18in). If, like me, you are a garden delinquent, it is very tempting to pop open the buds, just as I cannot resist touching the squirting cucumbers to see if they will explode. Childishness aside, *P. grandiflorus* is available in white, pink, blue and bluish-purple – single or double flowers and dwarf varieties that only grow to 30cm (12in). Charming members of the *Campanula* family. **Z4.**

Plectranthus (LAMIACEAE)

Related to *Solenostemon* (syn. *Coleus*), these plants are good container subjects with handsome foliage. They originate from Australia, Asia and Africa, and are tender perennials requiring frost-free conditions. **Z10.**

One of the most familiar is *P. argentatus* from Australia, with its softly hairy, tactile silvery foliage and spires of pale blue and white flowers in late summer. I grow *P. neochilus* with its green leaves and late spikes of lavender-blue flowers. It is a compact plant to 60cm (24in) and a good subject for an autumn-flowering container plant, but it will not tolerate frost. Another *Plectranthus* with brilliant blue flowers is *P. thyrsoideus*, which will flower all winter in a cool conservatory kept above 5 degrees C (41 degrees F).

Podophyllum hexandrum 'Majus' (BERBERIDACEAE)

Flowering in late spring, this choice woodland plant produces dramatic egg-shaped scarlet fruits in late summer and early autumn. It thrives in rich, damp soil in dappled shade. 45cm (18in). **Z6.**

Polemonium (POLEMONIACEAE)

The flowers are held aloft on stems rising above fine clumps of pinnate green foliage. Some are tubular, such as *P. pauciflorum,* while others are more open and cup-shaped, like *P. foliosissimum*. This genus is well represented in North America, the two species mentioned both hailing from there. *P. foliosissimum* has bluish-violet blooms, rarely white, and starts to flower in summer, continuing into the autumn. 60cm (24in). It requires moisture-retentive soil with good drainage in sun or dappled shade. *P. pauciflorum* prefers drier conditions and has tacky foliage, a slightly foxy scent and yellow-green purple-flushed tubular flowers. 50cm (20in). There are several lovely hybrids, which make good garden plants but many of them flower in early summer such as 'Sonia's Bluebell' an exquisite cup-shaped pale blue, 'Northern Lights' a powdery pale blue on upright growth and 'Glebe Cottage Lilac' a lilac-blue. 'Lambrook Mauve' AGM is a cup-shaped bluish-mauve, which reliably flowers into late summer. **Z3–7.**

Rodgersia (SAXIFRAGACEAE)

A first-class foliage genus for cool, moisture-retentive soils and light shade, with bold palmate leaves and flowering stems to 1.8m (6ft). This genus gives a strong structural form and impressive foliar effects. **Z5–6.**

R. aesculifolia **AGM** This has leaves reminiscent of a horse chestnut (*Aesculus*) and emerges in spring with bronzed foliage, bearing white flowers through summer.

P. pinnata **'Superba' AGM** There are several named forms of this species and 'Superba' has substantial pink flower spikes over handsome bronzed foliage. Unfortunately not all the plants under this name are correct and it is best to purchase it in flower. 'Elegans' may be a hybrid but is distinctive, with rosy red flowers in dense plumes to 90cm (36in).

R. podophylla **'Rotlaub'** An excellent form with bold, bronzed foliage tinged with red, turning green in summer, with loose panicles of white flowers and brilliant autumn bronze and red leaves.

Romneya coulteri 'White Cloud' AGM (PAPAVERACEAE)

A native of Mexico and California, this almost woody member of the poppy family has large white tissue-paper quality flowers with a bold boss of yellow stamens in late summer, over glaucous grey-green toothed foliage to 1.8m (6ft). It is one of those plants that, if happy, is rampant and a thug, spreading vigorously and invasively. If conditions are not suitable it sulks, gradually dwindling to nothing. There appear to be no halfway measures. I have at last succeeded with it by providing a deep gravel-rich bed in full sun – it despised my wet clay. 'White Cloud' AGM is a hybrid with especially large, scented flowers. **Z7.**

Left: *Rodgersia aesculifolia* AGM
Opposite, top: *Romneya coulteri* 'White Cloud' AGM
Opposite, bottom: *Rudbeckia hirta* 'Toto' AGM

Rudbeckia (ASTERACEAE)

Another stalwart of the daisy family, hailing from North America. They bloom from late summer and into the autumn with rich yellow, golden and orange flowers in a variety of shapes and sizes. They are easy to grow provided with a humus-rich, moisture-retentive soil in sun or light shade. *R. fulgida* var. *deamii* AGM can thrive in drier conditions whereas *R. maxima* prefers a damper environment despite having glaucous blue-green foliage, which often indicates a preference for hot and dry soils.

There are a number of perennial species, which can be flowered from a spring sowing and are often used for annual displays, such as *R. hirta* and its named seed strains. 'Indian Summer' AGM: large golden daisies to 80cm (32in); 'Marmalade': single golden orange and dark eye; 'Toto' AGM: single golden yellow and 'Prairie Sun': a recent Fleuroselect Gold Medal winner with light yellow flowers and a green eye. Other good seed strains are currently being introduced. **Z4.**

A recent trial by the RHS of perennial *Rudbeckia* species provided a brilliant and cheerful display on the trials grounds at the RHS garden at Wisley during 1999 to 2002. Seeing plants en masse is valuable in assessing the individual merits of different named forms. *R. fulgida* var. *sullivantii* 'Goldsturm' and *R. fulgida* var. *speciosa* both received an AGM, the former with large flowers of golden yellow to 60cm (24in) and the latter with orange-yellow ones to 75cm (30in). They both tolerate drier conditions and form neat mounds with a profusion of flowers. **Z4.**

Quite different is *R. laciniata* 'Herbstsonne' AGM with its dark green serrated foliage and flowering stems to 1.8m (6ft) or more. It has sunny yellow daisies with drooping petals and a greenish-yellow cone. It makes a good back of the border plant and tolerable for those who do not appreciate brassy yellows. *R. l.* 'Goldquelle' AGM is an old variety with double bright yellow flowers with a hint of green. The petals are so numerous that they obscure the greenish cone. 90cm (36in). **Z3.**

Rudbeckia maxima has almost ovate, handsome, glaucous blue-grey foliage and in late summer the flower stems elongate to 1.5m (5ft), producing lemon-yellow flowers with drooping ray petals, which contrast well with the pronounced black cones. Beautiful when grown well, this is not the easiest species to please with a high moisture requirement and a tendency to dwindle rather than thrive. **Z7.**

Salvia (LAMIACEAE)

The diversity of form and colour in this genus rivals and exceeds that of the hardy geraniums and few gardens will be devoid of at least one representative. Many of the more showy and brightly coloured sages are tender but their long flowering period offers tremendous value even if they do need to be replaced on an annual basis. Many of the species are increased easily by seed and named cultivars are propagated by cuttings or division. Most prefer full sun to maximize flowering potential and detest winter wet, but a few will tolerate and even favour partial shade. They are particularly important to pollinating insects in the latter part of the year as they provide nectar. Bees are very partial to sages and are even provided with a landing pad by the lower petals of the tubular flowers. Hummingbirds normally pollinate the vivid red and orange Mexican species in their native habitat.

There is an abundance of excellent sages for late-summer and autumn flowering so I have attempted to divide them into distinct groups. Annual and biennial salvias can be treated together and are easily grown from seed. Many salvia species have relatively large seed, which is a pleasure to harvest when ripe. Each fertilized flower produces a cluster of four seeds that turn from white or green to brown or black as they ripen. Squeezing the papery calyx when the seeds are mature will allow them to tumble out into your hand – so satisfying.

Seed usually germinates readily in good seed compost and can be handled at an early stage because the cotyledon leaves are large. I have been most impressed with *S. algeriensis,* an annual with large lavender-blue flowers and sage green leaves to 60cm (24in). A late spring sowing will ensure flowering in early autumn.

BIENNIALS

These include *S. aethiopis* and *S. argentea* AGM, which have lovely ornamental silvery rosettes in the first year and branched flowering stems with white flowers and pale bluish-purple spotting on the throat the following season. The latter has dense silvery hairs and produces lusty mounds of wavy edged foliage, which a nursery friend likens to a sheep. *S. aethiopis* is not so silvery, has more lobed leaves and is not as tall at 60cm (24in) while *S. argentea* attains 75cm (30in) in flower and is hardier. They detest winter wet and are best grown in sharply drained soil on a lean diet and full sun. *S. sclarea* var. *turkestanica* is another biennial with large greenish-purple bracts around its flowers. The flower spikes are hop-like as they emerge, becoming erect as the flowers open and the plants make substantial and imposing clumps to 1.5m (5ft). The foliage has a rather unpleasant odour so it is best placed in part of the garden where it will not get bruised when passing. There is a white-flowered form offered under the name of 'Vatican White'. **Z5–7.**

TENDER PERENNIALS

The next fairly distinct groups of salvias are tender perennials that are usually produced from seed each year and treated as annuals. This includes the familiar *S. patens* AGM and its colour forms. A mature plant has swollen tubers similar to a dahlia and should be likewise lifted for frost-free winter storage or mulched in situ to prevent frost damage. In milder areas *S. patens* is reasonably hardy. This sage has slightly clammy, triangular leaves and large deep

Opposite, right: *Salvia patens* 'Cambridge Blue' AGM
Opposite, far right: *Salvia uliginosa* AGM

blue flowers to 60cm (24in). 'Cambridge Blue' AGM is paler, a clear sky blue, 'Chilcombe' is lavender blue and 'White Trophy' is white. The plant originates in Mexico and in the early '90s, Compton, D'Arcy and Rix discovered an imposing giant new form, which they named 'Guanajuato' after the place of origin. This is larger in all its parts than *S. patens,* to 1.8m (6ft), and has dark markings on its foliage – a truly handsome plant. It produces little seed compared with the other named forms. **Z8.**

S. coccinea, S. farinacea and S. splendens are also usually grown as annuals and have been subjected to intensive breeding regimes. The wild species are often considered to be lax and untidy with a small proportion of flower to foliage. Forms have been selected that have more compact growth, congested spikes of flowers and earlier flowering especially in the case of *S. splendens*, which starts to flower in August until the frosts. The mass bedding schemes of parks and gardens are often centred on the highly bred forms of *S. splendens* with their rigid form and white, pink and red flowers. *S. farinacea* is also popular with a range of colour through white, pale blue, blue and purplish-blue and contrasting silvery green foliage. *S. coccinea* is found in white, coral, salmon, pink and red, another plant pollinated by hummingbirds. I am not fond of the compact congested varieties, preferring the more elegant and graceful appearance of the species. *S. splendens* 'Van Houttei' AGM is a selected form with deep wine-red flowers over light green foliage to 90cm (36in) and prefers a moisture-retentive soil in sun or light shade. It is propagated by cuttings not seed. **Z9–10.**

Tender sages that are not grown annually from seed each year include *S. corrugata* from Ecuador, with its deep green corrugated foliage and brown felty undersides. It has terminal congested spikes of deep blue flowers that continue for many weeks. I have grown it to 90cm (36in) but have heard that it can grow to 1.5m (5ft) kept in a cool conservatory. **Z10.**

For all the really tender sages it is necessary to take late-summer cuttings to provide material for the following season or keep the plant in frost-free conditions over winter. These salvias make excellent container specimens. *S. buchananii* AGM has furry cerise-purple flowers and glossy dark green leaves but its stems are very brittle and it needs to be placed where it will not get knocked. 60cm (24in). **Z10.**

S. 'Indigo Spires' is an especially fine *S. longispicata* x *S. farinacea* hybrid with spikes of penetrating blue flowers on erect dark stems. A purple infusion to the stems and leaves occurs in cooler temperatures and at dawn and dusk the colour saturation of the blooms is almost luminous. 1.5m (5ft). **Z9–10.**

The following salvias can withstand a bare minimum of frost provided it is not prolonged and they will survive in the warmer counties unscathed. Free-draining soil suits most of these sages best as most detest winter wet. I have grown *S. azurea* from several seed sources and find that some are much more winter hardy than others. (I suspect that winter wet is more the deciding factor than the cold.) This has silvery green leaves, rather lax growth to 1.5m (5ft) and azure-blue flowers that continue until the frosts. **Z9–10.**

S. candelabrum AGM is an imposing sage and I think it is shown to its best as a single specimen. It attains 90cm (36in) in height and similar in width with grey-green leaves and terminal spikes of bluish-purple blooms. **Z8.**

S. chamaedryoides is a charming, small-leaved, woody sage with bright blue flowers, which is seen at its best when tumbling out of a pot. Prune regularly for a good shape. *S. chamaedryoides* silver-leaved form has good silver foliage. **Z8.**

Opposite, top left: *Salvia darcyi*
Opposite, top right: *S. guaranitica* 'Blue Enigma'
Opposite, bottom: *Salvia* 'Indigo Spires'

S. darcyi is named after John D'Arcy and was found on a Mexican collecting trip by Compton, D'Arcy and Rix in 1991. It is 1.8m (6ft) tall with scarlet flowers and clammy green foliage. **Z9–10.**

S. guaranitica and its named forms and hybrids are some of the best tall sages for the late-summer garden. They grow to 1.5m (5ft) or more with long flower spikes held well above the foliage. 'Argentine Skies' is a clear pale blue, 'Black and Blue' makes an imposing leafy clump with pure blue flowers enclosed in contrasting near black calyces. 'Blue Enigma' AGM is a large-flowered, sumptuous blue and *S.* 'Purple Majesty' is reputed to be a hybrid between *S. guaranitica* and *S. gesneriiflora* with deep velvety-purple flowers. **Z9.**

S. involucrata AGM and its named forms are also on the borderline of hardiness. They form substantial clumps of foliage, often with purple-suffused undersides to the leaves, and stems with vivid magenta-red flowers and coloured bracts. They grow to 1.5m (5ft) tall, and almost as wide, and will tolerate some shade. 'Bethellii' AGM is the best-known cultivar with more rounded and congested spikes than the species with pink flowers and bracts. 'Hadspen' has darker, larger more spaced flower spikes of deep pinkish-purple. **Z9–10.**

S. uliginosa AGM is either a thug or a wimp and, when happy, can over-run a border in a season. It is autumn flowering with sky-blue flowers on long wand-like stems. Beautiful. 1.5m (5ft). **Z9.**

SHRUBBY SALVIAS

There is a number of species and hybrids, which form woody growth and are generally hardy if provided with good drainage and sun. In some cold winters they may be cut to the ground but emerge from basal growth in spring. This includes *S. greggii* and *S. microphylla* and hybrids between the two, *S.* x *jamensis*. In recent years there has been a large number of introductions from these species as they easily hybridize, and there is an excellent colour range. These sages produce rounded, woody subshrubs with small leaves and flowers. Some of the hybrids have very small blooms and not enough flower to foliage ratio to be first-rate garden plants. I have just selected a few to indicate the range of leaf and colour form. *S. greggii* 'Peach' AGM, orangey-red flowers, 'Sungold' a clear pale yellow and 'Silas Dyson', a resonant crimson-red. *S. microphylla* var. *microphylla* 'Newby Hall' AGM has bright apple green leaves and vivid scarlet flowers whereas *S. m.* var. *m.* 'La Foux' has a dash more blue in the flowers than the above but still a strong red. *S.* x *jamensis* 'Raspberry Royale' AGM is floriferous with blooms of reddish-purple, not like any raspberry I have seen. 'Pat Vlasto' is a peachy orange, 'Los Lirios' AGM is orangey-red and 'La Luna' is pale yellow with a flush of pink. Another species with slightly woody growth but more lax in habit is *S. lycioides* from Mexico, with scented foliage and a profusion of violet-blue flowers from June until the first hard frosts. It grows to 45cm (18in). **Z6–9.**

HARDY SALVIAS

Several hardy sages form foliage rosettes followed by tall, branched flowering stems that are wider at the top than the base. Flowers are well spaced and the plant has an airy disposition. I find these types more graceful and elegant than some of the mound forming hardy varieties. A notable species in this group is *S. pratensis,* the meadow clary, a British native. There are several named forms and possible hybrids that must be vegetatively propagated such as *S. pratensis* 'Indigo' AGM has deep blue spikes on lax stems to 90cm (36in). There is some indication that this may be a hybrid. 'Lapis Lazuli' is a pink form but it is difficult to know the true plant as it is often propagated by seed. A white seed strain, 'Swan Lake', has pale green leaves and pure white flowers. Seed is produced in quantity so to prolong flowering it is necessary to remove the spent flower spikes to get successive flushes. **Z3.**

Salvia verticillata 'Purple Rain' was selected by Piet Oudolf and has soft hairy mounds of grey-green foliage with purple flowers in whorls up the stem to 60cm (24in). Another of Piet's selections is *S. v.* 'Smouldering Torches' with more upright growth and a purple suffusion to the leaves, stems and calyces. They flower in early summer and if pruned back severely after the first flush is over, they will reliably flower again in early autumn. **Z6.**

Perhaps the most important group of hardy salvias to be used in gardens includes *S. nemorosa, S.* x *superba* AGM and *S.* x *sylvestris*. They are indisputably hardy given good drainage and a sunny position flowering for many weeks. Give them a good haircut after the first flush, which will encourage a second flowering well into autumn. The species and the hybrids have rugose leaves and form bushy mounds covered with flowers. Breeding work has resulted in a good range of colour and size to suit any garden. *S.* x *sylvestris* is a hybrid between *S. nemorosa* x *S. pratensis* while *S.* x *superba* is

Left: *Salvia verticillata* 'Purple Rain'

considered to be progeny of *S.* x *sylvestris* with *S. amplexicaulis* (syn. *S. villicaulis*). Whatever the parents these are good reliable perennials, which look fairly similar. **All Z5.**

S. nemorosa and *S. n.* subsp. *tesquicola* are species and can be propagated by seed – they are both garden-worthy, the latter taller and more elegant than some of the cultivars with less congested spikes of lavender-blue with reddish-purple calyces. 1.2m (4ft). Many named forms have been bred to be more compact for the smaller border – I am not convinced by some of these dwarfs as I find their appearance rather unnatural and dumpy. A recent introduction is *S. n.* Marcus ('Haueumanarc), growing to 30cm (12in) with deep purple-blue flowers and a spreading habit. *S. n.* 'Amethyst' AGM was bred by Ernst Pagels and has tall spikes of pink flowers with a darker purple calyx to 90cm (36in). I selected *S. n.* 'Phoenix Pink' from a large number of seedlings derived from 'Amethyst', which is shorter in stature at 60cm (24in) with a lighter pink flower and a warm reddish-pink calyx. *S. n.* 'Caradonna' is a recent introduction with purplish-blue flower spikes and blue-black suffused stems to 50cm (20in). *S. n.* 'Pusztaflamme' (syn. 'Plumosa') AGM is quite distinct with a mass of lasting purplish-pink bracts on congested spikes. It is not altogether to my taste but it is a very different form and persists for many weeks. 60cm (24in).

S. x *superba* 'Superba' flowers later than *S. nemorosa* and *S.* x *sylvestris* with vigorous growth to 1.5m (5ft) and long spikes of large lavender-purple flowers with a pleasing contrasting calyx of reddish purple. *S.* x *superba* 'Rubin' AGM is shorter at 60cm (24in) with rather lax growth, reddish-pink flowers and maroon calyces. *S.* x *s.* 'Dear Anja', formerly thought to be a *S. pratensis* hybrid, has large bluish-purple flowers with contrasting white lower lips. 90cm (36in).

S. x *sylvestris* 'Blauhügel' AGM was bred by Ernst Pagels and, although short at 50cm (20in), has the purest blue flowers of all the cultivars. A white sport from 'Blauhügel' has lighter green leaves and pure white flowers and is offered as 'Schneehügel' or sometimes 'Adrian'. 'Mainacht' AGM is one of the earliest to flower and occasionally blooms towards the end of April but always by mid-May. It has deep blue-violet flowers with darker calyces. 60cm (24in). 'Tänzerin' AGM is more erect and taller at 90cm (36in) with small violet-blue flowers with warm reddish-purple calyces on slender spires while 'Viola Klose' is more compact at 50cm (20in), with deep indigo-blue flowers and mounds of dark green foliage.

Sanguisorba (ROSACEAE)

I am prepared to stick my neck out by stating that the burnets will rapidly increase in popularity in the next few years and become stalwarts of naturalistic planting schemes. In the majority of species the flowers are not particularly large or showy, although this is certainly not true for *S. menziesii* and *S. hakusanensis* with their magnificent, pendent pink and burgundy catkins, which waft in the slightest breeze. Also *S. canadensis* has erect spikes of white flowers, not too dissimilar from that of *Actaea*. The pinnate foliage is particularly pleasing throughout the season and many species and cultivars also display yellow and red autumn colour. The taller members of this genus have wiry, willowy stems and move gracefully in gentle air currents, adding a diaphanous curtain to other elements of the late-summer and autumn border.

William Robinson mentions a handful of burnets in *The English Flower Garden* and the first *Plant Finder,* published in 1987, listed a mere six species and no distinct cultivars, supplied by a limited number of nurseries. The most recent RHS *Plant Finder,* published in 2005, lists no fewer than 40 sanguisorbas, including many named cultivars, froma large number of suppliers (although some of the plants are being sold under erroneous names and a few are duplicated). The increase in availability of sanguisorbas in nurseries has

resulted in the proliferation of many named distinct cultivars. It appears that burnets readily hybridize and a wide range of different-shaped flowerheads, colours and sizes has occurred in recent years.

I participated in a plant hunting expedition to Korea in 1993 with Dr James Compton, John Coke and John D'Arcy, collecting a small selection of sanguisorba seed, among other treasures. All the Korean burnets flowered later than forms already available in the trade, so the season can be extended by several weeks into the autumn months.

Burnets prefer moisture-retentive soil in sun or light shade, often found in their natural habitat in damp meadows. *S. minor*, the salad burnet, is a British native and tolerant of drier conditions, being the first to flower in May with abundant, globular greenish-red heads and long, straggly stamens. It is wind-pollinated and has a subtle charm. Burnets are pollinated by the wind (like *S. minor*), flies (as in all forms of *S. officinalis)* or butterflies (as in *S. hakusanensis)*. They are easy to grow and suffer little from pests and diseases although vine weevil grubs are attracted to the roots of this rosaceous herb. In a garden situation, vine weevil is not the devastating pest it becomes with container grown material. **All Z3–8.**

S. armena I have grown this plant under the name of *S. caucasica* but as I can find no confirmation of the name it is possible that it is *S. armena.* It produces striking clumps of glaucous green foliage slightly reminiscent of *Melianthus major* but with the added bonus of being totally hardy. Attains 90cm (36in) in flower with fat, dangling whitish caterpillars with pink stamens from June to August.

S. canadenis An imposing burnet standing a good 1.5m (5ft) in late summer with striking erect, shaggy white bottle-brushes over green pinnate foliage. Native to eastern North America, it grows best on

Top left: *Sanguisorba canadensis*
Left: *Sanguisorba* 'Korean Snow'
Opposite: *Sanguisorba officinalis* 'Red Thunder'

moisture-retentive soils. It mixes well with umbellifers and grasses, lending a strong vertical accent to a planting and flowering from July to September.

S. hakusanensis This is believed to be pollinated by butterflies and is certainly one of the most decorative species with its arching rose-red tassels on slender wiry stems to 90cm (36in). Native to Japan and Korea this flowers from June to August and prefers a moisture-retentive soil in sun or dappled shade.

S. 'Korean Snow' (CDC Korean collection) This majestic, willowy burnet attains at least 1.8m (6ft) during the year and flowers in early September. It has fresh bright- green pinnate foliage and would look well reflected in water. It would appear to be a relative of *S. tenuifolia* 'Alba'.

S. obtusa Striking pendent flowers of vivid pink over *Melianthus*-like grey-green foliage to 1.2m (4ft). *S. albiflora* (syn. *S. obtusa* var. *albiflora*) has grubby white dangling flowers, which I remove before

flowering, as it is the attractive foliage that is its best feature. It is a robust plant with a vigorous running habit and is useful for covering large areas with a foliage effect.

S. officinalis 'Red Thunder' (syn. *S. o.* 'CDC 262') One of the sanguisorba collections from Korea which does not require staking. It is elegant and graceful at 1.2m (4ft) and flowers in late August and September with swarms of red bobbles on thin springy stems.

S. o. 'Tanna' This diminutive burnet forms a mound of tight grey-green pinnate foliage with a froth of burgundy buttons waving aloft at 30cm (12in).

S. 'Pink Brushes' This is a seedling from *S. hakusanensis* raised and named by Coen Jansen, a Dutch nurseryman in Dalfsen. It is a handsome hybrid, taller than its parent at 1.5m (5ft), with long, dangling, brush-like pink catkins.

S. 'Pink Tanna' This arose as a seedling from *S. o.* 'Tanna' on the nursery of Coen Jansen. It is 90cm (36in) or more with pale pink cylindrical flowerheads.

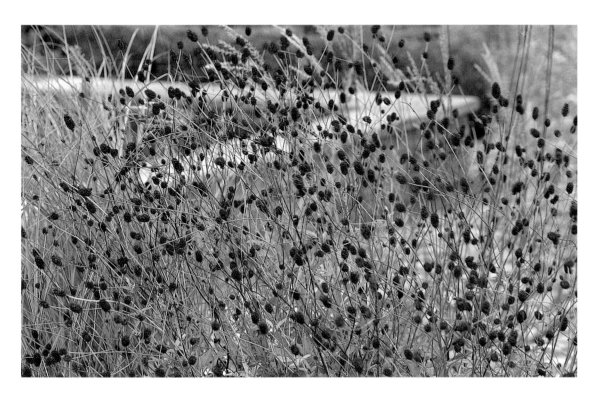

It is undoubtedly a hybrid but the provenance of the other parent is unknown and does not detract from its worth as an excellent garden plant.

S. tenuifolia Fine, divided, pinnate foliage and slender growth is characteristic of this species but I feel there is some confusion with the nomenclature between the white and coloured forms. Although they all have elegant foliage, the flower spikes of all the white forms I have seen are pendulous, but the pink and purple types are usually erect or semi-pendent. They are all attractive with slender cylinders of flowers in profusion to 1.5m (5ft) and flowering late in the season from July to September.

***S. t.* 'Alba'** There is quite a lot of variation in the white forms available, with some possessing attractive pink-flushed foliage in spring. The flowers are held on slim pendulous catkins to 1.5m (5ft) in summer to autumn.

There are many interesting hybrids appearing on the market as the interest in sanguisorbas gains momentum. I am working towards a deep burgundy-red erect taper (such as the flower form in *S. canadensis)* or maybe one in vivid pink. Any takers?

Saponaria x *lempergii* 'Max Frei' (CARYOPHYLLACEAE)

Soapworts have a bad reputation for being vicious thugs, colonizing an area with impunity. *S.* x *l.* 'Max Frei' is a well-behaved plant that does not run but forms a low mound studded with pink flowers, enclosed in purple *c*alyces all summer. It is 15cm (6in) in height and 60cm (24in) in breadth. It thrives in well drained soil in sun. **Z7.**

Scabiosa (DIPSACACEAE)

A magnet to bees, butterflies and hoverflies, this is an essential genus for any gardener wishing to encourage beneficial insects into the garden, providing them with nectar from late in the season until the first frosts. Most scabious species prefer a slightly alkaline soil, good drainage and full sun, when they will flower profusely for many months.

There is a range of sizes, foliage and flower colour to add interest to the late-summer border.

***S. atropurpurea* 'Chile Black'** I first grew 'Chile Black' many years ago not long after its introduction by the Hannays of Bath, who received seed of this plant. It was propagated by cuttings and had glorious purple-black pin-cushion flowers with contrasting white stamens. A short-lived plant but much admired, at up to 90cm (36in) in height. A recently introduced range of independent origin, with flowers in shades of red, deep red and burgundy, are marked under the names of 'Chilli Pepper', 'Chilli Red' and 'Chilli Sauce'. It is probable that all these forms are relatively short-lived. **Z8.**

S. caucasica I used to cut flowers for the original Covent Garden Market and in summer I was sent out to harvest the blue and white "scabs", as we called

Above: *Saponaria* x *lempergii* 'Max Frei'
Opposite: *Schizostylis coccinea* cv

them on the small-holding. Since those days I have found out that I was cutting the blooms of *S. caucasica* 'Clive Greaves' AGM (pale lavender-blue) and *S. c.* 'Miss Willmott' AGM (white). They last well in water when cut just as the first petal is beginning to unfurl, but I prefer to see them in the garden with strong wiry stems to 60–90cm (24-36in) over grey-green mounds of foliage. Other forms are available, some grown as seed strains, but selected cultivars must be propagated from division. **Z4.**

S. cinerea A subject for the raised bed or gravel border with tight rosettes of silvery grey-green foliage and lavender pink button-like flowers. 30cm (12in). **Z6.**

S. columbaria subsp. ***ochroleuca*** This is a charming small-flowered scabious with creamy white flowers and grey-green foliage, to 60cm (24in). **Z6.**

S. japonica var. ***alpina*** Compact mounds of softly hairy grey-green foliage and a profusion of small flowers of lavender blue or lavender pink all summer. Good frontal plant. 45cm (18in). **Z7.**

S. j. var. ***acutiloba*** Altogether different from the above with finely cut, shiny green foliage with pale lavender-blue flowers. Taller at 60cm (24in). **Z7.**

S. tenuis Filigree grey-green leaves and wiry stems to 90cm (36in), with typical scabious flowers in white, pale pink and dusty rose. Flowers all summer in sun with good drainage. Its only drawback is that it is annual, but it happily seeds around in favourable conditions. **Z7.**

Schizostylis (IRIDACEAE)

A useful South African genus of rhizomatous herbs that begin to flower in late summer and continue until the first major frosts. They require moisture-retentive soil that does not dry out during the summer months and, when happy, can grow into good-sized colonies. The named forms available are derived from *S. coccinea,* with spikes of salver-shaped flowers, to 60cm (24in) tall. There are several cultivars including *S. c.* 'Mrs Hegarty' a good pale pink, *S. c.* 'Sunrise' AGM, which has bright pink flowers, *S. c.* 'Tambara' soft rose-pink and *S. c.* 'Viscountess Byng' with late-flowering red flowers. Reasonably hardy in the milder parts of southern England but possibly tender further north. **Z6.**

Scutellaria (LAMIACEAE)

The skullcaps have relatively small flowers but a subtle charm, and some species are particularly useful in that they flower late in the season. They prefer well-drained soil in sun or dappled shade. Attractive to bees.

S. baicalensis Small, clump-forming perennial to 30cm (12in) with multiple spikes of purplish-blue flowers from July to September. **Z5.**

S. incana Native to eastern North America and reliably hardy, given good drainage, this late-flowering perennial has spires of large violet-blue flowers over grey-green foliage. 60cm (24in). **Z5.**

Sedum (CRASSULACEAE)

There are a good many excellent garden plants to be found within this genus, their fleshy foliage contrasting strongly with most other herbaceous perennials. From succulent buds in spring, their leaves and stems elongate to terminal clusters of small flowers in summer and early autumn. Leaf colour varies from jade green, through glaucous grey and greyish-pink to purple, often providing a colourful focal mound before the flowers have even developed. After flowering, the faded flower stems persist to give good winter silhouettes and are magical when covered with hoarfrost, the sun glinting off the ice particles like jewels. Sedums thrive in poor soil with good drainage and full sun. **All Z3–8 except S. altum.**

S. altum An unusual high-rise sedum, its growth habit is unlike any other with whorls of greenish-yellow flowers in tiers one above the other. 60cm (24in). Distinct and subtle. **Z6–10.**

S. **'Bertram Anderson'** AGM A low-growing stonecrop with small rounded leaves suffused with purple, increasing in depth of colour to almost purple-black as the strength of the sun increases and the season progresses. Deep-crimson flowers in late summer. 15cm (6in) tall, with 45cm (18in) spread.

S. **'Dentate'** Excellent hybrid from Graham Gough with reddish purple-black foliage and dark crimson flowers. Stunning, clump-former to 40cm (16in).

S. **'Karfunkelstein'** A recent German introduction with smoky purple foliage and dark flowers. 60cm (24in).

S. **'Purple Emperor'** A fine purple-leaved selection from Graham Gough, admired by all who see it. Clump-forming to 45cm (18in) with straw-yellow flowers from pink buds.

S. **'Red Cauli'** This is yet another of the spectacular stonecrops raised by Graham Gough with metallic blue-green foliage and clusters of ruby-red flowers. 45cm (18in).

S. spectabile **'Iceberg'** Pale green leaves (as with so many albinos) and cool white flowers. Occasional pink reversions do occur and must be removed immediately as they possess more vigour and will rapidly convert your cool, quiet sedum to a hot-pink clump. 45cm (18in).

S. telephium **'Gooseberry Fool'** Huge mid green fleshy mounds of foliage with creamy green plates of flowers. 60cm (24in).

S. t. **'Matrona'** A substantial sedum, to 90cm (36in) with large pinkish-green-suffused leaves and an upright habit. Large flat plates of rose-pink flowers in summer, which persist well into autumn.

S. t. **'Munstead Red'** Attractive toothed foliage in spring and dusky rose-red flowers in late summer. 45cm (18in).

S. t. **subsp.** *ruprechtii* This stonecrop is quite variable from seed with foliage that ranges from glaucous

blue-green to pink-suffused purple. The flowers are a subtle shade of pale greenish-yellow. 45cm (18in).

Selinum (APIACEAE)

Finely dissected mid-green foliage is characteristic of this genus of "refined" cow parsleys. They tend to flower late in the season from July to September, adding quiet charm and a cooling effect to the busy summer border. *S. carvifolium* is a rare British native and perhaps not so showy as *S. tenuifolium* and *S. wallichianum,* as it does not have such showy flowering bracts. It prefers a moisture-retentive soil and sun or dappled shade. **Z6–9.**

In the RHS *Plant Finder*, *S. tenuifolium* is described as synonymous with *S. wallichianum*. I grow two distinct plants under the two names, so I choose to keep them defined as such. By far the most regal to my mind is *S. tenuifolium* with extremely fine ferny foliage and green stems. Flowering starts earlier (in June) than with *S. wallichianum* and the large white umbels are held

horizontally in stiff tiers up the stem. The structure persists well into late summer after the flowers have finished. I have never found viable seed on this plant and it has to be propagated by division. 1.2m (4ft). *S. wallichianum* has a more lax habit, the ferny foliage is slightly more rounded and there is distinct purple suffusion to the flower stem and leaf petioles. The umbels flower almost a month later than *S. tenuifolium* and are not held so rigidly erect. Seed is produced in quantity. 1.2m (4ft). All three species are worthy of garden space, creating an elegant and graceful transparent effect.

Serratula (ASTERACEAE)

The saw-worts are so-named owing to the toothed nature of their foliage. This is another member of the daisy family, flowering late into the autumn. It prefers good drainage and needs full sun to perform well. **S. seoanei (syn. S. shawii)** More often seen as a subject for the rock garden or gravel border, this makes a fine front-of-border plant. It has neat, deeply cut dark green foliage with erect flowering stems and multiple heads of fuzzy purple-mauve knapweed-like blooms. Seldom in flower before the end of August, it continues until the first heavy frosts. 45cm (18in). **Z7.**
S. tinctoria A taller plant better suited to the wilder part of the garden or a naturalistic planting. It has toothed foliage and rather lax habit. 90cm (36in). **Z6.**

Seseli (APIACEAE)

I love the ferny and airy foliage of many members of the umbellifer family and this genus has many species that provide a good foil for other late-flowering plants. If happy, they are rather too eager to seed about. They prefer calcareous soils in sun with good drainage.
S. globiferum Filigree foliage, forming an almost spherical mound in early summer, followed by the

developing flowerhead appearing deep within the leaves. As time progresses this erupts from the sanctity of the foliage to 1.8m (6ft) with creamy white flower umbels. It is monocarpic but will normally seed around. Highly ornamental. **Z6.**

S. gummiferum Glaucous grey-green foliage with circular umbels of white pink-tinged flowers in summer. Usually a biennial that relishes full sun, a lean diet and good drainage. 60cm (24in). **Z6.**

S. hippomarathrum Enjoying similar conditions to *S. gummiferum,* this plant has finer dissected green foliage and is altogether smaller, at 30–45cm (12–18in), with small umbels of pink-tinged white flowers. Perennial and a quiet charmer. **Z6.**

S. libanotis An infrequent British native, the moon carrot is more suitable for the wild garden, with dark green ferny leaves contrasting well with the white flowers through summer. 90cm (36in). **Z4–9.**

Sesleria autumnalis (POACEAE)

Autumn-flowering as the name suggests, this clump-forming grass has striking bright green foliage throughout the season and stiff silvery -green flowers with white anthers in later summer, giving a shaggy appearance. 45cm (18in). Calcareous soils in sun suit it best. **Z5–10.**

Setaria (POACEAE)

Another group of grasses with ornamental flowers.

S. macrostachya AGM An annual fun grass with reddish caterpillar-like heads, which wave in the breeze (syn. *S. glauca* in RHS *Grasses,* 2005). Once grown, it seeds prolifically so you can give it to all your friends! Easy to weed out and a good clump-former. 60cm (24in). The drier the season, the redder the flowers. **Z6.**

S. palmifolia Not hardy, but with elegant evergreen pleated leaves and rather insignificant flowers. Good as a large container plant as it can grow to 2.7m (9ft) in time. It will perish with the first sniff of frost and requires winter protection with temperatures above 4.5degrees C (40 degrees F). **Z9.**

Sidalcea (MALVACEAE)

This is a member of the mallow family with relatively large blooms of flared, funnel-shaped flowers in pink or white over rosettes of attractive green foliage. Hailing from western North America, the most ornamental forms for garden use are selected from forms of *S. malviflora*.

Erect plants grow to 60–90cm (24-36in) with terminal spikes of flowers. They prefer well-drained soil in sun or light shade, but tend to have a fairly short flowering season. To prolong flowering, some or all of the stems could be pruned back in late May or early June to give either later colour or a succession of flowers over several weeks. Cutting back to ground level immediately after the first flush will occasionally succeed in producing a second flowering in autumn but this is rather weather-dependent. Cut stems last well in water.

S. candida A species with rather small, pristine white flowers over green shiny foliage. Planted en masse this can effectively cool a hot summer border. 75cm (30in). **Z5.**

S. malviflora A range of colour, form and size has been selected from the original species. 'Elsie Heugh' AGM has sugar-pink flowers with notched or fringed petals, 'My Love' is a recent selection by Piet Oudolf with longer-lasting pale pink blooms and 'William Smith' AGM has deep pink open trumpets. **Z5–10.**

Silene virginica (CARYOPHYLLACEAE)

Native to eastern North America, this is a fine species that is all too seldom seen in cultivation. Clump-forming with lax stems and true red flowers with long narrow petals. 45cm (18in). Best suited to a well-drained position in dappled shade. Summer to late autumn flowering. **Z5.**

Silphium (ASTERACEAE)

Giant yellow daisy relatives from North America, flowering late in the season at 1.8m (6ft) or more, with rather coarse foliage. Useful for naturalistic plantings where height is required and the stems supported with other tall perennials such as eupatorium and vernonia. They prefer a moisture-retentive soil in sun or light shade and are only suitable for the larger border or naturalistic garden.

At a recent trial of perennial yellow daisies at the RHS Wisley garden, *S. perfoliatum* was awarded the coveted AGM for its green perfoliate leaves which clasp the flower stalk and the multitude of bright yellow daisies on 2.4m (8ft) stems. Other silphiums grown as ornamental garden plants include *S. integrifolium* with coarse lanceolate foliage, *S. laciniatum*, the compass plant with narrow deeply pinnatifid (lobed) leaves and a preference for light shade, and *S. terebinthinaceum*, with huge leaves resembling an elephant's ear. All of them have bright-yellow daisy flowers in late summer and autumn, combining well with the deep purple flowers of *Vernonia crinita*, a giant aster relative of 1.8m (6ft) or more. **Z4–5.**

Sinacalia tangutica (ASTERACEAE)

This is another daisy relative (for the larger garden or naturalistic planting), as it has an invasive rootstock. It is a genus from China and *S. tangutica* is the only species commonly used for its ornamental value. Like ligularias and senecios, under which it has been classified in the past, it prefers a moisture-retentive soil and will tolerate sun or partial shade. Handsome **pinnate** foliage in early summer gives rise to erect red-suffused flowering stems with conical airy inflorescences, which are widely spaced along the stem. Small narrow-rayed yellow daisies followed by fluffy seed-heads throughout autumn complete the season. This is a good subject for the edge of a lake or large pond, associated with rheums, ligularias, gunnera and rodgersia, which add to the tropical look of these big foliage plants. 1.5m (5ft). **Z4–5.**

Top right: *Silphium perfoliatum* AGM
Right: *Sinacalia tangutica* seed-head

Solidago (ASTERACEAE)

Here is yet another North American genus with yellow flowers. Out of favour with British gardeners for many years, this genus may be making a small revival with the interest in naturalistic planting as its members combine seamlessly with grasses, asters and echinaceas. I have always found the more mustard-yellow forms not entirely to my taste but the paler yellow cultivars are effective with blue and purple flowers and foliage, as well as providing nectar for late-flying insects. **Z3–8.**

S. **'Goldenmosa' AGM** Many of the named forms originated from *S. canadensis* and this form has yellow stems with paler yellow flowers to 75cm (30in) from July to September.

S. rugosa Clump-forming perennial with small green leaves cladding the gently arching wiry dark stems to 1.2m (4ft). Small golden-yellow flowers in early autumn.

x Solidaster luteus 'Lemore' AGM (ASTERACEAE)

Intergeneric hybrids are uncommon but this naturally occurring hybrid materialized on a nursery in France almost a century ago. It is thought to have *Aster ptarmicoides* as one parent and a *Solidago* species as its other. It is an attractive perennial and in the form 'Lemore' has 60cm (24in) stems of pale lemon-yellow ray florets with a darker disc. The foliage is not so coarse as many other golden rods. It is sterile so it must be propagated from cuttings or division. **Z4–9.**

Sphaeralcea (MALVACEAE)

This is an attractive genus in the mallow family with more unusual colours of pale orange and tangerine as well as pink flowers. Hailing from arid parts of North and South America, often with hirsute silvery grey foliage, many are not hardy in our wet winters. Sharp drainage and the protection of a frame or alpine house are usually sufficient to keep most of these species alive and they are suitable for containers. They flower over many months often up

to the first major frosts by which time they should be tucked away in warmer conditions; alternatively, late-summer cuttings provide an insurance policy for the following season.

S. ambigua Multi-stemmed perennial with greyish-white hairy stems and grey-green foliage. Orange chalices open all the way up the stem. Sharp drainage and sun essential. 45cm (18in). **Z4.**

S. fendleri Taller than the above at 1.2m (4ft) with whitish hairy stems and foliage. Orange-red mallow flowers in congested terminal spikes. **Z4.**

S. munroana **pale pink** Good ground cover for a hot dry spot or on a raised bed, where it is happy tumbling over a wall; has pale pink mallow flowers and grey-green soft foliage. This is reasonably hardy given sufficient drainage. **Z4.**

Sporobolus heterolepis (POACEAE)

Known as the prairie dropseed, this North American grass has a curious odour although many people are unable to detect it. At 45cm (18in) this beautiful grass has multitudes of small flowers that catch the dew, covering it in the smallest droplets which reflect the light. **Z4.**

Stachys (LAMIACEAE)

There is a tremendous range of size and colour form in this large genus of labiates with many species performing well into late summer and autumn. Several have silvery grey foliage and prefer well-drained soils in full sun while others are green leaved and perfectly happy in most garden borders. Beloved by bees.

S. albotomentosa I first grew this plant as *S.* 'Hidalgo' and was entranced by the furry grey-green leaves with a white reverse and spikes of peachy orange flowers, which are produced successively over the summer months. I grow it on a gritty raised bed where it has reached 45cm (18in) but it may grow taller on a richer diet. **Z7.**

S. byzantina 'Big Ears' Quite different in character is this typical "lamb's ears" type with large, woolly silvery leaves on a virtually non-flowering clone; it makes an excellent edging plant and also provides a good foil for other plants. It needs full sun. 45cm (18in). **Z5.**

S. coccinea A native of Mexico and Texas with green, triangular foliage and vivid spikes of scarlet-orange flowers. Forms a spreading mat but can reach 45cm (18in) in height. **Z7.**

S. macrantha 'Robusta' AGM Large rose-purple flowers over attractive mounds of corrugated green foliage. 45cm (18in). **Z5.**

S. officinalis 'Hummelo' Abundant, 60cm (24in) tall spikes of reddish-purple flowers on this neat clump-forming *Stachys* selected by Ernst Pagels.

S. o. 'Spitzweg' A pale pink form, also selected by Ernst Pagels, with long flower spikes tipped with green; to 60cm (24in). **Z5.**

Opposite: x *Solidaster luteus* 'Lemore' AGM
Right: *Stipa gigantea* AGM

Stemmacantha centaureioides (syn. Leuzea centauroides) (ASTERACEAE)

The globular, papery bracts are the most striking feature of this bold lilac-purple knapweed, once known as *Centaurea* 'Pulchra Major'. Sporting silvery grey foliage, it performs best in full sun with good drainage and attains a height of 1.2m (4ft). The spent flowerheads persist well into autumn. **Z6.**

Sternbergia lutea (AMARYLLIDACEAE)

A cheerful yellow goblet-shaped flower for uplifting the spirit in early autumn. This is a Mediterranean bulb and requires long hot baking in summer in well-drained neutral or calcareous soil where it will gradually increase to form a small colony. Bulbs are often shy to flower here. 15cm (6in). **Z7.**

Stipa (POACEAE)

This genus of grasses contains many species that are widely used for ornamental planting and form an

important group for the landscaper. In general, feather grasses prefer well-drained soils in sun. Currently, many nomenclature changes are occurring in *Stipa* as there are quite distinct groups of grasses with varying characteristics within the genus. *Achnatherum, Anemanthele, Austrostipa, Calamagrostis, Hesperostipa, Macrochloa* and *Nassella* have all been suggested for dividing this genus into more discreet groupings. In this book I have tended towards clumping the various species under the *Stipa* umbrella. The majority are medium-sized grasses up to 90cm (36in) and do not form dense blocks like *Miscanthus*, but have a more mobile and transparent look. Two extremes of the genus are the most widely used in gardens – *Stipa gigantea* AGM at 1.8m (6ft) tall, with oat-like awns in midsummer, is a striking feature of many sunny borders while *S. tenuissima* at 45cm (18in) is a diminutive and graceful grass.

Below: *Stipa calamagrostis*

S. barbata, S. pennata, S. pulcherrima and **S. tirsa**
I have grouped these species together as they all require sharp drainage and sun, producing exquisite long feathery awns after flowering, which is their prime ornamental feature and gives them the colloquial name of feather grasses. They are some of the most elegant of grasses in flower, with long silvery flower plumes that shiver in the slightest breeze. When ripe, the plume behind the seed spirals, pulling it off the plant and propelling it head first into the ground. These grasses can be slow to establish and are not highly ornamental when out of flower with rather grey-green narrow leaves. 90cm (36in). **Z6–8.**

S. brachytricha (now often listed as *Calamagrostis brachytricha*) I have been fascinated to discover that there are definite differences in popularity of grasses between the sexes. I have led many grass workshops and on asking for a preference between this species and the next, find that most women like

S. brachytricha while the men plump for
S. calamagrostis. They are of a similar height, to
90cm (36in), and both start into flower during July
and into September. *S. brachytricha* is sometimes
called diamond grass – there you are, diamonds are
a woman's best friend! On emergence the flower
plume is a silvery purple-grey with an airy, gauzy
appearance. Early dew glistens like jewels on the soft
plume-like flowers. It requires a moisture-retentive
soil that does not dry out too much in summer.
Sadly, the flowerheads do not persist through winter,
collapsing with the onset of frost. Grown on poor soil,
the grass is more erect. **Z4.**

S. calamagrostis The men's choice. A dense clump-
forming grass with successive arching flower plumes
that begin silvery green, quickly fading to straw and
buff. Sometimes this is referred to as needle grass.
The variety 'Lemperg' is more compact at 60cm
(24in). I find this grass is too lax in many reasonable
garden soils and will perform better on a lean diet.
Z6–10.

S. capillata, S. offneri and **S. turkestanica** This group
are about 60cm (24in) tall with graceful flower
plumes in July and August, requiring sharply drained
soil in sun. They appear to be rather short-lived but
this is made up for by their fecundity. Copious
seedlings are produced and unwanted juveniles
should be removed before they colonize the border.
Differences between the species is most obvious in
the ripened seed; *S. offneri* has brownish-buff seeds
and awns whereas *S. turkestanica* is greener.
S. capillata falls between the two. These grasses are
very effective as small clumps in a gravel border so
long as they are kept under control. **Z6–10.**

S. gigantea AGM Referred to as giant feather grass or
Spanish oat grass, this makes a handsome specimen
in a sunny border and should be given enough space
around it to show it to best effect. It is one of the
most beautiful of all hardy grasses, especially if
backlit by the early morning or late evening sun.
Arching stems make 1.8m (6ft) fountains bedecked
with long-awned oat-like flowers. 'Gold Fontaene' is a

superb cultivar selected by Ernst Pagels for its
larger, flamboyant golden oat panicles and 'Pixie' is
a dwarf selection which is more suitable for smaller
gardens at 90cm (36in). **Z6.**

S. tenuissima Only 30–45cm (12–18in) with tightly
packed silky inflorescences all summer. It prefers
sun and sharp drainage, and it will grow into a more
compact, dense clump if starved. A short-lived plant
especially if well fed – a leaner diet will increase
longevity. Replacement plants are often available
from gentle seeding around. **Z6.**

Stokesia (ASTERACEAE)

Stokes' aster resembles a large cornflower with
green strap-shaped leaves and rather lax stems. It
is native to the south-east United States, thriving in
moist, acid soil among pines. I am able to grow it
successfully in neutral soil and I have seen healthy
flowering clumps on chalky soils, so I am not sure
whether the pH of the soil is of great importance.
It is a magnet to bees and butterflies through the
summer months with a range of colour through
white, yellow, pink, blue and purple. All those below
are to 30cm (12in). **Z5.**

S. laevis 'Alba' Large white cornflowers with a trace
of pink over green lanceolate foliage.

S. l. 'Blue Star' A good mid blue with a paler centre.

S. l. 'Mary Gregory' An introduction in the late
1990s with soft yellow flowers. It complements the
blue perfectly.

Strobilanthes (ACANTHACEAE)

This genus belongs to the acanthus family and
revels in rich moist soil in dappled shade. Many
gardeners are familiar with *Strobilanthes attenuata*
with its softly hairy, nettle-shaped leaves resembling
a salvia more than an acanthus. It flowers during
late summer and early autumn with blue-violet
funnel-like blooms, which fade to purple after mid-
day and shrivel by evening. It is good in moist fertile
soil but has a rather straggly habit to 1.2m (4ft).
Z7–9.

There are other neater members of the genus such as *S. wallichii* at 30cm (12in), forming a tight clump of pale green foliage with pale violet flowers. **Z7–9.**

I have recently been given *S. rankanensis*, which I am told will grow to 1.5m (5ft) in a huge dome and will be covered with pale purple flowers throughout autumn. In the mild climes of the Isle of Wight this continued to flower sporadically all winter. I am looking forward to observing its progress here in my cold frost pocket. **Z9–10.**

Succisa (DIPSACACEAE)

The scabious family generally prefers an alkaline soil with good drainage, producing abundant flowers which are a magnet to bees, butterflies and hoverflies. Chalky soils are particularly suitable for these plants. However, my nursery is on a thick clay cap a few hundred yards from chalk outcrops and scabious and knautia grow but reluctantly on my soil, which can be fairly wet in the winter months. For someone who is as passionate about attracting beneficial insects to the garden as I am, this was a bit of a drawback until I discovered *Succisa* and *Succisella*. Both of these genera are easily grown on heavier soils and produce swarms of round button-shaped scabious flowers in August and September. Neat mounds of dark green foliage are produced early in the season, erupting into an explosion of deep blue or indigo pin-cushions in autumn. Rarely, pink-flowered forms are found, such as *S. pratensis* 'Peddar's Pink' and the similar 'Forest Pink'. A creamy yellow form, 'Buttermilk' is also available. The plants can grow to almost a metre, although usually to 60cm (24in) with me, and will tolerate full sun or dappled shade. **Z5.**

Succisella (DIPSACACEAE)

S. altissima Deep blue pin-cushions on wiry branched stems to 90cm (36in) in August.
S. inflexa Leafy rosettes with myriads of small white pin-cushion flowers in August and September with pink-washed buds and pale blue anthers to 80cm

(32in). It can also be used as a cut flower. It will tolerate full sun or dappled shade. **Z6.**

Teucrium hircanicum (LAMIACEAE)

Muted purple spikes, reminiscent of a penstemon, on this sturdy 60cm (24in) tall, clump-forming perennial from July to September. Will gently seed around if happy and prefers a reasonably well-drained soil in sun or partial shade. **Z6.**

Thalictrum (RANUNCULACEAE)

A much under-represented genus in gardens with innumerable small petal-less flowers on tall, often wiry stems up to 1.8m (6ft) or more. Meadow rues are generally found in the wild in meadows, scrub or open woodland often in moisture-retentive soil. They are pollinated by wind, flies or bees and have differing floral structures depending on the pollination method. Wind-pollinated species tend to have green or yellowish hanging filaments held well above the foliage while those pollinated by flies usually have a slightly unpleasant odour. Bee-pollinated plants often have attractive coloured filaments and a pleasant scent, with flowers held closer to the foliage. There are about 300 species of thalictrum, many of them being rather weedy with little or no ornamental garden value. However, recent collections by Dan Hinkley and Crûg Farm Plants have introduced some fine garden-worthy species such as *T. finetii* and *T. decorum*. Most *Thalictrum* species have fine delicate foliage but are sturdy enough to withstand the onslaught of battering gales. They are at their most susceptible in spring, when tender early foliage can be burnt by blistering winds.
T. chelidonii A notable species from the Himalayas with a whitish bloom on the sturdy stems to 2.1m (7ft). Panicles of flowers with lilac-pink sepals. **Z7.**
T. decorum This is one of the most attractive species I grow with relatively large lilac-mauve blooms resembling a jester's cap. Sprawling when young,

Right: *Thalictrum delavayi* AGM

but becomes more erect with age to 90cm (36in). **Z7.**

T. delavayi **AGM** Fine exquisite foliage and late-summer flowering lilac bells with protruding creamy yellow stamens to 1.5m (5ft). Best in dappled shade and a moist soil. There is a clean white-flowered form, 'Album', with pale green foliage and a charming double form, 'Hewitt's Double' **AGM**. This tends to be a rather sprawling, weaker plant but delightful for foliage and flower. **Z7.**

T. **'Elin'** A giant at over 2.4m (8ft) and a natural hybrid discovered in Sweden between *T. flavum* subsp. *glaucum* and *T. rochebrunianum*. It starts to flower at the end of June and through July, but its strong stems and foliage persist well into autumn. **Z5–9.**

T. flavum With a gently running habit and dark green glossy leaves, it looks totally unlike its subspecies *glaucum*, which does not run. Reaching 1.2m (4ft) with pale yellow filamentous flowers. **Z6.**

T. f. **subsp.** *glaucum* **AGM** Mainstay of many a

herbaceous border with glaucous stems and foliage attaining 2.1m (7ft) or more in stature. Yellow filamentous flowers. The form 'Illuminator' was a selection from the above with creamy yellow emergent leaves that persist for the first couple of months of growth before taking on a greener hue. **Z6.**

T. kiusianum A miniature form for the cool, humus-rich shady border with a froth of delicate leaves and clouds of lilac-mauve flowers hovering over the foliage all summer.10cm (4in). **Z8.**

T. lucidum Tall at 2.4m (8ft) with shining green dissected leaves topped by branching sprays of fluffy yellow flowers through July. Pleasing through the autumn and into winter as a striking silhouette. **Z7.**

T. pubescens (syn. T. polyganum) Elegant stems reaching 2.4m (8ft) with bright green foliage and covered in a diaphanous cloud of creamy flowers through July. The seed-heads persist well. **Z4.**

T. punctatum Small at 60cm (24in), with pretty purple-pink filamentous flowers in late summer. **Z7.**

T. rochebruneanum A mere dwarf at 1.5m (5ft), this meadow rue flowers through June with sprays of lilac-purple inverted, cup-shaped flowers with protruding yellow stamens. Its skeleton and developing seed-heads look good in late autumn. **Z8.**

Trifolium rubens (PAPILIONACEAE)

Neat sheaves of foliage under plump madder-red flowers in July and August. An unusual clover for the front of the border, enhancing any "naturalistic" planting. Sun and good drainage suit this plant best and bees adore the flowers. 45–60cm (18–24in). There is also a pink form, which is slightly less vigorous, with smaller flowers and an even rarer white form with pale green leaves. All of them have interesting seed-heads that remain intact through the autumn months. **Z5–9.**

Tulbaghia (ALLIACEAE)

A South African genus closely allied to the ornamental onions and sometimes referred to as society garlic. Dividing plants certainly releases a strong onion-like odour that lingers for days. They provide interesting subjects for containers although some species can be grown successfully outside in the mildest areas in a sheltered well-drained site with plenty of sun. Flowering may continue for several months of the year if it is kept frost free. **Z8.**

T. cominsii Evergreen clumps of narrow leaves with sweetly scented white (with a touch of pink) pendent flowers. 20cm (8in). Excellent for pot culture.

T. 'Fairy Star' A natural hybrid selected by Cotswold Garden Flowers, with a profusion of delicate flowering stems of small, starry, tubular pink blooms. T. violacea is one of the parents and the small flower size is reminiscent of *T. cominsii*. A lovely introduction. 25cm (10in).

T. natalensis One of the hardiest species, not dissimilar to *T. violacea* but with pinker flowers and the foliage is deciduous. 30cm (12in).

T. violacea Vigorous evergreen foliage and strong stems with sprays of pendent violet-pink tubular flowers. 'Silver Lace' has similar flowers contrasting well with clean white and green variegated foliage. Great for containers. 30cm (12in).

Tweedia caerulea (syn. *Oxypetalum caeruleum*) (ASLEPIADACEAE)

None too hardy, this unusual subshrub has a twining, scrambling habit in its native South America but demonstrates a more sprawling tendency in Britain. Although I garden in a frost pocket I am able to grow *Tweedia* outside on my raised gravel bed, where it has survived -10 degrees C (14 degrees F). Again I am reminded that many plants are cold-tolerant but cannot survive winter wet. The foliage and stems are covered with soft hairs, and it is a delightfully tactile plant with caerulean-blue star-shaped flowers, which fade to a pinkish hue. Its rapid growth in late spring enables it to be grown and flowered as an annual in colder areas. Given frost-free winter protection, it will flower throughout the winter months producing long hairy pods that burst open to reveal flattened brown seeds attached

to a silky parachute to enable wind dispersal. 60–75cm (24–30in). **Z10.**

Uncinia (CYPERACEAE)

The New Zealand hook sedges have richly coloured red and mahogany brown leaves that provide a good foil for other plants. They are only hardy in the more southerly counties preferring a rich moist soil in partial shade. Too much shading will result in a greening of the foliage. Attaining 30cm (12in) or so in height, these sedges form robust clumps and would combine well with autumn-flowering bulbs such as *Colchicum* or *Crocus speciosus*. They look at their best when low light passes through them, enhancing the red and russet tones. *U. rubra* and *U. egmontiana* appear to be the hardiest species. **Z8.**

Veratrum (MELANTHIACEAE)

Highly poisonous but creates imposing vertical accents in flower, to some 150cm (5ft) or more.

Ignored by rabbits and deer, they can make useful structural clumps in gardens ravaged by voracious mammalian wildlife. They prefer a deep, moisture-retentive soil in partial shade and erupt in Spring with spectacular pleated leaves that are worthwhile for foliage alone. Somewhat similar in appearance to a Hosta, they also suffer the depredations of slugs and snails. A plant from seed will usually take at least six years to flower while building up its reserves in a large subterranean storage organ. There are several species available and more being introduced by Daniel Hinkley and Crûg Farm from their travels in the Far East. *V. nigrum* AGM may flower as early as five years old with stems clothed in dense branches of almost waxy, reddish-black starry flowers. *V. album* has white flowers but will probably take seven years to bloom and *V. album* var. *flavum* has greenish-yellow flowers. *V. viride* is another green- flowered species and *V. californicum* is taller at 1.8m (6ft) with greenish-white petals. Mature stands of these choice plants make an impressive display in flower throughout late summer and into autumn with their ripening seed-pods. **Z5–6.**

Verbascum (SCROPHULARIACEAE)

Hailing from the same family as *Digitalis*, many verbascums similarly offer a strong vertical accent to a planting with their elegant spires of flowers. There have been many new hybrids discovered and bred in the last few years and I predict that verbascums are destined to become some of the most popular perennials in the next decade.

Verbascums may be annual, biennial or perennial with either a herbaceous or woody sub-shrub growth habit. The majority of the species are biennial, producing a rosette of leaves during their first season. In the second year the flower spike emerges from the leaf rosette often attaining 2m (6ft 6in) or more usually with spires of yellow five-petalled flowers. There are occasionally white-flowered forms

Left: *Veratrum album*

of the species but only a small number of verbascums, notably *Verbascum phoeniceum*, exhibit a good colour range through white, pale pink, lilac, rose to deep purple. By chance or by design, many of the best hybrids are produced with *Verbascum phoeniceum* as one of the original parents. Many of the hybrid verbascums begin to send up flower spikes in mid-May and will remain in bloom for several weeks. So far there have been no records of hybrids setting seed, so the flowering season is greatly extended, as the plant is not using up valuable resources in seed production. Spent flower spikes should be cut down to ground level as soon as possible to encourage a second flush in late summer. In very mild seasons when there are no significant frosts until well into late autumn, some of these hybrids will favour us with yet a third blossoming as indeed happened in 2003 and 2004. The majority of large yellow species commence flowering in midsummer and are at their peak in July and August with secondary spikes lasting well into September. If left intact these tall architectural skeletons will persist through the winter months providing a framework for spider's webs and the jewel-like effect of hoar-frost.

Verbascums prefer an alkaline free draining soil with low nutrient – a lean diet suits them best. The yellow and white flowered verbascum species and their hybrids do perform well in full sun especially those with silver felty leaves. However, they also grow well in light shade especially if they do not receive early morning sun. In fact almost all the coloured hybrids and species (not white or yellow flowered) look better in a site where early morning sun does not bleach their petals. Hoverflies and bees are good pollinators of mulleins and it is likely that moths also play a part in the pollination process. Many verbascums are scented in the early hours of the morning, attracting moth pollinators. Most of the coloured flowered hybrids shrivel quickly in early morning sun which would inhibit pollination by day flowering insects, so it is possible that moths may have a more important pollinating role than is generally suspected.

Several of the popular hybrids introduced into the commercial market in the last few years have been discovered by observant gardeners and nurserymen. There are many species of mullein which are easily grown from seed such as *V. chaixii*, *V. chaixii* 'Album' AGM, *V. blattaria*, *V. b.* f. *albiflorum*, *V. phoeniceum* and *V. bombyciferum* which make fine garden-worthy plants. Natural hybrids arising from these species especially those with *V. phoeniceum* as one of the parents have produced some attractive colour forms. Any progeny, which has a seriously perennial parent, will produce long-lived plants. Unfortunately, many of the verbascum hybrids offered in the commercial market have arisen from non-perennial parents, resulting in progeny lacking longevity. The best example of a popular hybrid of this type is *V.* 'Helen Johnson', a plant that has featured in large numbers at all the major flower shows for almost a decade. It has large flowers of a muted brownish-pink but its life expectancy seldom exceeds one season. In the autumn of 2001, the plant had its AGM (Award of Garden Merit) revoked. Sadly, many people who have purchased this attractive mullein and failed to keep it alive believe that the whole genus behaves similarly. I hope that by introducing seriously perennial hybrids this experience can be reversed and that the pleasure of this group can be truly appreciated.

I have had the privilege of launching some of the new perennial hybrids in the last couple of years, starting in 2001 when I met fellow nurserywoman Patricia Cooper from Magpies Nursery in Mundford, Norfolk. I had seen some of her new hybrids at the Gardeners' Fair at the Pensthorpe Waterfowl Park near Fakenham. After some discussion it was decided that we would launch nine new hybrids, The Breckland Verbascums, that Patricia had grown at her nursery which all exhibited longevity, flowered prolifically and more than once during the season, ranging in colour through yellow, cream, buff, biscuit, apricot, pink and pinkish-mauve. An added bonus was a sweet scent reminiscent of *Mahonia*, only noticeable in the early hours of the morning. Their ability to repeat flower through the season makes them good contenders as late summer perennials. The reception of these new hybrids was so enthusiastic that I was delighted when the NCCPG National Plant Collection holders of *Verbascum* since 1999, Claire Wilson and Vic Johnstone, offered me the chance to launch some of the exquisite hybrids they have raised at their site

Left: *Verbascum bombyciferum*
Opposite: *Verbascum* 'Patricia'

in Whitchurch. It is thanks to my discussions with Claire and Vic over the past couple of years that my knowledge of mulleins has increased so radically. Their perennial hybrids increase the colour range with wonderful shades of tangerine orange, deep coppery brown, golden apricot yellow, deep coppery pink, pale peachy tangerine and rich reddish brown. Claire and Vic have selectively bred over a thousand verbascum hybrids with only the cream of their selections being offered for commercial purposes. These new hybrids (The Riverside Verbascums) are destined to enjoy a revived interest in this wonderful genus and will be enjoyed for many years to come.

THE BRECKLAND VERBASCUMS

V. **'Annie May'** Raised by Pat Cooper and named after her aunt. This has flowers of deepest damson, which do not appear to be so susceptible to the bleaching effect of the early morning sun as some of the range. Additionally the foliage and stems are suffused with deep reddish purple. 90cm (36in). Launched May 2003.

V. **'Apricot Sunset'** Apricot and pinkish shades with darker buds. Evocative of a fine Breckland sunset.

V. **'Brookside'** Rusty reddish bronze buds open to a muted mauvish-pink flower with hints of blue. An impossible colour to define. Named after the Essex house where Patricia's grandmother lived.

V. **'Charles Harper'** A delightful confection of soft pink and buff with a characteristic cream eye, this lovely verbascum was named in memory of a great gardening friend.

V. **'Daisy Alice'** A strong clear colour in deep pinkish-mauve, namesake of Patricia's grandmother.

V. **'Monster'** Different altogether with immense linear grey leaves and flower stems to 2.4m (8ft) covered in hundreds of large yellow flowers with a contrasting dark eye. If it can grow to this size on poor Breckland soil will it be a trifid on a more substantial diet? An architectural showstopper!

V. **'Norfolk Dawn'** The most vigorous and bold of the Breckland verbascums with substantial foliage rosettes; subtle shades of buff and biscuit in the large flowers. Unlike the others in the range this blooms in successive flushes up its stems whereas all the rest begin to open at the base of the flower spike and progress towards the top.

V. **'Patricia'** Not named after the proprietor of Magpies as you may suspect but after an aunt whose namesake Mrs Cooper became. One of my favourites with good green foliage and delightful flowers in rich biscuit, pink and buff with bronzed buds.

V. **'Primrose Cottage'** The palest in the collection with delicate flowers of pale cream and buff with a contrasting pink eye. Named from memories of childhood visits to her grandmother's cottage in spring when surrounded by a sea of primroses.

V. **'Valerie Grace'** A pleasing pastel combination of pale pink and buff named for Patricia's mother.
All Z7–9.

THE RIVERSIDE VERBASCUMS

V. 'Aurora' Pale peachy pink fading to a cream blush with violet filaments. Branched flowering stems. 1.2m (4ft).

V. 'Aztec Gold' Golden apricot yellow with light violet filaments. 1.2m (4ft).

V. 'Cherokee' A tone more reddish-orange brown than the fiery 'Phoenix'. Launched 2004.

V. 'Claire' Coppery, rose-pink flowers with purple filaments and much branched stems. 1.2m (4ft). Launched at Chelsea 2003.

V. 'Clementine' Tangerine orange petals with light violet filaments. 1.2m (4ft).

V. 'Hiawatha' Deep coppery brown petals with dark purple filaments. Best placed out of the early morning sun. 1.2m (4ft). Launched at Chelsea 2003.

V. 'High Noon' Tall at 1.8-2.7m (6–9ft) with branched stems and large yellow flowers with light purple filaments.

V. 'Ivory Towers' A superb new hybrid to 1.8m (6ft) or more with ivory white spires of large flowers. Similar to 'Virginia' in all but colour.

V. 'Kalypso' Branched flowering stems with blooms of pale purplish-pink with contrasting purple filaments. 1.2m (4ft).

V. 'Klondike' Clear light yellow flowers with pale violet filaments. Well-branched stems to 1.2m (4ft).

V. 'Moonshadow' Pale cream with a faint purple wash and light violet filaments. 1.2m (4ft)

V. 'Mystery Blonde' Cream with a hint of pale peachy tangerine. Light violet filaments. Well branched flowering stems to 1.2m (4ft).

V. 'Nimrod' Erect flowering stems to 90cm (3ft) with pale purple flowers and dark purple filaments.

V. 'Petra' A reddish-brown branching hybrid, with russet hues. 1m (3ft 6in). Launched Chelsea 2004.

V. 'Phoenix' I was flattered to have this, the first of Vic and Claire's reddish hybrids, to be named after my nursery. Well-branched stems are smothered with smouldering fiery red flowers with dark purple filaments. Up to 90cm (36in). Launched at Hampton Court 2003.

V. 'Virginia' Pure white flowers with a contrasting pale purple eye on long spikes opening in clusters up the stem. It produces a large basal rosette with flowering stems to 2.4m (8ft). Launched at Hampton Court 2003.

All Z6–9.

OTHER VERBASCUMS

V. 'Bridal Bouquet' Pure white petals on a compact small plant but rather short-lived. 60cm (24in). **Z7–9.**

V. creticum A handsome green-leaved mullein with slender spikes of large yellow sweetly scented flowers. Annual or biennial. Probably synonymous with 'Cotswold King' and 'Buttercup'. 90cm (36in). **Z7.**

V. epixanthinum Collected by an Alpine Garden expedition to the Vikos Gorge in Greece, this

Left: *Verbascum* 'Clementine'
Right: *Verbascum creticum*

perennial mullein has superb rosettes of silver to golden-grey felty leaves with short, stumpy spires of large yellow flowers. A good species to use as a parent in breeding programmes. 60–75cm (24in–30in). **Z7.**

V. **'Gainsborough'** AGM To my eye, still the most elegant and beautiful of the yellow verbascums with pale primrose flowers with greyish-green rosettes. Requires excellent drainage to remain perennial. 1.2cm (4ft). **Z7.**

V. **'Mont Blanc'** The white sibling to 'Gainsborough' , equally beautiful and short-lived with a pale eye. **Z7.**

V. olympicum The correct plant is seldom represented in the trade but hopefully this will be rectified by recent introductions of the true species. This impressive biennial mullein originates from a small area on Mt. Olympus with much branching stems to 1.5–1.8m (5–6ft). **Z6–9.**

V. phlomoides A large-flowered biennial species with robust rosettes and yellow flowers. There is also a

lovely white-flowered form. Large at 1.8–2.4m (6–8ft). There appear to be many synonyms including Harkness hybrids, 'Vega', 'Wega', 'Spica', 'Banana Custard' and 'Snow Maiden'. Flowering is from July to September. **Z6.**

V. phoeniceum A species with glossy rosettes and candles of dark-violet, purple, pink, rose and white. This species prefers dappled shade and more moisture than some of the yellow and white varieties. It has been used extensively for breeding programmes to produce hybrids in a wide variety of shades. *V. phoeniceum* tends to be short-lived although there are more perennial and robust populations and pollen from these is likely to produce the most sturdy hybrids. 90cm (36in). **Z6.**

V. rorippifolium Wiry stems and bright green foliage reminiscent of watercress with small bright yellow mullein flowers. Should have a similar effect to *Cephalaria dipsacoides* and *Verbena bonariensis* in the herbaceous border. Annual or biennial. 1.5m (5ft). **Z6.**

V. wiedemannianum A beautiful biennial species to 1.2m (4ft) from Turkey with dark violet-purple flowers and rosettes with a white cobwebby indumentum (leaves covered with dense white fluff). It requires superb drainage in dappled shade and is a truly beautiful species. The hard spherical seed-heads are produced in bobbles up the stem and the best way to obtain seed is with the aid of a hammer. It is a great pity that this species is biennial as it would be a superb breeding parent for perennial coloured hybrids if it had a greater longevity. **Z7.**

Verbena (VERBENACEAE)

A decade ago this genus was regarded as material for bedding out during the warm summer months, especially some of the attractive hybrids such as 'Gravetye', a pale purple spreading herb, 'Silver Ann' with pink flowers and 'Sissinghurst' with magenta-pink blooms. Milder winters have enabled many species and hybrids to survive as perennials. Z9. Most of the species originate in South America, the

most familiar being *V. bonariensis* AGM, an indispensible plant for the sunny border which attracts multitudes of butterflies and bees to its sweetly scented purple flowers. Tall and structural, at 1.2–1.5m (4–5ft), it is a useful for the front of a border to frame other subjects behind it. Flowering continues for many monthsuntil first hard frosts. **Z8.**

Other tall, slender species include *V. hastata* **Z3** and *V. macdougallii* **Z7–8** from N. America with spires of purple, pink or white flowers. They may be short-lived but, like *V. bonariensis,* have a propensity to seed freely in sharply drained, sunny positions.

Smaller species but no less floriferous include *V. rigida* AGM, a South American plant with stiffly erect stems to 60cm (24in) with a top-knot of small purple flowers. *V. r.* 'Polaris' is a smaller but delightful form of *V. rigida* with cool, globular heads

Left: *Vebena bonariensis* AGM
Below: *Verbena* 'Claret'

of icy blue. *V. corymbosa* has small bluish-purple flowers, spreads vigorously and flowers for several months. **Z9.**

This season I have experimented with *V. tenuisecta*, the moss verbena, with bright green dissected foliage and mauve, scented flowers. If it survives the winter it will be a useful addition to my perennial selection. **Z9.**

A number of hybrids consistently survive winter in the warmer counties provided with sharp drainage. 'Homestead Purple' is one example but with me in my frost pocket, *V.* 'La France' and *V.* 'Claret' have been the most successful. 'La France' has almost luminous purple-blue scented flowers at dawn and dusk, blooming from late spring until the first hard frosts. It has a spreading habit to 90cm (36in) and attains some 60cm (24in) in height. 'Claret' is more compact to 45cm (18in) in height and width with deep wine coloured rounded heads of flowers. **Z8–10.**

Vernonia crinita 'Mammuth' (ASTERACEAE)

One of the true splendours of the early autumn, with its tight clusters of aster-like flowers held in multiple-branched heads atop strong 2.4m (8ft) stems, of a rich violet-purple. A North American prairie plant with an epithet of ironweed that provides nectar for insects late on the wing. Try dividing an established clump – how true to name it is. **Z5.**

Veronica longifolia and V. spicata (SCROPHULARIACEAE)

Spires of blue, purple, rose, pink and white are available in varieties of *V. longifolia* and *V. spicata*.

The former tend to be slightly taller at 60cm–1.2m (24in–4ft) while the latter are generally no more than 60cm (24in). They are useful plants for slender vertical accents in late summer and ambrosia for bees and butterflies. 'Blauriesen' and 'Schneeriesen' are good named *longifolia* cultivars in blue and white while *V.* 'Pink Damask' is an excellent sugar pink and 'Lila Karina' has pale lilac-blue wands of flowers.

Other tones can be raised easily from seed. **Z5–8.**

V. spicata tends to produce more vividly hued flower spikes. 'Romiley Purple' has fine dark purple candles and 'Heidekind' rich wine-red flowers suitable for the front of a border or raised bed. 'Spitzentraum' has grey foliage with long pointed blue flower spikes. **Z4–8.**

These two species prefer sun and good drainage. Grown well, they are admirable components in the summer border but they tend to succumb to mildew. I have reduced the range I grow for this very reason but love to see them thriving in more suitable environments. Not all is lost, though, because a genus – veronicastrum – that was once included in *Veronica* provides me with the strong, willowy verticals without the threat of mildew.

Veronicastrum (SCROPHULARIACEAE)

These are quite different in effect to the shorter veronicas with strong erect stems to 1.8m (6ft) and leaves in whorls along their length. A strong perpendicular accent persists well into the autumn long after the flowers have gone. They do not suffer from the disfigurement from infection by mildew and seldom need staking if grown without too much added nutrients. Veronicastrums prefer sun or dappled shade with reasonably drained soil but not too dry. Most flower in midsummer with the occasional secondary spike later in the season.

Plants grown for ornamental use appear to fall into two groups. An earlier flowering category, which have occasionally been labelled as *V. virginicum* var. *sibiricum*, appear to be shorter at 1.2m (4ft) and more stocky. Some hybrids between *Veronica* and *Veronicastrum* may also fall within this collection. These include 'Apollo' with long wands of rosy lilac, 'Temptation', lavender-blue spires and 'Spring Dew' with pale silvery green foliage in early spring and long pipe-brushes of pure white flowers smothering the long stems in early summer. The seedheads persist as deep bronze architectural accents into late autumn. 'Inspiration', possibly a *Veronica* x

Veronicastrum hybrid has pure white flowers and green foliage.

The other group appear to flower consistently 2–3 weeks later than the first batch and are usually classified as *Veronicastrum virginicum*. These are in flower throughout late summer and often into the autumn with attractive, persistent seed-heads remaining through the winter season. I grow a white form of *V. v.* 'Album' that has red-tinged early foliage, which is unusual in white flowering plants. It is smaller than some of the other veronicastrums at 1.2m (4ft). Another white flowered form 'Diane' has pure white flowers and is a named cultivar that is propagated vegetatively. 'Fascination' is a fine colour with a touch of red in the lavender-mauve flowers but the flower stems have a tendency to fasciate (exhibiting abnormal fusion to give a flattened ribbon-like effect) which I find rather disfiguring. Staking is usually required. 'Lavendelturm' has branched spikelets of lavender flowers atop this stately cultivar that seldom requires support and grows to 1.8m (6ft). 'Pink Glow' and *V. v.* f. 'Roseum' are to my eye almost identical with pale pink spikes and flowering later in the season than the previous varieties. 'Pointed Finger' is a form with long purplish-blue flower wands that lie almost horizontally in one direction creating a rather windblown effect. Maybe more of an amusing curiosity than sheer beauty but attractive to insects nevertheless.

A more recent selection is *Veronicastrum* 'Erica' with deep reddish buds opening to pink flowers. This is a useful plant for late summer as it flowers a couple of weeks after the others. I have also grown 'Red Arrows' expecting a rosy hue to the inflorescence. The plant I flowered had pretty bluish purple spikes – am I missing something?

Veronicastrums combine superbly with many ornamental grasses , including *Miscanthus,*

Top left: *Veronicastrum virginicum* 'Fascination'
Left: *Veronicastrum virginicum* 'Spring Dew'

Calamagrostis and *Molinia*. Their vertical accent and willowy grace, combined with ease of growth and lack of disfiguring disease, make this genus indispensible in the naturalistic garden. **Z3.**

Watsonia (IRIDACEAE)

A South African genus with gladiolus-like corms and suitable for containers. Several of the larger species are hardy in warmer counties planted out in a sheltered part of the garden. There are several spectacular plants to choose from but I will cover two of the hardiest. **Z9.**

W. *borbonica* subsp. *ardernei* 'Arderne's White'
Vigorous to 90cm (36in) with sheaves of green leaves and spikes of large, pure white open flowers in late summer and autumn.

W. 'Stanford Scarlet' Stems of brilliant orange-scarlet flowers emerge from the sword-like foliage. Hardy with sun and good drainage but not too dry in early summer when the spectacular display is about to begin. 1.2–1.5m (4–5ft).

Zauschneria californica (ONAGRACEAE)

Flamboyant though diminutive members of the willowherb family hailing from the southern half of North America from California to Mexico. Classification wanders from *Epilobium* to *Zauschneria* but appears currently to be settled in the latter. The wild species produce vivid, fiery orange-red displays of trumpet-shaped flowers with exserted stamens that are pollinated by hummingbirds and insects with long tongues. In cultivation, varieties have been bred with a wider colour range varying from white, pale pink, deep pink, salmon through orange to red. They prefer a sunny position with excellent drainage and dislike intensely cold, wet winters. These plants are reasonably cold-hardy but succumb to excess moisture in their dormant season. A raised gritty bed, gravel or alpine garden in full sun would suit them best.

I have grown many species and cultivars over the years with varying degrees of success. Among the hybrids, 'Solidarity Pink', brought back from America by Graham Thomas, has shell-pink flowers set off by pale grey-green foliage while 'Sierra Salmon' has deeper pink tones and greener leaves. 'Alba', with its small white flowers, did not grow vigorously with me and the pink varieties fared little better. More vigorous by far, in fact a pest at times, was 'Western Hills', with large reddish-orange flowers, from Marshall Olbrich's famous Californian nursery. This grows to 45cm (18in) or more, spreading underground by runners and forming large clumps quickly. 'Olbrich Silver' has silvery leaves and red trumpets but is not so vigorous. 'Dublin' (syn. 'Glasnevin'), an old cultivar with tubular orange-red flared blooms, is still one of the most successful in British gardens growing to 20cm (8in) and flowering until the first hard frosts. Species such as *Z. arizonica* make large bushes to 90cm (36in) with vivid red flowers – a real show-stopper when grown well. **Z8.**

Zigadenus (LILIACEAE)

From North America, this genus encompasses some attractive bulbous plants with narrow linear leaves and racemes of star-like flowers in jade green, cream and white. They are also extremely poisonous: indeed one of the colloquial names used for one species (*Z. nuttallii)* is the "death-" or "poison camas". However, they are indisputably hardy and their subtle colour combination is much admired by gardeners. They prefer moisture-retaining soil in sun or dappled shade and in time produce clumps with several flowering stems. Many species are so similar in flower that only one or two would be necessary. *Z. elegans* grows to 60–75cm (24–30in) and *Z. nuttallii* is shorter at 30–45cm (12–18in). If growing any of these plants, do take care where they are sited if you have livestock or young children who might nibble the foliage. But if you have a problem with voracious wildlife such as rabbits or deer, you could use them as a boundary around your garden. **Z3–6.**

GLOSSARY OF BOTANICAL TERMS

Annual A plant which grows, flowers, seeds and dies in one year.

Axis The main stem of a plant or the receptacle of a flower.

Biennial A plant sown in one year and flowering or fruiting in the next.

Bract A leaf-like structure arising from the stem of a flower, often where the flower is insignificant.

Burr Hooked or barbed flowerhead or fruit.

Calyx (calyces) The group of modified leaves enclosing a flower bud.

Capitulum A cluster of small, stalkless flowers.

Colour break A mutation caused by a spontaneous change in the chromosomes or genes of a plant, affecting the colour of the flowers.

Cordate Said of leaf that is heart-shaped.

Corolla The inner whorl of a flower.

Crenulate Finely toothed margins.

Cultivar A cultivated variety.

Decussate Leaves arranged in pairs on the opposite sides of a stem.

Disc floret The centre part of a flower (eg a daisy) where the outer florets join to the central cushion.

Guttation Droplets of water found on the margins of leaves.

Inflorescence The flowering part of a plant that can be made up of different types of flower eg spikes, panicles, umbels etc.

Lanceolate Leaves shaped like a lance, ie wider below the middle and tapering at both ends.

Monocarpic Used to describe a plant that dies after flowering.

Panicles A flowerhead with several branches. They can be opposite or alternate.

Pedicel The stalk of a flower contained in an inflorescence.

Peltate Term used to describe a shield-shaped leaf, where the leaf-stem joins the leaf near the centre on the underside.

Perennial A plant that flowers annually but usually lives for two or more seasons. Applied to non-woody plants (known as herbaceous perennials).

Perfoliate Said of a pair of leaves that completely encircle the plant stem.

Petiole The stalk of a leaf where it joins the plant stem.

pH The degree of acidity or alkalinity of soils. A soil with a pH of 7 is neutral. Lower figures denote the degree of acidity; higher figures the degree of alkalinity.

Pinnate Used to describe a leaf which has its leaflets arranged in pairs on both sides of the leaf stalk.

Pinnatifid A leaf divided in a pinnate manner but into lobes rather than leaflets.

Ray The outer petals of certain flowers, such as daisies.

Ray floret A ring of strap-shaped petals, as in daisies.

Remontant Said of a plant that produces a second crop of flowers in the same year.

Receptacle The thickened stalk carrying the parts of a flower.

Rugose Corrugated or wrinkled.

Spathulate Said of leaves that are broader at the tip than the base.

Umbel A flowerhead where the individual flower steams radiate from a central point.

Variety Said of plants that have distinctive features yet not distinct enough to be classed as a species. Variety applies to naturally occurring varieties; cultivar to cultivated ones.

Zygomorphic Said of a flower that is divisible into two equal parts in one plane only (eg an antirrhinum).

FURTHER READING

Baumgardt, J.P., *How to identify Flowering Plant Families,* Timber Press, ISBN 0-917304-21-7

Bendtsen, B.H., *Gardening with Hardy Geraniums,* Timber Press, ISBN 0-88192-716-3

Bryan, J.E., *Bulbs,* Timber Press, ISBN 0-88192-529-2

Clebsch B., *A Book of Salvias,* ISBN 0-88192-369-9

Cloyd, R.A., Nixon, P.L. & Pataky, N. R., *IPM for Gardeners – A Guide to Integrated Pest Management,* Timber Press, ISBN 0-88192-647-7

Cooke, I., *The Plantfinder's Guide to Tender Perennials,* David & Charles, ISBN 0-7153-0635-9

Darke, R., *The Colour Encyclopaedia of Ornamental Grasses* Weidenfeld & Nicolson, ISBN 0-297-82531-3

Davies, B., Eagle, D. & Finney, B., *Soil Management: A Farming Press Book,* ISBN 0-85236-053-3

DiSabato-Aust, T., *The Well-Tended Perennial Garden,* Timber, ISBN 0-88192-414-8

Elliott, J., *The Smaller Perennials,* Batsford, ISBN 0-7134-7799-7

Flora Europaea, Vol.1–5, Cambridge University Press, ISBN 0-521-08489-X

Gerritsen, H. & Oudolf, P., *Dream Plants for the Natural Garden,* Frances Lincoln, ISBN 0-7112-1737-8

Grenfell, D., *The Gardener's Guide to Growing Daylilies,* David & Charles, ISBN 0-7153-0695-2

Griffiths, M., *The New RHS Dictionary Index of Garden Plants,* Macmillan, ISBN 0-333-59149-6

Grounds, R., *Grasses – Choosing and Using these Ornamental Plants in the Garden,* Quadrille, ISBN 1-84400-159-8

Harmer, J. & Elliott, J., *Phlox,* Hardy Plant Society, ISBN 0-901687-18-9

Hinkley, D.J., *The Explorer's Garden,* Timber Press, ISBN 0-88192-426-1

Ingram, D.S., Vince-Prue, V. & Gregory, P.J., *Science and the Garden,* Blackwell Publishing, ISBN 0-63205-308-9

King, M. & Oudolf, P., *Gardening with Grasses,* Frances Lincoln, ISBN 0-7112-1202-3

Lloyd, C., *Christopher Lloyd's Garden Flowers,* Cassell & Co., ISBN 0-304-35427-9

Miller, D., *Pelargoniums,* Batsford, ISBN 0-7134-7283-9

Nold, R., *Penstemons,* ISBN 0-88192-429-6

Oudolf, P. & Gerritsen, H., *Planting the Natural Garden,* Timber Press, ISBN 0-88192-606-X

Phillips, R. & Rix, M., *The Botanical Garden Volume II,* Macmillan, ISBN 0-333-74890-5

Phillips, R. & Rix, M., Annuals, Pan, ISBN 0-333-74889-1

Phillips, R. & Rix, M., *Bulbs,* Pan, ISBN 0-330-30253-1

Phillips, R. & Rix, M., *Conservatory Plants, Vol. 1 & 2,* Pan, ISBN 0-330-37375-7/0-330-37376-5

Phillips, R. & Rix, M., *Perennials, Volume 1 & 2,* Pan, ISBN 0-330-30926-9/0-330-29275-7

RHS Plant Finder, Dorling Kindersley, ISBN 1-4053-0736-6

Rice, G., *Discovering Annuals,* Frances Lincoln, ISBN 0-7112-1293-7

Rice, G., *Hardy Perennials,* Viking, ISBN 0-670-84371-7

Schmid, W. George, *An Encyclopedia of Shade Perennials,* Timber Press, ISBN 0-88192-549-7

Sutton, J., *The Plantfinder's Guide to Daisies,* David & Charles, ISBN 0 7153 0973-0

Sutton J., *Gardener's Guide to Growing Salvias,* ISBN 0-7153-0803-3

Thomas, G.S., *Perennial Garden Plants,* Dent, ISBN 0-460-86048-8

Way, D. & James, P., *Gardener's Guide to Growing Penstemons,* ISBN 0-7153-0803-3

White S., *Origanum,* ISBN 0-9518623-9-1

Yeo, C., *Salvias I & II,* Pleasant View Nursery, ISBN 0-9529954-0-9/0-9529954-1-7

INDEX

ACKNOWLEDGMENTS

This book would never have been written without the encouragement and support of friends, family and nurserymen. At times it has been exhilarating, inspiring, exhausting and occasionally frightening, when the words ceased to flow, but my overall impression is that I have just participated in a most wonderful experience.

My special thanks to Susan Berry, my editor, who not only proposed the idea of this book but has steadfastly guided me through the trials and tribulations of this manuscript and helped to assemble the words into some semblance of order; to Anne Wilson, the designer, who has laid out the pages so elegantly; to the team at Frances Lincoln, who have been so helpful and friendly; to Tony Lord (Consultant Editor of the RHS Plant Finder) who has helped me to get my plant names correct – any errors are mine alone; to Dan Hinkley for writing such a generous foreword and offering me his friendship.

Last, but not least, my thanks to Steven Wooster, whose stunning photographs enhance and clothe my words.

Marina Christopher's nursery
   Phoenix Perennial Plants,
   Paice Lane,
   Medstead,
   Alton,
   Hampshire GU34 5PR,
   Tel: 01420 560695
   Fax: 01420 563640

The nursery is open from late March to October on Thursday, Friday and Saturday from 10 a.m. to 6 p.m. To receive a catalogue, please send 4 x 1st class stamps loose in an envelope with your name and address.